EDEXCEL

# AS AND A LEVEL MUSIC TECHNOLOGY

# Listening Tests

To acces audio visit:
**www.halleonard.com/mylibrary**

**3744-5596-6507-8472**

ISBN 978-1-78558-632-3

RHINEGOLD EDUCATION

EXCLUSIVELY DISTRIBUTED BY

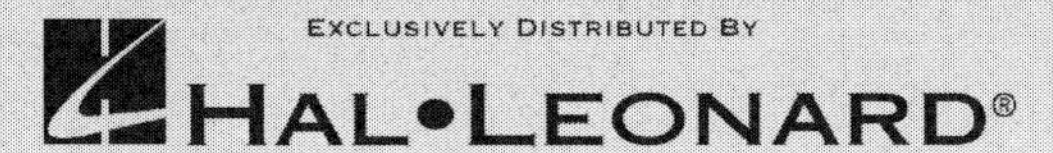




Visit Hal Leonard Online at
**www.halleonard.com**

World headquarters, contact:
**Hal Leonard**
7777 West Bluemound Road
Milwaukee, WI 53213
Email: info@halleonard.com

In Europe, contact:
**Hal Leonard Europe Limited**
1 Red Place
London, W1K 6PL
Email: info@halleonardeurope.com

In Australia, contact:
**Hal Leonard Australia Pty. Ltd.**
4 Lentara Court
Cheltenham, Victoria, 3192 Australia
Email: info@halleonard.com.au

You should always check the current requirements of your examination, since these may change.

Editors: Elisabeth Boulton and Katharine Allenby
Cover and book design: Fresh Lemon Australia

# EDEXCEL

# AS AND A LEVEL MUSIC TECHNOLOGY

## Listening Tests

JAMES REEVELL

# The author

**James Reevell**

is a teacher, author and examiner with extensive experience in delivering Music and Music Technology A Level courses. He studied Music at Durham University, completed a Masters at Manchester Metropolitan University, and has experience teaching in sixth form colleges across the north of England.

James has worked as a Subject Leader for Visual and Creative Arts with responsibility for courses in Art, Dance, Drama, Music and Music Technology. He has contributed to study and revision guides for A Level Music, Music Technology and GCSE Music as both author and consultant. James delivers nationwide training to teachers with a particular focus on Music Technology and Popular Music.

## Acknowledgements

The author would like to thank Elisabeth Boulton for her editorial work, Katharine Allenby for her support and guidance in putting this book together, and Phil Gambrill of Fresh Lemon Australia for his patience and the extensive work he has put into the diagrams and page setting.

# Contents

# Introduction

## Congratulations on choosing to study Music Technology for AS or A Level!

The course is challenging, but it is a rewarding way of developing your practical skills, theoretical knowledge and ability to apply what you learn to a variety of situations. In doing so, you will build your skills in aurally identifying processes, problem solving and critical thinking. The course is designed to introduce you to the skills and techniques required to progress into the music technology industry, and for further study in higher education.

This book is designed to give you opportunities to practise your listening, analysing and production skills for the Edexcel AS and A Level written exam papers for **Component 3** and **Component 4**. These are collectively worth 60% of your entire grade, so it is really beneficial for you to practise the skills you will need to apply and prepare yourself for what to expect before you enter the exam room.

## Good luck with your exam practice!

# General guidance on answering exam questions

**This section offers guidance on how to best address what the exam question is asking you to do. There is also a brief topic overview of the era and style content that make up Components 3 and 4, along with a discussion of Assessment Objective 3 (AO3) and Assessment Objective 4 (AO4) to help you understand the mark schemes that are included later in the book.**

### AS LEVEL AND A LEVEL

Throughout this book, the questions are written to help you prepare for both levels of the course. Question numbers with an * next to them indicate that you need to be able to answer them for both AS and A Level. Those without an * are for A Level only. This means that the total marks available for the AS questions are not always the same as in the exam. Look at the bottom right of each page to see how many marks are available for each level.

## Musical styles and eras

**In both Component 3 and Component 4, you will need to demonstrate your knowledge and understanding of the music technology associated with eras and styles.**

**You need to know about five different eras in music technology:**

- Direct to tape mono recording (c.1930–1963)
- Early multitrack recording (c.1964–1969)
- Large-scale analogue multitrack recording (c.1969–1995)
- Digital recording and sequencing (c.1980–present)
- Digital audio workstations (DAW) and emerging technologies (c.1996–present).

The Rhinegold Education *Edexcel AS and A Level Music Technology Study Guide* (2017) by Tim Hallas provides a detailed discussion of each of the eras above to help you with your exam preparation. You will also find useful the Rhinegold Education revision guides for both AS and A Level Music Technology.

**You also should have an understanding of the following styles, the instruments and sounds associated with them, and the combinations of instruments and voices used:**

- Jazz
- Blues
- Rock 'n' roll
- Rock
- Metal
- Reggae
- Punk
- Soul
- Disco and Funk
- Commercial pop
- Urban
- Electronic and Dance
- Acoustic and Folk
- Music for the media: film and computer games.

## Understanding the questions

- A 'command word' is the word in the question that tells you exactly what you need to do to answer it fully
- The table below lists the key command words used in the exam; as we move down the list they assess deeper levels of learning
- You can refer back to the table if you are unsure on how to answer fully any of the questions in the practice papers, or in your general exam preparation
- In Component 4, you will also have to answer questions and complete practical tasks related to the specific effects and processes in your DAW, for example 'compress the vocal part'.

| | |
|---|---|
| **State, give, name, list** | ■ Give one or more points<br>■ Recall or find facts |
| **Identify** | ■ Give one or more points<br>■ Find information in a stimulus (e.g. an audio track or picture/diagram) |
| **Complete, label, draw** | ■ Fill in the gaps in a table<br>■ Label, draw or complete a graph or diagram |
| **Calculate** | ■ Do a calculation to find an answer |
| **Describe** | ■ Make one or more points |
| **Explain** | ■ Make one or more points that are justified or extended |
| **Compare** | ■ Make points about the similarities and differences<br>■ Make relative judgements |
| **Discuss** | ■ Identify the situation<br>■ Explore all aspects of the situation<br>■ Investigate the situation by reasoning/justification |
| **Analyse** | ■ Examine or dissect the elements in detail<br>■ Focus on individual elements and how they combine to create an effect or achieve a purpose |
| **Evaluate** | ■ Make judgements against parameters<br>■ Draw conclusions<br>■ Justify your opinions or make comparisons. |

# Assessment objectives (AO3 and AO4)

- Because they are referred to in the practice papers and mark schemes, along with the Edexcel Sample Assessment Materials, it is useful for us to think briefly about assessment objectives.

**There are further materials to help you prepare for your exams on the Edexcel Music Technology (2017) website: www.qualifications.pearson.com/en/qualifications/edexcel-a-levels/music-technology-2017.html**

- The assessment objectives are the overarching things that Edexcel must assess you on in your coursework and exams.
- In the mark schemes for some longer answer questions, you will be shown a split for AO3 and AO4 marks.
- At A Level, this is often heavily weighted towards AO4. You will need to demonstrate these skills to score highly on the extended response questions for Component 3 and Component 4.

| | |
|---|---|
| **AO3** | Demonstrate and apply knowledge and understanding of music technology |
| **AO4** | Use analytical and appraising skills to make evaluative and critical judgements about the use of music technology |

- The easiest way to think of it is that AO3 marks are awarded when you demonstrate your knowledge and understanding of music technology.
- However, to achieve marks for AO4, you need to apply this knowledge, evaluating the effectiveness of something (for example an audio track, a picture or diagram), or making links between something and other relevant material (for example when identifying the wider context for the production of a track).
- It's not possible to access AO4 without using AO3 to get there (because as part of AO4, you already have to show your knowledge and understanding).
- At the bottom of the command words table, terms like 'compare', 'analyse' and 'evaluate' tell you that you will need to demonstrate AO4 skills.

## Types of questions

**It is useful to take a brief look at the types of question you might have to answer in your exams.**

### Gap fill, line matching and multiple-choice questions

- For some questions on the paper, you might have to fill in a missing word in a sentence. For example: Pad is used on the condenser microphone because of the trumpet's high ________. ('SPL' would be a suitable answer.)
- You also might have to match up information by drawing a line between related words or phrases.
- Multiple-choice questions will give you options from which you have to pick the correct answer. You might, for example be asked to identify one specific instrument from a list, identify a decade of a song's release, or identify the correct effect applied to an instrument in the mix.

### Short answers

- These questions ask you to provide information but you don't have to write it into a complete sentence.
- You might be asked to identify how a vocal line is made thicker in the mix. (Doubletracking might be an appropriate answer.)
- You should make sure you answer the question clearly and using the correct terminology, and beware of using abbreviations or providing two contradictory answers. If you do this, you are unlikely to score credit for your answer, even if part of it is correct.
- The key thing to remember is to answer the question by making the appropriate number of points.
- If a question has one mark available, then a single answer will suffice.
- However, if the question has two or three marks available, then it will require multiple points to achieve full marks.

### Tables and diagrams

- You may have to complete a table.
- This may include information about device parameters, or provide space for you write a specific number of points.
- In some tables, there might be space for you to make a point and another for you to justify it.
- You might be presented with a half-completed table in which you have to provide missing information, or as a table with a series of headings in which you are expected to fill in the gaps.
- You could also be asked questions involving a small amount of drawing.
- For example, you might have to complete a graph of a filter and label the axes.
- You can also use diagrams to illustrate your points in other questions – for example when drawing a microphone polar pattern or filter graph in a longer answer question.
- When sitting the exam, you should make sure you have a pencil ready to help you sketch out a diagram question.
- The examiner is looking for you to demonstrate your knowledge of music technology, and will not be judging your artistic ability.
- Remember to label your diagram and make it as accurate and as clear as possible, in order to make your meaning apparent to the examiner.

### Open questions

- It can be trickier to answer open questions because there are more possible responses than a single word or other short answer questions.
- It is useful to keep yourself on track by using bullet points, or by writing subheadings to keep your answer focused.
- Make sure you've looked at the mark allocation for the question; it's important that you have supplied enough detail for you to gain the maximum number of marks.
- For some questions, you may have to provide a point and a justification, so it is important that you expand each of the points you make.
- For example, in suggesting how a vocal part could have been recorded more effectively, you might write 'use a pop shield'. This could be expanded to identify that you know this 'because there are a number of plosive sounds in the recording'.
- You could even suggest a further solution, for example 'you could use a high pass filter to reduce the effect of the plosive sound when mixing'.

### Practical questions

- As part of Component 4, you will have to demonstrate various practical skills, and bounce/mix down the resulting audio to be submitted at the end of the exam.

Find out more about the structure of Component 4 on page 27

- These are skills that you will have used extensively in preparing your work for Component 1 (recording) and Component 2 (technology-based composition).
- You may be asked to, for example, remove noise, apply an effect or processing to a track, or to synthesise a sound based on another audio file.

### Extended response questions

- For the longer extended response questions in the exam, you will need to draw upon your knowledge and understanding of music technology and apply this in order to make a judgement or reach a conclusion.
- You might also need to analyse a stimulus (like a picture of a synthesiser or a photo of a microphone placement) or make comparisons between different pieces of audio (like discussing the differences in production between two tracks).
- The focus for these questions is you demonstrating your higher level skills in application, analysis, connection, logical thinking and conclusion.
- You can structure your answers as you wish, but make sure you stay focused on what the question is asking – for example, if it specifies a date, stay within the range in the question.

## GENERAL ADVICE ON WRITING YOUR ANSWERS

- **Remember to use the spaces provided for your answers. There is often more space provided than you need to fully answer the question - don't feel you have to fill all the lines! Instead, focus on answering the question clearly and concisely, to the best of your ability.**
- **It's much better to try and keep your answers concise, rather than to repeat the same thing lots of times.**
- **Bullet points can be a really good way of doing this, keeping your answer focused and detailed. You can then make sure you extend and add detail to each point you write.**
- **You should look carefully at the number of marks each question carries; for shorter answers, this will be the number of relevant points you need to make to achieve full marks in the question.**
- **For the extended response questions, your answer will be given an overall level band (1-4 at AS Level, 1-5 at A Level) based on the quality of your response. This will relate to a number of marks, as you will see in the mark schemes provided later on.**
- **Concentrate on answering the question asked on the exam paper; not the one you've prepared a perfect answer for!**
- **It's fine to leave a rough essay plan for the longer response questions; it may even score some credit if you've not managed to include all the points in your final answer!**
- **However, do make sure you cross through any work you don't want the examiner to mark and make sure you show your working if asked to in the question.**
- **Keep your answers as specific as you can. General responses like 'use of effects', 'delay' or 'reverb' probably won't give the examiner enough information. Providing more detail will help you to gain credit for all of the points you make.**
- **A good example would be saying that 'a crotchet delay with a high level of feedback has been used on the lead vocal', or that 'the reverb on the snare drum has a 2 second reverb time'. These statements tell us a lot more about what you are hearing.**
- **Make sure that your handwriting is clear and legible; if the examiner can't read your answer, they can't give it credit.**

**COMPONENT 3:**

# Listening and analysing

## Overview

**Component 3 at both AS and A Level assesses your knowledge and understanding of recording and production technology, techniques and principles. During the exam, you will answer questions that are related to recordings of songs, provided by the Edexcel exam board.**

| **Summary of Component 3** | |
|---|---|
| **AS Level Component 3** | **A Level Component 3** |
| 1 hour 15 minutes exam paper | 1 hour 30 minutes exam paper |
| **Section A (44 marks)**<br>■ Three questions worth **10 marks each** and one question worth **14 marks** | **Section A (40 marks)**<br>■ Four questions worth **10 marks each** |
| **Section B (16 marks)**<br>■ One extended comparison question focusing on the production features of two tracks worth **16 marks** | **Section B (35 marks)**<br>■ One extended comparison question focusing on the production features of two tracks worth **15 marks**<br>■ One further extended response question placing a track into its wider technical context worth **20 marks** |
| **Total: 60 marks**<br>**25% of your total AS Level** | **Total: 75 marks**<br>**25% of your total A Level** |

## What will I have to do for Component 3?

**You will be expected to apply the knowledge you have gained through your recording and composition work in Components 1 and 2, along with your study of music technology theory that relates to:**

- Recording and production techniques for both corrective and creative purposes
- The principles of sound and audio technology
- The development of recording and production technology.

**In doing so, you will need to demonstrate your ability to:**

- Comment on the music production tools and techniques used to capture sounds, including musical instruments
- Use your aural skills to identify and evaluate how music technology elements are used in unfamiliar works
- Critically analyse and make perceptive comments about music production techniques in a range of music and assess the impact of these techniques on different styles
- Apply language associated with musical elements in the context of music technology; for example, structure, timbre, texture, tempo, rhythm, melody, harmony, tonality and dynamics
- Give written responses about the equipment used in a recording by identifying the effects used and commenting on specific parameter settings
- Understand the wider context of music technology and how it has influenced musical trends.

You will have your own copy of the recordings in the exam, so you can skip to the specific time references in the questions, or just replay a certain section if you need to listen to it again. Your school or college will provide you with a means of listening to the recordings in the exam. You might use a computer to do this. If you do use a computer, you are not permitted to access any other software like a DAW, or use other equipment like MIDI keyboards.

## What will the exam look like?

### Section A questions

- **For AS Level**, Section A will consist of three questions worth 10 marks and one question worth 14 marks
- **For A Level**, Section A will consist of four questions worth 10 marks each; all of these will be related to unfamiliar commercial recordings
- These tracks will be chosen by Edexcel and could be from any of the genres listed in the exam specification (see page 7); all the eras in the specification will be covered in each paper
- The questions will get more challenging as the paper progresses, and later questions will require you demonstrate your comparison and evaluation skills.

### Section B questions

- As part of Section B, you will demonstrate your knowledge of different production techniques, how they compare and how they fit into the wider context of music production
- **For AS Level**, you will complete one extended response question worth 16 marks, which compares the production techniques used in two different tracks
- These tracks will share some sort of connection; they might be cover versions, or songs by the same producer
- **For A Level,** you will complete one extended response comparison between the production features used in two different tracks (as for AS Level), worth 15 marks
- You will also complete a final extended response question worth 20 marks, which requires you to use your evaluation skills and fit a track into its wider context related to music production
- The extended response questions require greater planning, and it will be beneficial for you to practise constructing an appropriate answer that addresses all parts of the question
- Use the practice questions at the end of each section in this book to help you prepare.

## Using this book to prepare for Component 3

- When practising, try to answer the questions in the same conditions as you would experience during the exam
- You should listen on good quality headphones and check that the left and right sides are the correct way around
- Beware of using different versions of the tracks specified in this book; this may make the questions not applicable
- To stream or download the audio tracks, simply go to www.halleonard.com/mylibrary and enter the unique code found on page 1 of this book.

**TIPS FOR COMPONENT 3**

- **Remember that you have control of the music in the examination; you can skip directly to a specific time or replay things**
- **This is great because you can easily focus in on what you need to listen to – but be careful not to spend too much time repeating the audio for a single question**
- **Keep an eye on the clock to make sure you are using your time effectively**
- **Remember to use appropriate music technology terminology in your answers.**

# Component 3

**AS LEVEL AND A LEVEL**

The questions that follow are written to help you prepare for both levels of the course. Question numbers with an * next to them indicate that you need to be able to answer them for both AS and A Level. Those without an * are for A Level only.

## Practice Paper 1

## SECTION A

**Answer ALL questions.**

**Write your answers in the spaces provided.**

## Question 1

**Track 1 – Ultravox: 'Vienna' (1981)**

***a.** The sound of the snare drum on this recording is quite characteristic of 1980s production. Describe three features of the production of the snare drum before 1'20". **(3)**

1. ______________________________

2. ______________________________

3. ______________________________

***b.** Despite being recorded in the 1980s, this track uses a variety of 1970s analogue synthesisers and drum machines. Describe the challenges when working with 1970s analogue synthesisers in a live situation compared to a software synthesiser on a DAW. **(3)**

______________________________

______________________________

______________________________

***c.** Identify an appropriate time in seconds for a vocal reverb, as used on this recording from 0'56". **(1)**

| **Reverb time** (s) | |
|---|---|

***d.** Describe how you would recreate the sound audible between 1'16" and 1'21" using:

i. Modern DAW technology. **(1)**

______________________________

ii. Analogue technology/tape. **(2)**

______________________________

______________________________

**Total for AS Level: 10 marks/Total for A Level: 10 marks**

# Question 2

**Track 2 – The Beatles: 'In My Life' (1965)**

***a.** Identify two features of the production of this track that show it was produced in the 1960s. (2)

1. ............................................................

2. ............................................................

**b.** The electric guitar on this recording is slightly distorted.

*i. Describe two different ways distortion could have been produced in the 1960s. (2)

............................................................

............................................................

ii. Draw a distorted version of the clean wave shown below. (1)

| Clean | Distorted |
| --- | --- |
| | |

**c.** The electric guitar in the opening of this track was recorded using a microphone. Draw a cross to identify where you would place the microphone on the speaker to create the brightest guitar sound. (1)

**d.** Doubletracking is used in this track to thicken the lead vocal. Explain how automatic doubletracking (ADT) could be achieved using DAW technology today. (4)

............................................................

............................................................

............................................................

............................................................

**Total for AS Level: 4 marks/Total for A Level: 10 marks**

# Question 3

**Track 3 – Billie Holiday: 'On The Sunny Side Of The Street' (1944)**

***a.** The vocal part in this recording is significantly louder than the other parts in the mix. Suggest two ways this could have been achieved in the 1940s when this track was recorded. **(2)**

1. ______

2. ______

***b.** A student wishes to re-record the lead vocal of this track to modern standards. They have chosen a condenser microphone in order to do so. Explain three reasons why the student might have made this choice. **(6)**

______

______

______

______

______

______

***c.** Due to limitations in the technology of the time, there are some problems with the capture in this recording. Two of the issues are given in the table below. State how the issues could be avoided if re-recording the track using modern equipment. **(2)**

| Problem with the capture | How could it be avoided? |
|---|---|
| **Piano sounds muddy** | |
| **Drums are not well balanced** | |

**Total for AS Level: 10 marks/Total for A Level: 10 marks**

## Question 4

**Track 4 – Galantis: 'Runaway (U&I)' (2014)**

***a.** Describe how the vocal parts have been processed to maintain interest between 0'35" and 1'11" in this track. (4)

***b.** Aside from dynamic processing, describe three processes the engineer might have used on this track during mastering. (3)

1.

2.

3.

**c.** Describe how compression has been used to add interest to the synth pads between 1'07" and 1'36". (3)

**Total for AS Level: 7 marks/Total for A Level: 10 marks**

---

**Total for AS Level Section A: 31 marks/Total for A Level Section A: 40 marks**

## SECTION B

**For AS Level answer Question 5 only; for A Level answer both Questions 5 and 6.**

**Write your answers in the spaces provided and use extra paper if required. In the actual exam more space will be provided in the answer booklet.**

At AS Level the extended response comparison question (question 5) is worth 16 marks. At A Level the question is worth 15 marks.

## *Question 5

**Track 5 – Avicii: 'Levels' (2011)**

**Track 6 – Avicii: 'Levels' (Skrillex remix) (2012)**

Compare the production techniques used in both versions.

**Total for AS Level: 16 marks/Total for A Level: 15 marks**

## Question 6 (A Level only)

**Track 7 – Jimi Hendrix: 'Purple Haze' (1967)**

Jimi Hendrix was a virtuosic performer and pioneer of the electric guitar.

Evaluate the impact of the electric guitar technology used in the production of this track and how it influenced electric guitar music through the 1970s.

**Total (A Level only): 20 marks**

**Total for AS Level Section B: 16 marks/Total for A Level Section B: 35 marks**

**Total for AS Level paper: 47 marks/Total for A Level paper: 75 marks**

## Practice Paper 2

# SECTION A

**Answer ALL questions.**

**Write your answers in the spaces provided.**

## Question 1

**Track 8 – Charlie Parker: 'Ornithology'**

***a.** When was this track recorded? Put a cross in the correct box. (1)

☒ **A** 1946

☒ **B** 1956

☒ **C** 1966

☒ **D** 1976

***b.** This recording uses a piano.

i. Identify three potential issues you might encounter when recording an upright piano. (3)

ii. Describe how you would use EQ to replicate the sound of the piano on this recording. (2)

***c.** Explain two processing techniques that could be used when remastering, to improve the sound of this track. (4)

1.

2.

**Total for AS Level: 10 marks/Total for A Level: 10 marks**

## Question 2

**Track 9 – Crowded House: 'Don't Dream It's Over' (1986)**

***a.** Other than reverb, identify two effects that are audible on the electric guitar in the introduction. (2)

1. ______________________________

2. ______________________________

***b.** This track was recorded on analogue multitrack tape in the late 1980s. There is audible hiss in the introduction.

i. Describe a precaution the engineer would have taken during recording in the 1980s to reduce this issue. (1)

______________________________

ii. Explain why the hiss on the recording gets worse at 0'10". (2)

______________________________

______________________________

***c.** Describe how the guitarist has created the sound audible at 1'12". (1)

______________________________

***d.** Identify the instrument playing the melody in the solo at 1'46". (1)

☒ **A** Rhodes piano

☒ **B** Clavinet

☒ **C** Hammond organ

☒ **D** Theremin

**e.** Describe how the player of the instrument above (identified in question d) changes the sound of the instrument when the chords start at 2'10". (3)

______________________________

______________________________

______________________________

**Total for AS Level: 7 marks/Total for A Level: 10 marks**

## Question 3

**Track 10 – Jean-Michel Jarre: 'Oxygene Part II' (1976)**

***a.** Many of the instrumental parts on the recording use delay.

i. Identify two ways of creating delay in 1976. **(2)**

1. ______________________________

2. ______________________________

ii. Describe two ways Jean-Michel Jarre could have used a single delay unit to apply delay to multiple instruments in 1976. **(2)**

1. ______________________________

2. ______________________________

***b**. Describe how Jean-Michel Jarre creatively uses synthesis in the unpitched sound effects audible between 0'11" and 0'37". **(6)**

______________________________

______________________________

______________________________

______________________________

______________________________

______________________________

**Total for AS Level: 10 marks/Total for A Level: 10 marks**

## Question 4

**Track 11 – Massive Attack: 'Angel' (1998)**

***a.** In this recording the snare drum plays on crotchet beat 3.

i. Identify an appropriate quantise resolution for the **bass part** between 0'10" and 0'19". (1)

☒ **A** 1/4

☒ **B** 1/8

☒ **C** 1/12

☒ **D** 1/16

ii. Identify a way you could use quantise to tighten the rhythm of a part while maintaining a natural sound. (1)

***b.** Complete the table below to describe how Massive Attack uses the stereo field to add interest to the recording. (2)

| Time reference | Use of stereo field |
|---|---|
| **0'10"–0'14"** | |
| **0'51"–0'56"** | |

***c.** Explain how Massive Attack uses ambience as a creative device in this extract. (6)

**Total for AS Level: 10 marks/Total for A Level: 10 marks**

**Total for AS Level Section A: 37 marks/Total for A Level Section A: 40 marks**

## SECTION B

**For AS Level answer Question 5 only; for A Level answer both Questions 5 and 6.**

**Write your answers in the spaces provided.**

At AS Level the extended response comparison question (question 5) is worth 16 marks. At A Level the question is worth 15 marks.

## *Question 5

**Track 12 – Nancy Sinatra: 'Bang Bang (My Baby Shot Me Down)' (1966)**

**Track 13 – Audio Bullys: 'Shot You Down' (2005)**

Compare the production techniques used in both versions.

**Total for AS Level: 16 marks/Total for A Level: 15 marks**

## Question 6 (A Level only)

**Track 14 – Daft Punk: 'One More Time' (2001)**

Evaluate the impact that dynamic processing technology has had on the production in this track, and the wider impact dynamic processing has had on electronic dance music since 2001.

**Total (A Level only): 20 marks**

**Total for AS Level Section B: 16 marks/Total for A Level Section B: 35 marks**

**Total for AS Level paper: 53 marks/Total for A Level paper: 75 marks**

## *Additional practice Question 5

Remember that Question 5 is worth 16 marks at AS Level and 15 marks at A Level.

**Track 15 – Pink Floyd: 'Another Brick in the Wall, Pt. 2' (1979)**

**Track 16 – Eric Prydz, Floyd: 'Proper Education' (radio edit) (2007)**

Compare the production techniques used in both versions.

**Total for AS Level: 16 marks/Total for A Level: 15 marks**

**COMPONENT 4:**

# Producing and analysing

## Overview

**Component 4 at both AS and A Level assesses your knowledge and understanding of editing, mixing and production techniques. During the exam, you will have to apply these skills to answer questions that are related to stem audio files and a MIDI file provided by the Edexcel exam board.**

**Summary of Component 4**

| AS Level Component 4 | A Level Component 4 |
| --- | --- |
| 1 hour 45 minutes exam paper<br>(with 10 minutes setting up time) | 2 hours 15 minutes exam paper<br>(with 10 minutes setting up time) |
| **Section A (68 marks)**<br>■ Five questions related to the audio and MIDI materials provided, which include both written questions and practical tasks<br>■ You will produce three bounces of the tasks you have completed on specific instrumental/vocal parts<br>■ One of these questions will be a guided mixdown of the materials to produce a final bounce | **Section A (85 marks)**<br>■ Five questions related to the audio and MIDI materials provided, which include both written questions and practical tasks<br>■ You will produce three bounces of the tasks you have completed on specific instrumental/vocal parts<br>■ One of these questions will be a guided mixdown of the materials to produce a final bounce |
| **Section B (16 marks)**<br>■ One extended response question focusing on a specific signal process, effect or music technology hardware unit | **Section B (20 marks)**<br>■ One extended response question focusing on a specific mixing scenario, signal path, effect or music technology hardware unit |
| **Total: 84 marks**<br>**35% of your AS Level** | **Total: 105 marks**<br>**35% of your A Level** |

## What will I have to do for Component 4?

**You will be expected to apply the knowledge and skills you have built up through your recording and composition work in Components 1 and 2, along with your study of music technology theory that relates to:**

- Editing, mixing and production techniques
- Recording and production techniques for both corrective and creative purposes
- Principles of sound and audio technology.

**In doing so, you will need to demonstrate your ability to:**

- Comment on the music production tools and techniques used to capture sounds, including musical instruments
- Use music production tools and techniques to create new sounds
- Use processing techniques to edit, correct and process audio and MIDI tracks

- Use your aural skills to identify and evaluate music technology elements in unfamiliar work and refine recordings
- Use processing techniques to produce a final balanced mix
- Apply language associated with musical elements in the context of music technology - for example, structure, timbre, texture, tempo, rhythm, melody, harmony, tonality and dynamics

**Additionally, at A Level you will need to demonstrate your ability to:**

- Make informed decisions about equipment by analysing and interpreting data, graphs and diagrams - in relation to, for example, frequency response, polar patterns and dynamic response
- Apply technical numeracy to make calculations in the context of music technology.

As part of the exam you will have access to your own computer, DAW, MIDI keyboard and headphones. You will not be able to access anything else on the computer, and you will have no access to the internet or local network. You will not be able to use a calculator or calculator software on the computer you are working on. You will be provided with your own copy of the stem files and an exam paper with instructions to tell you what you need to do.

**Stem files are the individual MIDI or audio files that make up a mix.**

You will bounce your work during the course of the exam. At the end of the session, your bounces and exam paper will be submitted to Edexcel.

## What will the exam look like?

### Section A questions

- **For both AS and A Level**, Section A will consist of five questions related to the audio and MIDI files provided, which will include both written responses and practical tasks
- You will be guided through a variety of processes, which require you to demonstrate both your practical and theoretical knowledge of music technology
- This will require you to problem-solve, think logically and find solutions as part of the tasks on the paper
- At the end of Section A, you will be provided with a number of tasks that you will have to complete in order to create an effective mix of the materials you have been given
- This will ultimately involve you combining all of the instruments/vocal parts to create a finished stereo mix
- This mix will be submitted to Edexcel at the end of the exam, along with your exam paper.

### Section B question

- **For AS Level**, you will answer an extended response question that will focus on a specific signal process, effect or music technology hardware unit
- **For A Level**, you will answer an extended response question that will focus on a specific mixing scenario, signal path, effect or music technology hardware unit
- As part of the question, you will be provided with a diagram, photograph or other stimulus; you will need to apply your knowledge of music technology to the scenario given in the question
- To achieve top marks, you will need to examine and dissect it, commenting on how it achieves (or does not achieve) its purpose, making judgements and presenting your own conclusions
- In doing this, you will justify your statements with the knowledge and understanding you have built up while completing your coursework and study as part of the course.

## Using this book to prepare for Component 4

- There are eleven Section A practice questions, and three Section B practice questions with mark schemes
- The questions for Section A will have audio associated with them in the actual exam, but in this book they are designed to help you assess your knowledge and understanding of the specification content for Component 4
- Use the mark schemes and indicative content provided to help you measure your progress and prepare yourself for the real exam.

### TIPS FOR COMPONENT 4

- You have a lot of control over the timings in this exam, so keep an eye on the clock
- Make sure you are using your time effectively, and that you are allocating enough time to the parts of the exam that are worth more marks
- Be careful not to focus too much on one task, trying to make your work perfect at the cost of running out of time for other questions
- Leave enough time for your question 5 final mix and question 6 extended response
- Include diagrams and graphs in your answers, as they provide detail and can score plenty of credit, especially if you label them with units and other annotations
- Make sure that if discussing controls on equipment you don't just reword the question – for example, you won't get any credit if, for a control labelled 'threshold' you write 'the threshold changes the threshold'
- Remember that in Component 4, the extended response question is worth just under 20% of the available marks on the paper. That relates to around 20 minutes of the exam time at AS Level and around 25 minutes of exam time at A Level
- Try to complete the extended response questions in this book within 20–25 minutes, to get a feel for exam conditions
- For your bounce of the final mix, make sure you follow the instructions in the final part of question 5 as to how your track should start and finish, being careful not to cut off the last note or the reverb tail
- Focus on what the question asks you to do and remember that you are sitting an exam, not trying to add whatever effects you want
- Adding extra effects or processes not required in the question might mask what the examiner is listening for and mean that you are not awarded marks for the work you have done. Equally, applying the wrong effects can mean that full credit might not be given, so marks could be lost
- Remember that you are demonstrating your ability to perform the specific effects and processing asked for
- The stem files are often mastered at deliberately varying volumes, so balance with your ears, not with your eyes on the faders!
- Listen to the overall mix: aim for loud drums with an audible kick, ensure you can hear all of the words in the vocal part; then gradually bring in the other tracks to produce an effective overall mix
- Watch your output level – use the mixer faders to set up your mix so it's sufficiently loud but not distorting
- You must not use any processing to master the track unless the question asks you to do so

**AS LEVEL AND A LEVEL**

The questions that follow are written to help you prepare for both levels of the course. Question numbers with an * next to them indicate that you need to be able to answer them for both AS and A Level. Those without an * are for A Level only.

# SECTION A

## Practice questions

**The questions on the next few pages are designed to help you prepare for Component 4. They will help you to apply your music technology skills, by discussing a diagram or other stimulus.**

**Try to complete the questions without reference to the mark scheme, then carefully review it afterwards to identify areas where you are less certain about the content or how to apply it. Then, make sure you know how to adapt or develop your answers to score full credit in an exam situation.**

## Question 1

### Microphones

The table below shows the position of the switches on a condenser microphone used to record a snare drum.

**a.** Identify the function of each switch and explain why each setting is being used. **(8)**

| Switch | Function | Justification |
|---|---|---|
| | (1) | (1) |
| | (1) | (2) |
| 0 -10dB | (1) | (2) |

**b.** The engineer plans to use a second microphone underneath the snare drum.
Identify an issue that they might encounter during mixing and suggest a possible solution. **(2)**

**Total for A Level: 10 marks**

## Question 2

### Capturing and editing sound

***a.** The diagram below shows a section of a vocal waveform captured using a microphone.

i. By drawing a cross on the wave below, identify appropriate start and end points to create a smooth loop so this sound sustains if a key is held. (2)

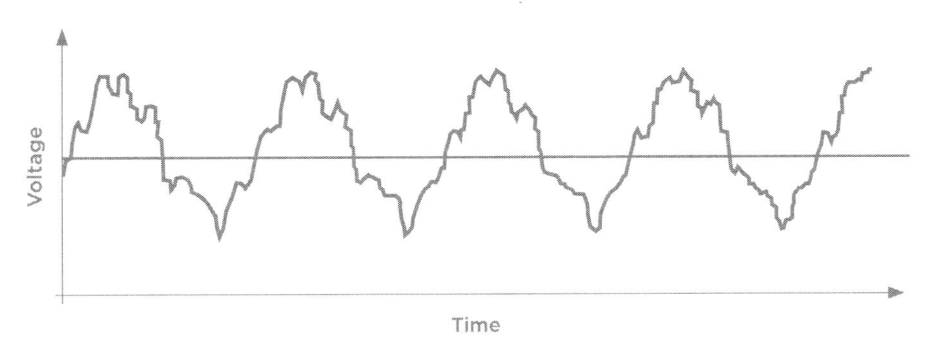


ii. Identify a way of avoiding a click when looping a waveform. (1)

*b.** Describe how compression could be used to increase a sample's sustain. (3)

**c.** A sound engineer wishes to capture a choir with a stereo microphone configuration. They have selected two possible microphone placements.

Compare the relative benefits and drawbacks of the following two microphone placements: (4)

**spaced pair/mid-side pair**

**Total for AS Level: 6 marks/Total for A Level: 10 marks**

## Question 3

**Synthesis – LFOs**

The diagram below shows the LFO section of a synthesiser.

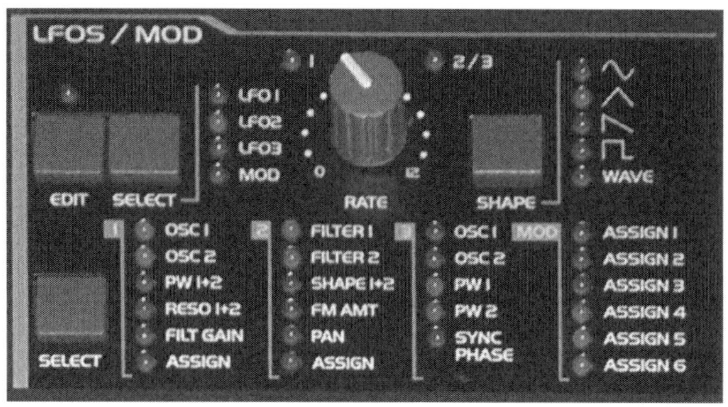


***a.** State the meaning of the term LFO. **(1)**

______________________________

***b.** Using LFO2, state how the synthesiser could be made to move from side to side of the stereo field. **(1)**

______________________________

***c.** Vibrato is a modulation effect. Identify the aspect of the sound that is modulated to create vibrato. **(1)**

______________________________

**d.** State the function of the depth and rate controls when creating a vibrato effect.

*Rate: ______________________________ **(1)**

Depth: ______________________________ **(1)**

**e.** Describe the difference in vibrato produced using square and sine wave shapes. **(2)**

______________________________

______________________________

**f.** i. Identify the function of the 'PW 1+2' parameter on LFO1. **(1)**

______________________________

ii. Draw a diagram to show the effect that altering this parameter would have on the waveform. **(2)**

**Total for AS Level: 4 marks/Total for A Level: 10 marks**

# Question 4

## Synthesis - Envelopes

***a.** The graph below shows the volume envelope of a sound produced on a synthesiser.

i. Label the sections of the envelope (4)

ii. Label the axes (2)

iii. Label when the key is pressed and released (2)

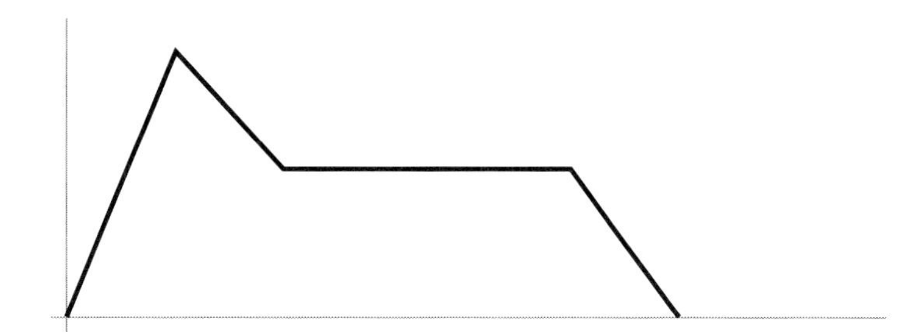

**b.** Describe the sound that would be created by the envelope drawn above when it is routed to the cut off frequency of a low pass filter on the synthesiser. (4)

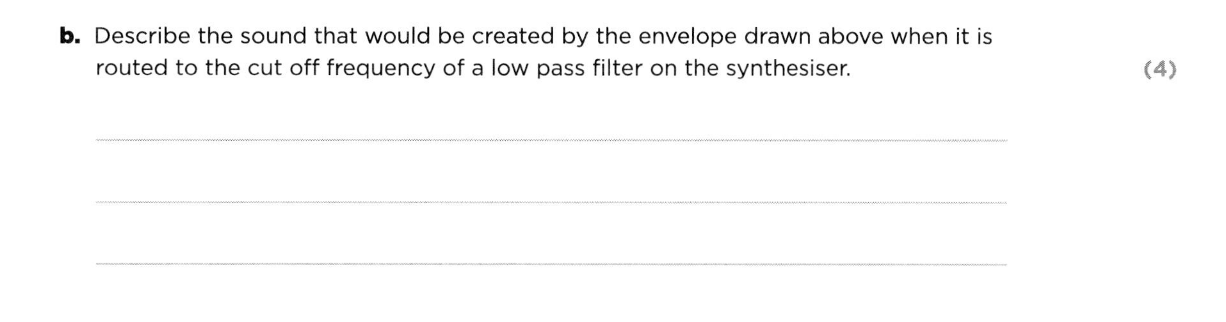

**Total for AS Level: 8 marks/Total for A Level: 12 marks**

# Question 5

## Equalisation

The parametric EQ plugin below has been used to process a vocal part.

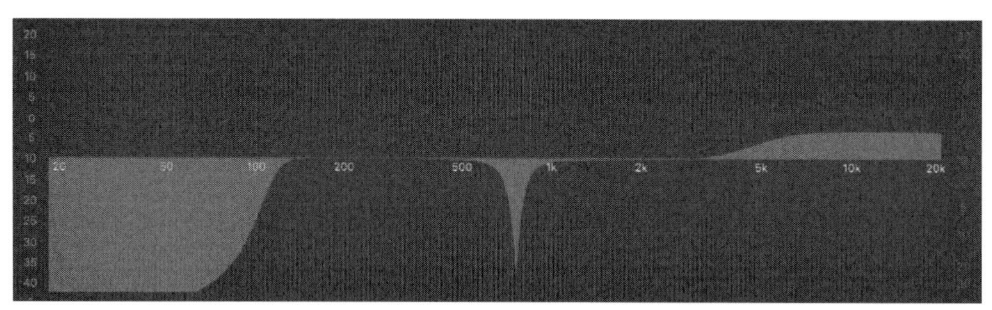


***a.** Describe three benefits of using a parametric EQ over a graphic EQ. **(3)**

1. ..........

2. ..........

3. ..........

***b.** In the table below, explain why the three EQ changes shown above have been chosen to process a lead vocal part. **(6)**

| Change | Justification |
|---|---|
| (1) | (1) |
| (1) | (1) |
| (1) | (1) |

***c.** Identify the centre frequency of the middle EQ change. **(1)**

..........

**Total for AS Level: 10 marks/Total for A Level: 10 marks**

## Question 6

### Delay

The picture below shows a plugin that recreates the sound of a Roland Space Echo analogue tape delay.

***a.** Describe five benefits of using a software plugin over an analogue tape delay unit. (5)

1. ______
2. ______
3. ______
4. ______
5. ______

***b.** Aside from using tape, identify another way delay could be added to a recording in the 1970s. (1)

______

**c.** Fill in the table below to describe the function of each feature of the plugin. (4)

| Plugin feature | Function |
|---|---|
| ***Peak level** | (1) |
| ***Repeat rate** | (1) |
| ***Input vol** | (1) |
| **Intensity** | (1) |

**Total for AS Level: 9 marks/Total for A Level: 10 marks**

# Question 7

## Dynamics processing

The picture below shows a noise gate.

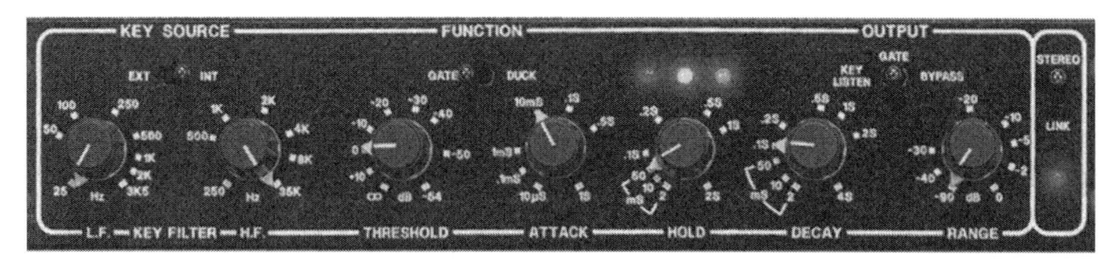


***a.** Describe the function of a noise gate. **(2)**

______________________________________________

______________________________________________

**b.** Describe the functions of the following noise gate controls. **(3)**

| Control | Function |
| --- | --- |
| ***Threshold** | (1) |
| **Gate/duck** | (1) |
| **Attack** | (1) |

***c.** Explain how you could use the controls on this gate to set up a synth part to play at the same time as the snare drum in a recording. **(5)**

______________________________________________

______________________________________________

______________________________________________

______________________________________________

______________________________________________

**Total for AS Level: 8 marks/Total for A Level: 10 marks**

## Question 8

### Reverb

A sound engineer is making a recording in a reflective space to create a convolution reverb.

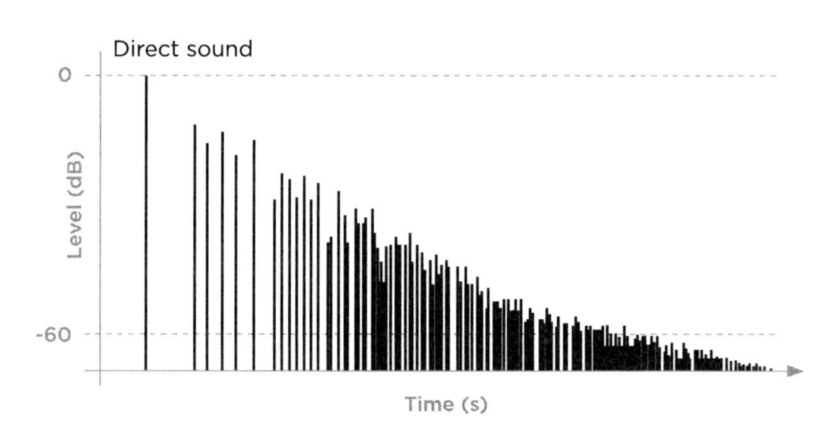


**a.** Label the following parameters on the graph: (4)

**$RT_{60}$** **pre delay** **early reflections** **reverb tail**

**b.** Describe how the graph would look different when recording an impulse response in a less reflective room. (1)

______________________________

**c.** State the meaning of the term 'convolution reverb'. (1)

______________________________

**d.** Describe four benefits of using a convolution reverb over an echo chamber. (4)

1. ______________________________
2. ______________________________
3. ______________________________
4. ______________________________

**Total for A Level: 10 marks**

# Question 9

### Numeracy and calculations

The frequency of wave 1 below is 100Hz.

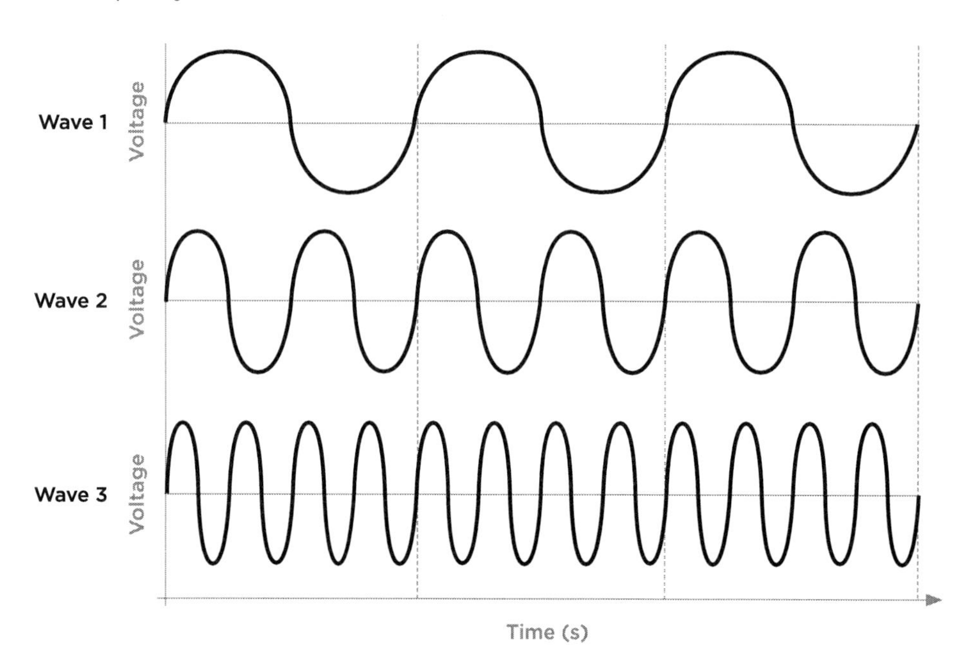


**a.** Label the amplitude of wave 1. (1)

**b.** Draw a wave that is 180 degrees out of phase with wave 1. (2)

**c.** Identify what you would hear if you played wave 1 and the wave you have drawn in part (b) at the same time, at the same amplitude. (1)

______________________________

**d.** Calculate the period of wave 1. Show your working. (2)

period ______________ s

**e.** Calculate the frequency of both waves below. Show your working.

i. Wave 2 (2)

frequency of wave 2 ______ Hz

ii. Wave 3 (2)

frequency of wave 3 ______ Hz

iii. Identify the musical relationship between waves 2 and 3. (1)

______

**f.** Calculate the frequency of a wave that is a perfect 5th above wave 1.
Show your working. (2)

frequency ______ Hz

**g.** Calculate the frequency of the sixth harmonic of wave 1. Show your working. (2)

frequency ______ Hz

**Total for A Level: 15 marks**

## Question 10

### Analogue and digital

**a.** Below is an analogue waveform. Label the axes on the waveform graph below. (2)

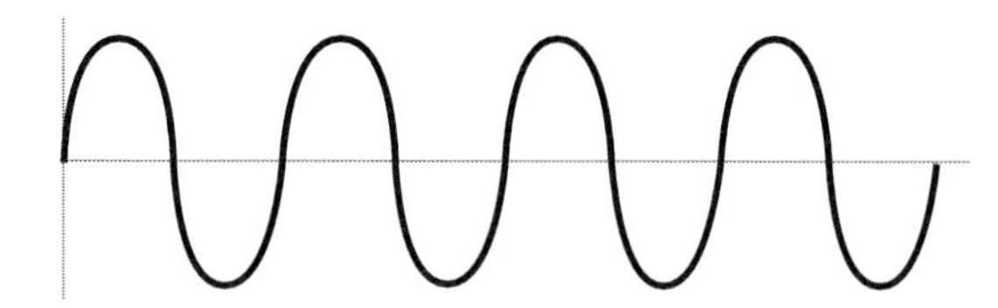

**b.** Give definitions for the following terms associated with digital audio.

Sample rate: ______ (1)

Bit depth: ______ (1)

**c.** The diagram below shows a small-scale digital sampling system.

i. Draw crosses on the diagram to indicate the digital samples that you would take if sampling the analogue wave at 2 bit/4Hz. The first one has been done for you. (3)

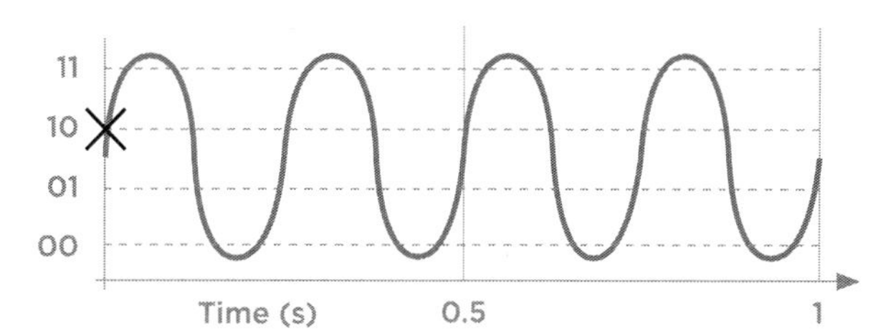


ii. Identify the binary values of the samples you have taken. (1)

______

iii. Given your answer to part i, evaluate why 4Hz is not a high enough sample rate to represent the analogue waveform and suggest a more appropriate value. (6)

______

______

______

______

______

iv. The bit depth used in part i is also too low. Identify the issue that arises in digital sampling when the bit depth is so low, and suggest a more appropriate value. (2)

______

______

v. A student has decided to record the sound at 96kHz. Explain why this is a poor choice. (2)

______

______

**Total for A Level: 18 marks**

# Question 11

### Drum machines and matrix editors

The matrix editor on the sequencer below shows a programmed drum beat.
The tempo is 120 bpm and the pattern lasts for two bars of $\frac{4}{4}$.

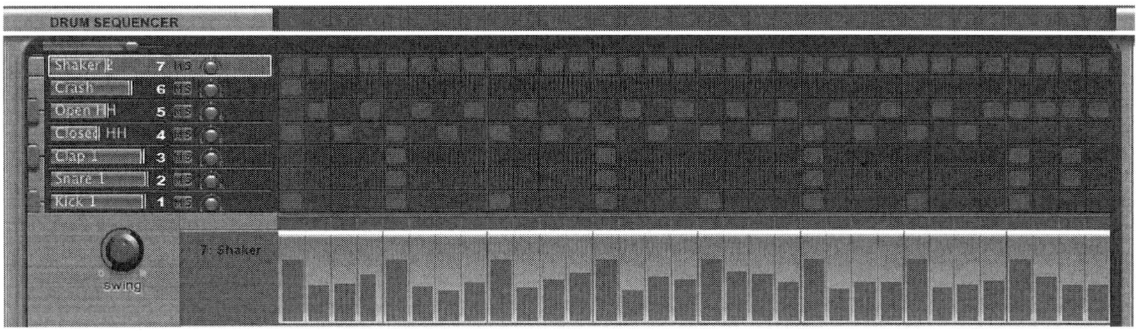

DRUM SEQUENCER
Shaker 2 7
Crash 6
Open HH 5
Closed HH 4
Clap 1 3
Snare 1 2
Kick 1 1
Swing
7: Shaker

***a.** In the pattern shown above, describe what is being played by each part of the drum kit by filling in the table below. **(5)**

| Part of Kit | Description |
|---|---|
| **Kick** | (1) |
| **Snare/clap** | (1) |
| **Hi-hat** | (1) |
| **Shaker** | (1) |
| **Crash** | (1) |

***b.** Identify two things that have been done to the drum beat to make it sound more realistic **(2)**

1. ............

2. ............

***c.** If the drum kit had been inputted live as MIDI data, explain how the rhythms of the part could be tightened up while maintaining some sense of freedom. **(3)**

............

............

............

**Total for AS Level: 10 marks/Total for A Level: 10 marks**

## SECTION B

### Extended response questions

At AS Level the extended response question is worth 16 marks. At A Level the question is worth 20 marks.

## *Question 12

**Recording vocals**

The picture below shows a microphone placement used to record a lead vocal part.

Evaluate the studio technique used.

**Total for AS Level: 16 marks/Total for A Level: 20 marks**

## *Question 13

### Compression

Evaluate the suitability of settings on the compression plugin below to control the volume of a vocal part in an electronic dance track.

**Total for AS Level: 16 marks/Total for A Level: 20 marks**

## Question 14 (A Level only)

**Synthesiser**

Evaluate the settings on this synthesiser plugin that make it suitable for use as a lead synthesiser in an electro track.

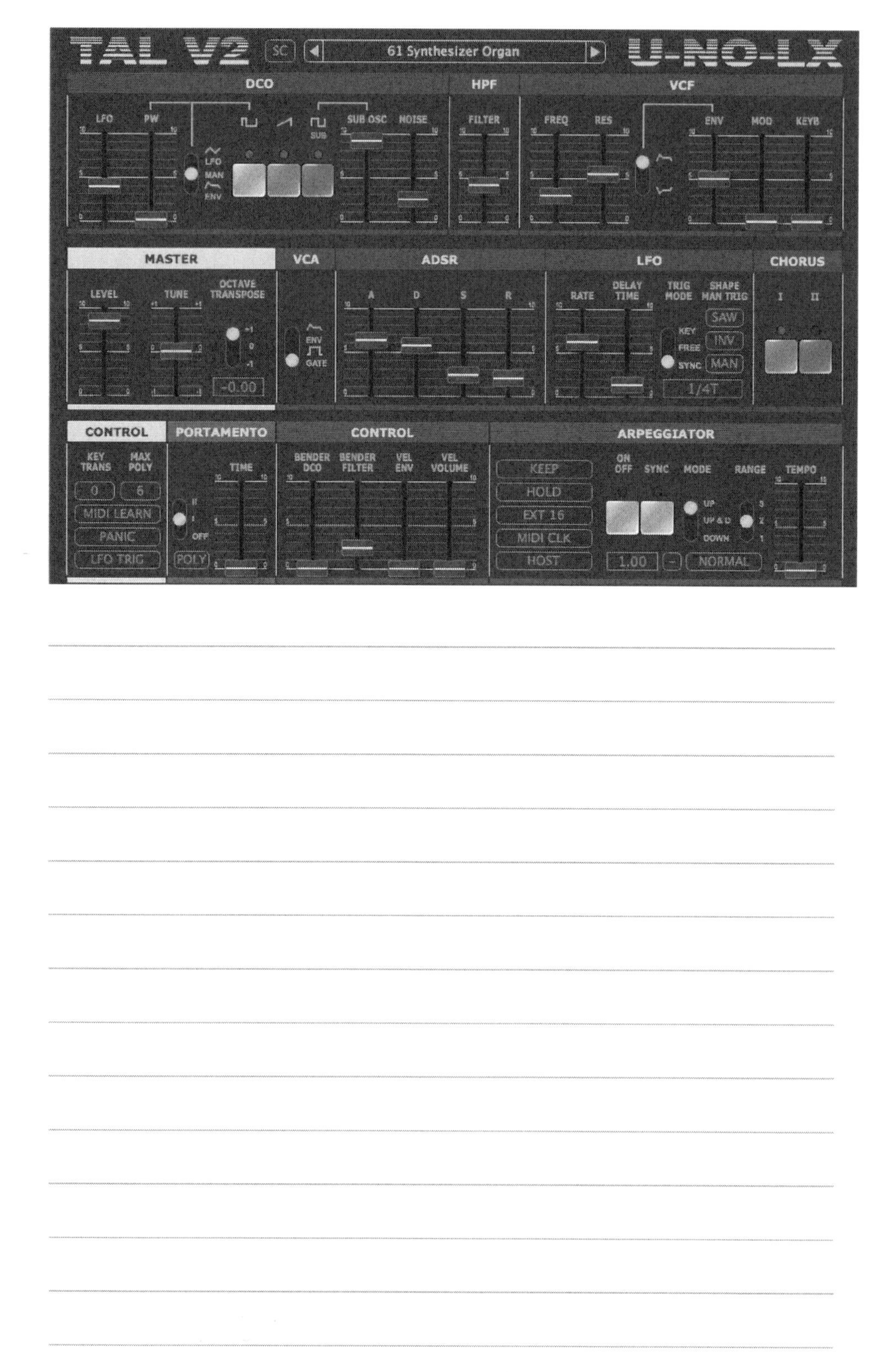


**Total for A Level: 20 marks**

# Answers

# Component 3

## Practice Paper 1

### SECTION A

Points in italic are for A Level only

## Question 1

**Ultravox: 'Vienna' (1981)**

***a.** Acceptable answers:

Electric/synthesised/white noise (1)

High reverb send amount (1)

Unusual panning/unconventional/R in intro and L in verse (1)

LFO/modulation used as sound decays (1)

**[max. 3 marks]**

***b.** Acceptable answers:

Analogue synthesisers often go out of tune in the heat (1)

Lack of presets/have to set up sounds manually (1)

Can't sync LFOs/have to listen to get them in time (1)

Can only have one synth unless you buy more/lack of multiple instances (1)

CV-gate more difficult to synchronise with other equipment (1)

**[max. 3 marks]**

***c.** Accept any value between 1 and 3 seconds (1)

***d.** i. Use DAW to reverse sample (1)

ii. Record cymbal onto tape (1)

Reverse tape/play tape backwards (1)

## Question 2

**The Beatles: 'In My Life' (1965)**

***a.** Acceptable answers:

Extreme/polarised panning/drums and vocals opposite (1)

Flange (allow phaser) (1)

Hiss/noise (1)

Plate reverb (1)

Constricted EQ on the vocal (1)

Clean/slightly overdriven/rhythm guitar (1)

Distant/muffled kick (1)

Jangly guitar sound (1)

**[max. 2 marks]**

**b.** *i. Acceptable answers:

Overdriving the amp (1)

Increasing the gain on the desk (1)

(Not slashing the cone)

**[max. 2 marks]**

ii.

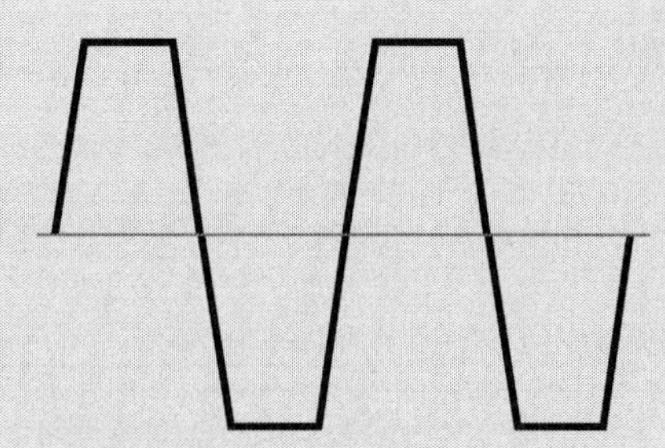

(Allow suitable soft clipped waveform) (1)

**c.** (1)

**d.** Acceptable answers:

Copy and paste the audio to another track (1)

Apply a short (1) 10–60ms (1) delay/time difference (1) to only one channel with no feedback (1)

Delay time shouldn't be too short otherwise phasing/flanging/comb filtering would occur (1)

**Allow:**

Apply slight (1) 5–15 cents (1) de-tuning/pitch shift (1) to one channel (1)

Pan (slightly) left and right (1)

**[max. 4 marks]**

## Question 3

**Billie Holiday: 'On The Sunny Side Of The Street' (1944)**

***a.** Spot mic on vocal, combine with other mics on a mixer and record to tape (1)

Move vocalist closer to single mic (1)

***b.** Acceptable answers:

See table on page 47: one mark is awarded for each point (max. 3) with a further mark for an explanation of the point (max. 3).

| | |
|---|---|
| Sensitive, giving effective capture of quiet sounds | Vocal is generally quietly delivered/quiet parts of vocal part |
| Flat/accurate/wide frequency response | To capture the full range of frequencies in the vocal part |
| Generally able to capture a brighter signal than dynamic microphones/ better high frequency response | Female voice has lots of high frequencies/ appropriate capture of high frequencies to give a breathy quality to the vocal |
| Good signal-to-noise ratio/high output volume | Low noise/reduce background noise/hiss |
| Wide dynamic response | Vocal has some louder bits so can capture full range of the part |

***c.**

| | |
|---|---|
| **Piano sounds muddy** | ■ Separate mic for piano<br>■ Record the piano on a separate track<br>■ Use two microphones on the piano for a stereo recording (1) |
| **Drums are not well balanced** | ■ Mic up each part separately<br>■ Multitrack individual drums (1) |

## Question 4

**Galantis: 'Runaway (U&I)' (2014)**

***a.** Acceptable answers:

Use of doubletracking/overdubbing multiple vocal layers (1)

Octaves (1)

Copy and paste of vocal syllables/repetition/samples (1)

Starts of words have reversed syllables (e.g. 0'49") (1)

Ambience effects (e.g. increased wet signal/send/reverb level at 1'03") (1)

Pitch shift across vocal gives artefacts (e.g. 0'51") (1)

Extreme pitch shifts of single words/phrases (e.g. pitch bend at 1'05") (1)

**[max. 4 marks]**

***b.** Acceptable answers:

Master EQ/match to commercial tracks/match other album tracks (1)

Control stereo width/mid side (1)

Radio edit/remove lengthy sections of drums at start/long solos (1)

Top and tail to leave short silence at the beginning and end without cutting reverb tail (1)

EQ/increase upper-mids and LFs to increase perceived loudness (1)

(Aural) exciter to increase brightness (1)

**[max. 3 marks]**

**c.** Acceptable answers:

Sidechain (1) compression/ducking – kick controlling ducking of bass/synths (1)

Mix compression/limiting (1) used to give high/loud overall master level (1)

Vocals/piano use heavy (1) compression/limiting (do not double credit 'limiting' unless reference to vox and mix) (1)

**[max. 3 marks]**

## SECTION B

Remember that in the exam you only have about 20 minutes for your essay for question 5. The mark schemes given in this book are more extensive, to cover as many points as possible and help you with your revision. At A Level make sure you allow enough time to answer both questions in this section.

## *Question 5

**Avicii: 'Levels' (2011)**
**Avicii: 'Levels' (Skrillex remix) (2012)**

**Total for AS Level: 16 marks – AO3 8 marks, AO4 8 marks**
**Total for A Level: 15 marks – AO3 5 marks, AO4 10 marks**

**Marking instructions**
Markers must apply the descriptors in line with the general marking guidance and the qualities outlined in the levels-based mark scheme below.

**Responses that demonstrate only AO3 without any AO4 should be awarded marks as follows:**

**AS Level:**

- Level 1 AO3 performance: 1-2 marks
- Level 2 AO3 performance: 3-4 marks
- Level 3 AO3 performance: 5-6 marks
- Level 4 AO3 performance: 7-8 marks.

**A Level:**

- Level 1 AO3 performance: 1 mark
- Level 2 AO3 performance: 2 marks
- Level 3 AO3 performance: 3 marks
- Level 4 AO3 performance: 4 marks
- Level 5 AO3 performance: 5 marks.

Content shown below is for AS and A Level. Content specific to A Level only is shown in italics.

**Indicative content guidance**
The indicative content below is not prescriptive and candidates are not required to include all of it. Other relevant material not suggested below must also be credited. Relevant points may include:

| AO3 | AO4 |
|---|---|
| **Capture** | |
| Avicii – sequenced on a DAW<br>Skrillex – sequenced on a DAW | Despite both being sequenced on a DAW, the two tracks are in different styles: the first evokes a commercial style of electronic dance music, the second is a dubstep remix |

| | |
|---|---|
| The vocal in the Avicii could be a sample or it could be sung live<br><br>The Avicii vocal part is sampled in the remix | New vocal recordings/samples are used in the Skrillex remix to lead into the drop. In the original, the sample for 'oh' is looped to create a sustained note underneath the vocal when it comes in (1'42"). The middle sustained part of the sample has been looped to create a sustained note where you can't hear a very obvious join |
| The vocal in the remix is pitch shifted (0'13") | Pitch shift means that the sampled vocal fits the key of the remix/vice versa. Extreme pitch shift can introduce artefacts to the sound. These are sometimes used creatively in electronic dance music (e.g. Galantis) |
| The instrumental parts in the remix are synthesised/electronic | The remix adds many new parts to create a new synthesised/ electronic accompaniment with a completely different musical structure to the Avicii track |
| **Sampling** | |
| The remix uses the vocal part of the original as a sample source | The original vocal could be a sample or recorded live.<br>If a sample, it has been cleaned up to better fit with the modern, synthesised parts. As the majority of other parts are electronic/sequenced, compression would be needed to ensure that the dynamic range of the vocal matches that of the electronic parts |
| The synthesiser riff also makes an appearance in the remix (could be replayed/interpolated) | The remix uses a small fragment of the synthesiser riff from the original at the start. The rhythm is changed and reverb is applied to integrate it into the mix. As a producer you could use a sample of the original to do this, or you could replay the synthesiser riff on a similar sounding bright synthesiser setting |
| Avicii is based on loops to build up textures and establish different sections | The Avicii track uses reverse cymbals as section transition effects, whereas the remix tends to use rhythmic build ups and progressive diminution |
| **Synthesis** | |
| The original uses an arpeggiator and bright synthesiser leads sound in octaves to create the hook | The synthesiser part is originally treated with a high pass filter, but low frequencies are gradually added back in as the cut off frequency is lowered. This creates a sense of build which is a common stylistic feature of electronic dance music, but a low pass filter is normally used rather than a high pass filter |
| The remix uses synthesis to create a 'wub'/'wobble' bass, with other synthesiser parts to create more interest | The Skrillex remix is in a dubstep style, and makes use of the characteristic 'wub'/'wobble' bass sound. The volume and filter cut off frequency of the synthesiser bass line have been manipulated, creating a repeated note/tremolo effect, which in this song is used to create a complex rhythm in the drops |
| *Many of the synthesiser notes have a short/clipped envelope in the remix* | *Many of the synthesiser notes here use envelopes with little or no release so they cut very suddenly/use gating to 'clip' synthesiser notes. This is a stylistic feature of dubstep, and is also true of the percussion sounds, and helps them to cut through the mix* |

| | |
|---|---|
| *The remix makes use of pitch bend* | *The Skrillex remix adds octave portamentos/pitch bends in the bass parts and synthesiser parts in the drop. Portamentos are also used towards the end of the extract on a high synthesiser part in the original* |
| **Effects** | |
| The original opening uses changing amounts of reverb on the arpeggiated synthesiser line | The synthesiser in the opening of the original changes in ambience over the whole section. It starts with less reverb, but the wet signal and reverb time are increased as the section progresses |
| Use of delay and reverb; the cymbal sound at the beginning of the original uses timed delay | Use of creative effects processing is stylistic of electronic dance music. There is timed delay at the start of the original, whereas the remix uses a very reverberant lead synth at the start to play the hook |
| Use of compression as a mix/creative effect | *Sidechain compression is used in the original to give rhythmic drive; this is a common feature of electronic dance music. It is audible on the synthesiser pads before the hook melody enters around 1'04". Use of compression here creates a ducking/pumping effect and gives rhythm for dancing* |

**AS Level: Levels based assessment grid:**

| Level | Mark | Descriptor |
|---|---|---|
| | **0** | ■ No rewardable material. |
| **Level 1** | **1–4** | ■ Demonstrates and applies limited knowledge and understanding of production techniques used, some of which may be inaccurate or irrelevant (A03)<br>■ Gives limited analysis and deconstruction of production techniques used, making limited comparisons between the two recordings and/or little attemot at chains of reasoning (A04) |
| **Level 2** | **5–8** | ■ Demonstrates and applies some knowledge and understanding of production techniques used, which is occasionally relevant but may include some inaccuracies (A03)<br>■ Gives some analysis and deconstruction of production techniques used, making some comparisons between the two recordings and/or simplistic chains of reasoninq (A04) |
| **Level 3** | **9–12** | ■ Demonstrates and applies clear knowledge and understanding of production techniques used, which is mostly relevant and accurate (A03)<br>■ Gives clear analysis and deconstruction of production techniques used, making clear comparisons between the two recordings and competent chains of reasoninq (A04) |
| **Level 4** | **13–16** | ■ Demonstrates and applies detailed knowledge and understanding of production techniques used, which is relevant and accurate throughout (A03)<br>■ Gives detailed and accurate analysis and deconstruction of production techniques used, making detailed comparisons between the two recordings and loqical chains of reasoninq (A04) |

**A Level: Levels based assessment grid:**

| Level | Mark | Descriptor |
|---|---|---|
| | 0 | ■ No rewardable material. |
| Level 1 | 1–3 | ■ Demonstrates limited knowledge and understanding of production techniques used, some of which may be inaccurate or irrelevant (AO3)<br>■ Gives limited analysis and deconstruction of production techniques used with little attempt at chains of reasoning (AO4)<br>■ Makes limited comparisons between the two recordings, with little or no conclusion. (AO4) |
| Level 2 | 4–6 | ■ Demonstrates some knowledge and understanding of production techniques used, which is occasionally relevant but may include some inaccuracies (AO3)<br>■ Gives some analysis and deconstruction of production techniques used with simplistic chains of reasoning (AO4)<br>■ Makes some comparisons between the two recordings, reaching unsupported conclusions. (AO4) |
| Level 3 | 7–9 | ■ Demonstrates clear knowledge and understanding of production techniques used, which is mostly relevant and accurate (AO3)<br>■ Gives clear analysis and deconstruction of production techniques used, with competent chains of reasoning (AO4)<br>■ Makes clear comparisons between the two recordings, reaching partially supported conclusions. (AO4) |
| Level 4 | 10–12 | ■ Demonstrates detailed knowledge and understanding of production techniques used, which is relevant and accurate (AO3)<br>■ Gives detailed and accurate analysis and deconstruction of production techniques used, with logical chains of reasoning on occasion (AO4)<br>■ Makes detailed comparisons between the two recordings, reaching well supported conclusions. (AO4) |
| Level 5 | 13–15 | ■ Demonstrates sophisticated and accurate knowledge of production techniques used throughout (AO3)<br>■ Gives sophisticated and accurate analysis and deconstruction of production techniques used, with logical chains of reasoning throughout (AO4)<br>■ Makes detailed comparisons between the two recordings, reaching sophisticated conclusions. (AO4) |

## **Question 6** (A Level only)

### Jimi Hendrix: 'Purple Haze' (1967)

**AO3 (5 marks)/AO4 (15 marks)**

**Marking instructions**
Markers must apply the descriptors in line with the general marking guidance and the qualities outlined in the levels-based mark scheme below.

**Responses that demonstrate only AO3 without any AO4 should be awarded marks as follows:**

- Level 1 AO3 performance: 1 mark
- Level 2 AO3 performance: 2 marks

- Level 3 AO3 performance: 3 marks
- Level 4 AO3 performance: 4 marks
- Level 5 AO3 performance: 5 marks.

**Indicative content guidance**
The indicative content below is not prescriptive and candidates are not required to include all of it. Other relevant material not suggested below must also be credited. Relevant points may include:

| AO3 | AO4 |
|---|---|
| Recorded on multitrack tape – audible hiss | While Hendrix would have recorded onto four-track tape, 1970s technology would allow for more guitar overdubs and 16/24 tracks. Bouncing down would have helped to give more flexibility in recording, but it would have built up hiss as tracks were bounced onto another |
| Some layering of guitar tracks/overdubs but limited tracks in 1967 | 16/24 track technology in the 1970s enabled the recording of more layers and avoided having to bounce down/gave more flexibility to mix after recording/bigger guitar sound by doubletracking and panning. Improved signal-to-noise ratio as avoided the need to bounce tracks |
| Stompboxes used to created distorted effects | Use of fuzz/distortion, stompboxes/Fuzz Face. Use of stompbox gives more flexibility with routing guitar effects. Modern guitar recordings could use similar technology as stompboxes have seen something of a resurgence in recent years, but amp integrated distortion and multi-effects units are also common |
| Fuzz/heavy distortion used on the guitar parts | In the 1970s distortion became easier to achieve; Hendrix tended to overdrive his amplifier to create distorted effects, whereas (e.g.) Marshall amps in the 1970s had a separate distortion channel |
| Although solid-state/transistor technology existed in the late 1960s and 1970s, transistor amps had reliability issues, and use of valve amplification and so soft clipping (for distortion), was common. In the 1970s transistor amps became more common | Valve amps have a 'warmer tone'; many experienced guitarists prefer this to the harsher, hard clipping exhibited by transistor amps that exhibit hard clipping<br>**Original signal** Threshold<br>**Soft clipping** Distortion<br>**Hard clipping** |
| Hendrix was a virtuosic guitarist and used many techniques to play the instrument | Hendrix uses a number of tremolo arm effects on the song. At the time, extensive tremolo arm use could lead to detuning of the instrument. Floyd Rose tremolo arm systems and locking nuts helped to remedy this |
| Hendrix uses an octave pedal in the solo | This could have been created in the 1970s (and 60s with varispeed) using a pedal, or using varispeed tape, where music is recorded with the tape machine slowed down or speeded up. This also would change the length of the solo/timbre (e.g. The Beatles, 'In My Life' piano solo) |

**Levels based assessment grid:**

| Level | Mark | Descriptor |
|---|---|---|
| | 0 | ■ No rewardable material. |
| Level 1 | 1–4 | ■ Demonstrates limited knowledge and understanding of production techniques/technology used, some of which may be inaccurate or irrelevant (AO3)<br>■ Applies limited analysis and deconstruction of production techniques/ technology used in the recording with little attempt at chains of reasoning (AO4)<br>■ Makes limited connections between the production techniques/ technology used in the recording and their wider impact (AO4)<br>■ Makes limited evaluative and/or critical judgements about the wider impact of the production techniques/technology used in the recording. (AO4) |
| Level 2 | 5–8 | ■ Demonstrates knowledge and understanding of production techniques/ technology used, which are occasionally relevant but may include some inaccuracies (AO3)<br>■ Applies some analysis and deconstruction of production techniques/ technology used in the recording, with simplistic chains of reasoning (AO4)<br>■ Makes some connections between the production techniques/technology used in the recording and their wider impact (AO4)<br>■ Makes some evaluative and/or critical judgements about the wider impact of the production techniques/technology used in the recording. (AO4) |
| Level 3 | 9–12 | ■ Demonstrates clear knowledge and understanding of production techniques/technology used, which are mostly relevant and accurate (AO3)<br>■ Applies clear analysis and deconstruction of production techniques/ technology used in the recording, which is mostly detailed, with competent chains of reasoning (AO4)<br>■ Makes valid connections between the production techniques/technology used in the recording and their wider impact (AO4)<br>■ Makes clear evaluative and critical judgements about the wider impact of the production techniques/technology used in the recording. (AO4) |
| Level 4 | 13–16 | ■ Demonstrates detailed knowledge and understanding of production techniques/technology used, which are relevant and accurate (AO3)<br>■ Applies detailed and accurate analysis and deconstruction of production techniques/technology used in the recording, with logical chains of reasoning on occasion (AO4)<br>■ Makes detailed and valid connections between the production techniques/ technology used in the recording and their wider impact (AO4)<br>■ Makes detailed and valid evaluative and critical judgements about the wider impact of the production techniques/technology used in the recording. (AO4) |
| Level 5 | 17–20 | ■ Demonstrates sophisticated and accurate knowledge and understanding of production techniques/technology used throughout (AO3)<br>■ Applies sophisticated and accurate analysis and deconstruction of production techniques/technology used in the recording and logical chains of reasoning throughout (AO4)<br>■ Makes sophisticated and valid connections between the production techniques/technology used in the recording and their wider impact (AO4)<br>■ Makes sophisticated and valid evaluative and critical judgements about the wider impact of the production techniques/technology used in the recording. (AO4) |

## Practice Paper 2

# SECTION A

Points in italic are for A Level only

## Question 1

**Charlie Parker: 'Ornithology'**

***a.** A (1)

***b.** i. Acceptable answers:

Hammer noise/pedal noise (1)
Distortion (1)
Spill from headphones (1)
Control of ambience (1)
*Phase problems/stereo image* (1)
**[max. 3 marks]**

ii. Cut/reduce volume of low frequencies (1)
Cut/reduce volume of high frequencies (1)
Band pass filter/(semi-)parametric EQ to remove high and low frequencies (1)
High shelf cut (1)
Low shelf cut (1)
Allow: high pass filter (1)
**[max. 2 marks]**

***c.** Acceptable answers:

One mark is awarded for each point/process (max. 2) with a further mark for an explanation of the point (max. 2).

| | |
|---|---|
| Use EQ/filtering | To alter the frequency range to compensate for the lack of low/high frequency content or to add clarity to different parts e.g. saxophone/piano |
| Use a high pass filter/EQ/ de-noiser | To reduce hum/rumble |
| Use a low pass filter/EQ/ de-noiser | To reduce hiss |
| Use compression | To make the overall track louder (reference to overall volume, not individual parts) |
| Use compression | To reduce the dynamic range |
| Use a stereo spreader/stereo reverb | To enhance the stereo image/add stereo to a mono recording |

## Question 2

### Crowded House: 'Don't Dream It's Over' (1986)

***a.** Delay (1)

Chorus (1)

(Light) distortion/overdrive (1)

**[max. 2 marks]**

***b.** i. High gain to achieve good signal to tape/signal-to-noise ratio when recording onto the tape (1) Leave little to no headroom (1) Drive the tape a little to ensure good level (1)

**[max. 1 mark]**

ii. Unused tracks (e.g. bass) muted in introduction (1)

Reduces the number of tracks producing hiss in the mix (1)

***c.** Tremolo arm/whammy bar (1)

***d.** C (1)

**e.** Acceptable answers:

Increases rate (1) and depth (1) of modulation (1)

Allow: more (1) modulation instead of rate/depth

Vibrato/chorale/tremolo/rotary (1)

Leslie speaker (1)

Drawbars opened up (1)

More harmonics/high frequencies (1)

**[max. 3 marks]**

## Question 3

### Jean-Michel Jarre: 'Oxygene Part II' (1976)

***a.** i. Tape delay (1)

Bucket brigade delay (1)

ii. Bus send from mixing desk channels (1)

Overdub each instrument with delay applied, maintaining same settings (1)

***b.** White noise (1) sweeps (1)

LFO (1) with changing rate (1)

Both effects control low pass (1) filter (1) cut off frequency (1) and are *resonant* (1)

Both effects rise and fall/increasing and decreasing rate and/or cut off (1)

**[max. 6 marks]**

## Question 4

**Massive Attack: 'Angel' (1998)**

***a.** i. D (1)

ii. Acceptable answers:

Percentage quantise (1)

Iterative quantise (1)

Include/exclude (1)

**[max. 1 mark]**

***b.** Acceptable answers:

| Time reference | Use of stereo field |
|---|---|
| **0'09" – 0'13"** | Delayed percussion/click sound panned L (1) |
| **0'50" – 0'54"** | Stereo effect on guitar/stereo reverb (1) |

***c.** Acceptable answers:

One mark is awarded for each point (max. 3) with a further mark for an explanation of the point (max. 3).

| | |
|---|---|
| Bass/electronic snare have no reverb | Opening is very dry (0'00") |
| Delayed signal has more reverb/fades into the distance by reducing high frequencies | Spot effects make sounds more distant (0'10", 0'38") |
| Guitar feedback has more reverb along with background FX | Background sounds are further back in the mix than the instruments, which creates a sense of space (1'00") |
| Longer decay time on the vocal reverb/ higher send amount | Lead vocal is more ambient (1'08") |

## SECTION B

**Extended response mark schemes**

Remember, the extended response and longer answer mark schemes in this book contain what we call 'indicative content'. This means that the answers given are not exhaustive, and that the examiner will also give credit for points that are valid but that are not listed in the mark scheme.

There are further practice questions in the *Rhinegold Education A Level Music Technology Revision Guide*, and the AS Level edition, along with model answers and guidance on improving your work.

## *Question 5

**Nancy Sinatra: 'Bang Bang (My Baby Shot Me Down)' (1966)**
**Audio Bullys: 'Shot You Down' (2005)**

**Total for AS Level: 16 marks - AO3 8 marks, AO4 8 marks**
**Total for A Level: 15 marks - AO3 5 marks, AO4 10 marks**

**Marking instructions**
Markers must apply the descriptors in line with the general marking guidance and the qualities outlined in the levels-based mark scheme below.

**Responses that demonstrate only AO3 without any AO4 should be awarded marks as follows:**

**AS Level:**

- Level 1 AO3 performance: 1-2 marks
- Level 2 AO3 performance: 3-4 marks
- Level 3 AO3 performance: 5-6 marks
- Level 4 AO3 performance: 7-8 marks.

**A Level:**

- Level 1 AO3 performance: 1 mark
- Level 2 AO3 performance: 2 marks
- Level 3 AO3 performance: 3 marks
- Level 4 AO3 performance: 4 marks
- Level 5 AO3 performance: 5 marks.

Content shown below is for AS and A Level. Content specific to A Level only is shown in italics.

**Indicative content guidance**

The indicative content below is not prescriptive and candidates are not required to include all of it. Other relevant material not suggested below must also be credited. Relevant points may include:

| AO3 | AO4 |
|---|---|
| **Capture and instrumentation** | |
| Nancy Sinatra version is captured using microphones/ Audio Bullys version is sequenced in a DAW | The Nancy Sinatra would have been recorded live, whereas the Audio Bullys version would have been sequenced in a DAW, using the vocal samples from the original, and recording more vocal samples. The original creates a 'live' feel by using only vocals and electric guitar with little overdubbing and processing. There is less hiss on the Audio Bullys version as it has been recorded digitally (audible at the start of each track). Digital recording has a greater signal-to-noise ratio than analogue tape. Sometimes hiss is used as a creative effect (see below, audible at the start of the remix), whereas in the original, it is a product of the recording process. The hiss on the remix is used to cover up the hiss of the original and to make it sound 'lo-fi' |
| There is no synthesis in the original; electric guitar and vocals/Audio Bullys version adds synthesiser layers and a new synthesiser bass line, with a number of synthesiser effects | The electric instruments/synthesisers in the remix could either have been recorded using DI techniques, or could have been DAW plugins. Both of these techniques would minimise unwanted noise in the mix. The instrumentation is indicative of each track's style; the original as a pop ballad and the remix as electronic dance music |
| Unwanted hiss and restricted frequency range is present in the original | The remix has more high and low frequency content; this is indicative of mixing trends in the 2000s when it was produced, compared to the restricted frequency range in the original, which is lacking these frequencies (most audible when comparing the start of the original with around 1'24" in the remix) |
| **Sampling** | |
| The Audio Bullys version repeats the word 'down' and uses it as a sample leading into the chorus<br>Other single words are sampled from the hook<br>'Shot me down' is used as a sampled hook in the remix | The remix is sequenced and makes use of both longer samples that are similar to the Nancy Sinatra version, and heavily edited samples where single words and phrases are repeated to create build ups and breakdowns. In the remix, these short vocal samples are used to create rhythmic effects ('down' – 1'24" onwards) whereas in the original the melody line uses a melodic and rhythmic hook ('bang bang' – 0'24"). The sample of 'down' is cut harshly in the remix and it clicks. Zero crossing editing or fading would remove this, but it might lose some rhythmic impact. Samples of gunshots (0'45") are used in the remix to reflect the lyrics of the original, and as rhythmic devices |

| **Effects** | |
|---|---|
| In the original an electric guitar is used with a tremolo effect | Tremolo is used on the electric guitar throughout the original, and this forms part of the sample in the remix. In the 1960s the tempo could not be tempo synced to the timing of the vocal; this is possible using the modern technology in the remix |
| Reverb is applied to the vocals in the original | The ambience in the original is inconsistent. The guitar part is quite dry whereas the vocal has lots of reverb (0'12"), whereas the Audio Bullys version mostly has more contemporary treatment of reverb/ambience. However, as the sample is taken from the original, the reverb is still present on the vocal (0'57") |
| The Audio Bullys remix uses delay as a creative effect | Some of the samples (e.g. gunshots) have timed delay applied (for example 0'45", with a *high level of feedback*). These create interesting rhythmic effects |
| The guitar and vocal in the original are panned left/central respectively | The panning in the original is unconventional and indicative of early stereo technology, whereas in the remix, the guitar's polarised panning is not present and vocal and guitar sit central (more conventional/contemporary standards - 0'46"). DAW technology enables greater control of the stereo image and effects/processing to use it creatively |
| There is more compression/a narrower dynamic range in the Audio Bullys remix | The sequenced drums in the remix are heavily compressed, which makes sure that the transients cut through the mix, as appropriate to an electronic dance style. There are no drums in the original track. Compression is prominent in the remix, giving a punchy dynamic/pumping (1'24") . The average volume of the remix is louder; this is indicative of the 'loudness wars' in music |
| In the remix, distortion is added to the samples from the original | There is an audible difference between the quality of the recording in the remix. This is used as a creative effect (e.g. hiss at start, sample at 0'46"). It is used to make the samples seem more 'retro'/to acknowledge they are old. Before we hear the vocal for the first time, hiss appears and disappears (0'56"). This is used to 'prepare' us for the sound of the sample from the Nancy Sinatra song. The sections are very different, and this is amplified rather than integrated, with a clear divide between the samples and the new material |

**The AS Level and A Level levels based assessment grids are given on pages 50-51.**

## Question 6 (A Level only)

**Daft Punk: 'One More Time' (2001)**

**AO3 (5 marks)/AO4 (15 marks)**

**Marking instructions**

Markers must apply the descriptors in line with the general marking guidance and the qualities outlined in the levels-based mark scheme below.

**Responses that demonstrate only AO3 without any AO4 should be awarded marks as follows:**

- Level 1 AO3 performance: 1 mark
- Level 2 AO3 performance: 2 marks
- Level 3 AO3 performance: 3 marks
- Level 4 AO3 performance: 4 marks
- Level 5 AO3 performance: 5 marks.

**Indicative content guidance**

The indicative content below is not prescriptive and candidates are not required to include all of it. Other relevant material not suggested below must also be credited. Relevant points may include:

| AO3 | AO4 |
|---|---|
| Compression to even out dynamic range/avoid distortion | Electronic instruments have a narrower dynamic range than acoustic instruments. Acoustic instruments therefore tend to need more compression in the mix. Vocals in this mix are heavily compressed to help them cut through the mix. It is very easy to change the amount of compression applied to any part, and the effect is relatively easy to add or remove/non-destructive |
| Too much compression/over compression can cause ducking on the mix | Sidechain compression is used creatively throughout the mix, with the kick drum creating a 'ducking' or 'pumping' effect across the mix. This is a characteristic feature of electronic dance music. It is particularly audible on the horn and pad parts around 0'47", and is stylistic to electronic music, providing rhythmic movement. Settings used to create this particular compression would need to be a low threshold and relatively high ratio, with quick attack and release. 'Peak' mode works more effectively than RMS. In this track the horns and pad(s) duck quickly in response to the kick drum four-to-the-floor pattern (e.g. 1'34"). Use of attack/release can help to make the music push forward or drag. A badly judged release time can destroy the rhythmic drive of a song. The sidechain compression does not cause this track to drag, so the attack and release times are well set. Artists such as David Guetta used sidechain gating and compression creatively, to create synthesiser lines and ducking effects from percussion rhythms/drum parts |
| Modern music is heavily compressed, which makes it seem louder overall/limiting<br>Volumes of album tracks can be matched using mix compression/limiting | A brickwall/∞:1 limiter at end of chain prevents clipping/going above threshold peaking at around -0.1dB to -1dB to allow headroom. There is a trend that masters are getting louder; this means they have less dynamic range and they stand out on radio. This is increasingly important when recordings are played on small/phone speakers. It is beneficial for low quality streamed audio to have a smaller dynamic range. Streaming became more popular from the late 2000s onwards as internet speeds increased. Listeners are used to hearing louder tracks, which means that producers aspire to do this, or compare their mixes to commercial masters to ensure comparable levels. 'Loudness wars'. Streaming services such as Spotify can automatically match the loudness of different tracks to maintain a comparable playback level. This means that streaming is reversing the trend of loud masters as track volumes are increased or decreased based on an average level, so a song with quieter sections might ultimately play back louder than a consistently loud master |

| | |
|---|---|
| Can be applied using plugins or hardware equipment | Compressors can be used as hardware units; producers have often favoured hardware compressors that can apply compression at a master stage. DAWs also come bundled with compressors and multiple instances of these can be used on one track. DAW plugins sometimes emulate hardware compressors and gates. Classic mix compressors/with valves/warm sound, e.g. Teletronix LA-2A |
| Noise gating to remove noise/ quiet sounds | In some electronic dance styles, gates can be sidechained/keyed gate to create synthesiser rhythms from drum/percussion parts etc. Silence is used in various places in the track, where parts drop out and the texture changes, so it is important that any quiet noise is removed (e.g. 0'59", 1'29"). The scissor tool could also be used to remove noise for greater control |

The A Level levels based assessment grid is given on page 53.

## *Additional practice Question 5

**Pink Floyd: 'Another Brick In The Wall, Pt. 2' (1979)**
**Eric Prydz, Floyd: 'Proper Education' (radio edit) (2007)**

**Total for AS Level: 16 marks - AO3 8 marks, AO4 8 marks**
**Total for A Level: 15 marks - AO3 5 marks, AO4 10 marks**

**Marking instructions**
Markers must apply the descriptors in line with the general marking guidance and the qualities outlined in the levels-based mark scheme below.

**Responses that demonstrate only AO3 without any AO4 should be awarded marks as follows:**

**AS Level:**

- Level 1 AO3 performance: 1-2 marks
- Level 2 AO3 performance: 3-4 marks
- Level 3 AO3 performance: 5-6 marks
- Level 4 AO3 performance: 7-8 marks.

**A Level:**

- Level 1 AO3 performance: 1 mark
- Level 2 AO3 performance: 2 marks
- Level 3 AO3 performance: 3 marks
- Level 4 AO3 performance: 4 marks
- Level 5 AO3 performance: 5 marks.

Content shown below is for AS and A Level. Content specific to A Level only is shown in italics.

**Indicative content guidance**

The indicative content below is not prescriptive and candidates are not required to include all of it. Other relevant material not suggested below must also be credited. Relevant points may include:

| AO3 | AO4 |
| --- | --- |
| **Capture** | |
| Original captured using mics and recorded live on analogue multitrack tape | A choir is recorded in the original (1'05"); multitracking could have been used to layer up a smaller group of singers to create this effect. *You could use an XY pair/coincident pair/other stereo mic technique to do this.* Layering lots of recordings could mean that the hiss builds up on the multitrack recording. The remix has less noise than the original because it uses a DAW/digital technology |
| Remix is faster than the original | Remix is faster than the original; the lead vocal and sampled guitar parts are time stretched to play them faster. This would be achieved now on a DAW, which means that pitch and time can be independently controlled. In the late 1970s when this track was originally released, it would have been achieved using tape, which would affect both pitch and time. The faster tempo in the remix makes the song more appropriate for the electronic dance music style and for dancing to |
| Live/recorded vocal in the original | The vocal stem part from the original is used to form the vocal for the remix. It is mostly used in order, with some phrases repeated or used in different places, particularly in the build up around 2'22". The use of the vocal stem in mostly the same order in the remix gives a clear musical link to the original |
| **Sampling** | |
| Original uses some sampled sound effects; these would have been recorded and replayed on tape | Sound FX used in original; created from tape-based sounds (playground noise, phone ringing at end 3'20" onwards). These are not reproduced in the remix, but small fragments of audio from the original are used and manipulated with spot effects (e.g. the delay/reverb on 'alone' at 2'57" and 'education' at 3'08" which is repeated and high pass filtered). The manipulation/processing of fragments of vocal from the original gives a musical sense of build in the remix |
| The remix is built upon a vocal stem from the original, along with parts of the guitar | The verse in the remix uses primarily new synthesised parts against the vocal stem file. At the beginning, some samples of the original are used, but these are removed gradually as the piece progresses, leaving mostly new synthesised parts and providing further opportunities for textural build in these parts. The new material is therefore further developed rather than simply relying on the original loop. This is a stylistic feature of electronic dance music and remixes, and, at the end of a track, can also facilitate mixing into the next song. The chorus brings some of the original guitar parts back. This maintains a strong link to the original track, and emphasises a catchy chorus hook |

| **Synthesis** | |
|---|---|
| Synthesiser pads replace the guitar chords in the remix<br>Synthesiser bass replaces the bass guitar in the remix | In the remix, synthesiser layers/pads added to replace the guitar in the original. These parts in the remix develop over the course of a vocal phrase; a low pass filter is used to make the sound gradually brighter by automating the cut off frequency. There is a syncopated synthesiser bass part in the remix that uses stereo delay effects/panned layers in the verse. This provides rhythmic interest and contrast |
| Hammond organ used in original at 2'14" to accompany the guitar solo | The Hammond organ is the solo of the original; a Leslie speaker is used to create a vibrato/tremolo/chorus effect that changes in rate during the solo to create different patterns of modulation. This gives a sense of movement to the timbre |
| **Effects** | |
| The remix uses filtering to create build and add interest | A low pass filter is used on the mix of the remix around 2'05", with the cut off frequency gradually increasing to add build. At the same time 'another brick in the wall' is used in isolation, delayed with a short delay time and high feedback level. This is the breakdown section, and the feedback creates a build into the final chorus. The use of filtering also gives a dynamic difference between different sections, and helps to give clarity to the structure of the electronic dance remix |
| There is a long audible reverb tail on the vocals at the ends of phrases in the original. This is more audible because the other parts drop out (e.g. 1'01")<br>The group vocal in the second verse/chorus of the original is more reverberant (1'06") | Long reverb at the ends of each section in the original; long reverb time. In 1979 this would have been produced using an echo chamber or a plate reverb. As this effect is on the vocal stem track, it also occurs in the remix. In the original, the guitar solo has a longer reverb than the other tracks and is lightly distorted. There is no guitar solo in the remix; the remix focuses on the verse/chorus music and changing instrumentation/effects/textures between sections. Choir vocal in verse 2 and chorus 2 of the original is very reverberant. As the stem track is used, this is also the case in the remix. A large choir would usually be recorded in a reverberant space to create this effect. These contrasts in ambience add musical interest |
| Distorted guitar in original | The same sampled (distorted) guitar part is used in the remix, but distorted synth layers are also added (e.g. synth bass note that fades in around 0'15"). The distortion makes the signal brighter and gives more power. It also brings the part forward in the mix, giving a fuller frequency spectrum and thus fuller mix |
| The average volume of the remix is much louder than the original | Modern masters are heavier in LFs and HFs compared to older masters. They are also more heavily compressed, and this is shown in the overall difference in dynamics between the two pieces of music. Compression is also used as a creative effect to add pumping/ducking to the mix. *Sidechain compression is stylistic to electronic dance music and provides rhythmic movement. This occurs on the filter sweeps before the chorus* |

**The AS Level and A Level levels based assessment grids are given on pages 50-51.**

# Component 4

## SECTION A

## Question 1

### Microphones

**a.** Acceptable answers:

| Switch | Function | Justification |
|---|---|---|
| ◯ ▭ ○ | Polar pattern switch (1) | Set to cardioid (1) to reduce ambience (1) from the room (1) to avoid background noise/ spill (1) **(max. 2)** |
| — ▭ ⌐ | Rumble filter/ high pass filter (1) | Removing spill/reducing capture of kick drum (1) |
| 0 ▭ -10dB | Pad/ attenuation/ sensitivity (1) | Snare has high SPL (1) so pad reduces microphone's sensitivity (1) **(max. 2)** |

**b.** Acceptable answers:

Phase problems/destructive interference/frequency cancellation/comb filtering/ would cancel out (1)

Invert phase on mixer/invert polarity/use DAW to flip phase during or after recording/ use phase reverse adapter (1)

## Question 2

### Capturing and editing sound

***a.** i. Example:

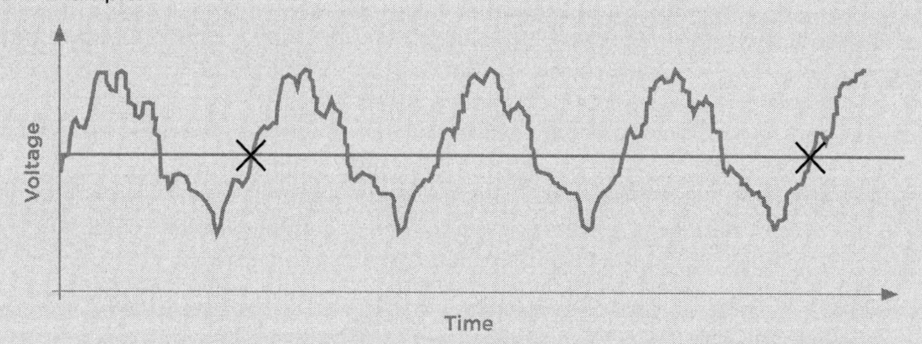


**Award 1 mark for two loop points chosen at zero crossing points at the same point in the wave cycle. Award 1 further mark for two loop points that include three wave cycles (an example of which is given above).**

The loop would sound most natural when more wave cycles are included. Because of the limited number of wave cycles in the question, the loop here might not sound very natural.

ii. Zero-crossing (detection) (1)

Cross-fade looping (1)

**[max. 1 mark]**

***b.** Acceptable answers:

Push down/decrease volume of initial transient (1)

Increase overall volume of sample, thus increasing the loudness of the decay (1)

High ratio (1)

Low threshold (1)

Short release (1)

**[max. 3 marks]**

**c.** Acceptable answers:

**Spaced pair:**

Exaggerated stereo image (1)

Poor mono compatibility (1)

Hole in the middle if too wide (1)

The distance between the microphones would define how evenly the singers are captured, e.g. if they were too far apart only the singers at the side would be captured (1)

**Mid side pair:**

Can adjust width of stereo image afterwards (1)

Requires phase inversion/processing (1)

Good mono compatibility (1)

Singers at the far ends of the choir would be far away so would not be picked up as well (1)

**[max. 4 marks]**

## Question 3

### Synthesis – LFOs

***a.** Low Frequency Oscillator (1)

***b.** Pan (1)

***c.** Pitch (1)

**d.** Acceptable answers:

| | |
|---|---|
| ***Rate** | Speed of the pitch change (1) |
| **Depth** | Amount of pitch change (1) |

**e.** Acceptable answers:

**Sine** – continuous gradual change (1)

**Square** – pitch instantly changes between two notes (1)

**f.** i. Modulate/select the pulse width (1)

ii. Diagram should demonstrate a pulse wave with a changing pulse width. Here is an example:

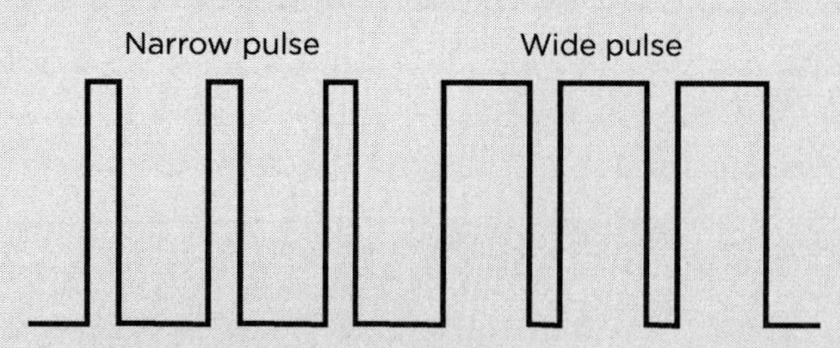


**Award 1 mark for a pulse wave**
**Award 1 mark for a demonstration that the width/mark-space ratio changes**

## Question 4

### Synthesis – Envelopes

***a.**

Volume/dB
Attack
Decay
Sustain (level)
Release
Key pressed
Time
Key released

Label correctly:

i. A/D/S/R (1 mark for each stage)

ii. Volume/dB (1) time axis (1)

iii. Key pressed/released labelled correctly (1 mark for each)

**b.** Acceptable answers

- Starts muffled and gets brighter/attack means that cut off increases gradually (1)
- The cut off frequency then slightly decreases (1)
- It holds at the sustain level (1)
- And then decreases so the sound is muffled again after the key is released (1)

**[max. 4 marks]**

## Question 5

### Equalisation

***a.** Acceptable answers:

- Flexibility to draw a curve rather than use individual band filters
- Variable Q/bandwidth
- Variable frequencies for each filter
- Store presets/revert to a previous setting
- Can be automated/MIDI controlled
- Better signal to noise ratio

- Better frequency response
- Multiple instances

**[max. 3 marks]**

***b.** Acceptable answers:

| Change | Justification |
|---|---|
| High pass filter (1) | Remove rumble (1) |
| (Narrow) parametric EQ cut (1) | Room resonance/standing wave/ unwanted single frequency (1) |
| Presence boost/high shelf filter (1) | Bring forward in mix (1) |

***c.** Accept answers between 700 and 800 Hz (1)

## Question 6

### Delay

***a.** Acceptable answers:

- Can be automated/MIDI controlled
- Stereo/more inputs and outputs
- Ping-pong/each tap can be panned differently
- Tempo sync
- Improved accuracy of delay time
- More parameters
- Better signal to noise ratio
- Better frequency response
- Presets
- Multiple instances with different parameters
- Greater number of taps available
- No maintenance issues/cleaning/new tape

**[max. 5 marks]**

***b.** Acceptable answers:

- Bucket brigade delay (pedal)
- Solid state delay (pedal)

Accept appropriate models/brand names, e.g. Electro-Harmonix Memory Man, MXR Analog Delay, Boss DM-1 **[max. 1 mark]**

**c.** Acceptable answers:

| Parameter | Function |
|---|---|
| ***Peak level** | Will illuminate if the signal clips/distorts (1) |
| ***Repeat rate** | Delay time/the amount of time between each repeat (1) |
| ***Input vol** | Used to set gain for a good signal-to-noise ratio (1) |
| **Intensity** | Feedback amount/number of repeats (1) |

**[max. 4 marks]**

## Question 7

### Dynamics processing

***a.** Acceptable answers:

Cuts out/turns down sound (1) below the threshold (1)

Expander (1)

**[max. 2 marks]**

**b.** Acceptable answers:

| Control | Function |
|---|---|
| ***Threshold** | The volume level below which sound does not pass through the gate (1) |
| **Gate/duck** | Controls whether the sound will be reduced in volume or to silence (1) |
| **Attack** | The amount of time taken, once the signal is above the threshold level, for the gate to open (1) |

**[max. 3 marks]**

***c.** Acceptable answers:

- Switch 'key source' to 'ext' (1)
- This is an external sidechain; the snare drum track would be connected to the sidechain input of the noise gate and control when the synth signal passes through the gate (1)
- When the snare drum level goes above the threshold value (0dB on this gate), it will open (1)
- The level of the threshold will depend on how loud the snare drum track is (1)
- Set the attack/hold/decay (release) so that the synth does not click (1)
- Use the filter to isolate the snare drum if recorded with other parts of the kit (1)
- 'Key listen' can be used to listen to the signal triggering the sidechain in order to do so effectively (1)

**[max. 5 marks]**

## Question 8

### Reverb

**a.**

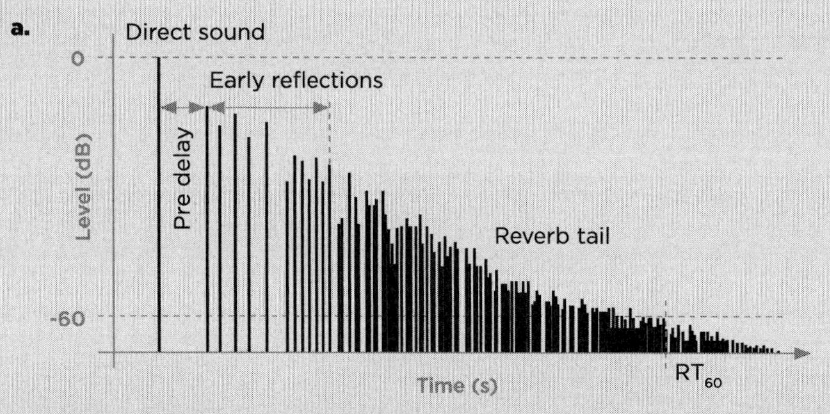


One mark for each correct label

**[max. 4 marks]**

**b.** Shorter reverb tail (1)

**c.** 'Samples' the reverb in a space. (1)

**d.** Acceptable answers:

- Can sample a variety of different spaces
- Presets are readily available/shareable
- Multiple (different) instances of reverbs
- Easy to alter parameters
- Award one mark for a parameter e.g. reverb time, pre-delay
- Can be automated/MIDI controlled
- Better signal-to-noise ratio
- Better frequency response

**[max. 4 marks]**

## Question 9

### Numeracy and calculations

**a.**

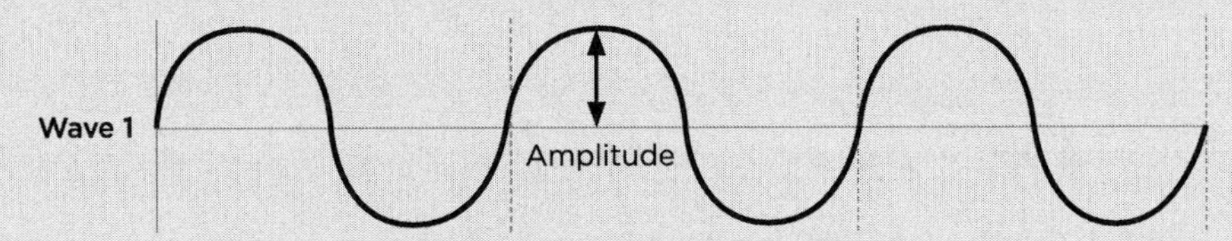


**1 mark for correct identification of amplitude**

**b.**

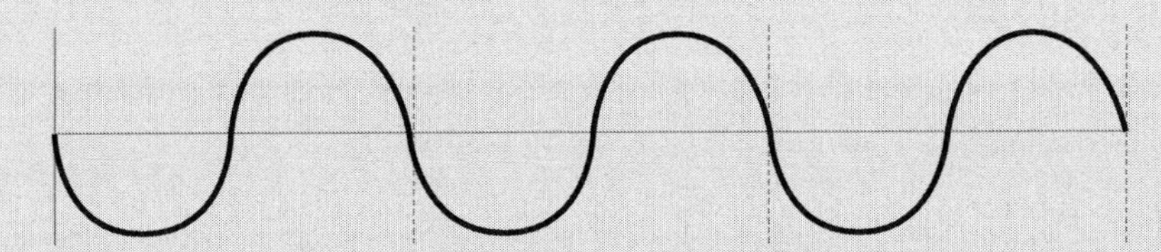

- Award 2 marks for a wave that follows the original closely with one full cycle in each section of the diagram.
- Award 1 mark for a wave that shows an understanding that the peaks become troughs and vice versa.

**c.** Silence/nothing/cancellation (1)

**d.** 1/100 = 0.01s

**1 mark for calculation; 1 mark for correct answer**

**e.** **1 mark for calculation; 1 mark for correct answer**

i. **Wave 2:** 100Hz x 2 = 200Hz

ii. **Wave 3**: 200Hz x 2 = 400Hz
or 100Hz x 4 = 400Hz

iii. **Musical relationship:** The waves are one octave apart (1)

**f.** Acceptable answers:

(100Hz/2) + 100Hz = 150Hz

or (100Hz + 200Hz)/2 = 150Hz

or (100Hz x 1.5) = 150Hz

**1 mark for calculation; 1 mark for correct answer**

**g.** 100Hz x 6 = 600Hz

**1 mark for calculation; 1 mark for correct answer**

## Question 10

### Analogue and digital

**a.** Voltage/V/ displacement (1)

Allow volume/ level/amplitude/ dB

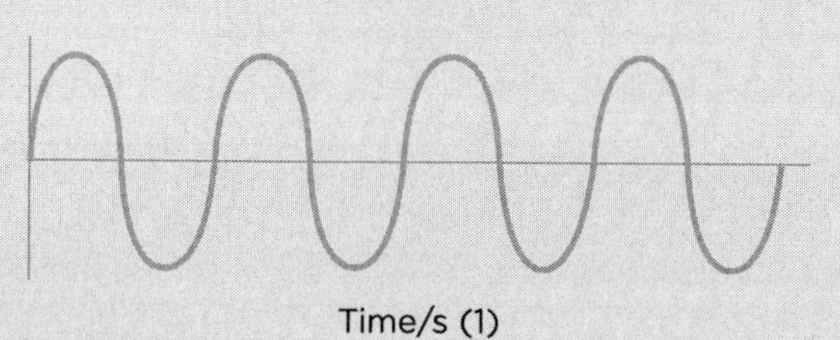

Time/s (1)

**b.** Sample rate: number of samples taken per second (1)
Bit depth: the accuracy that the amplitude/displacement is represented to (1)
The greater the number of bits, the better the signal-to-noise ratio (1) **[max. 1 mark]**

**c.** i.

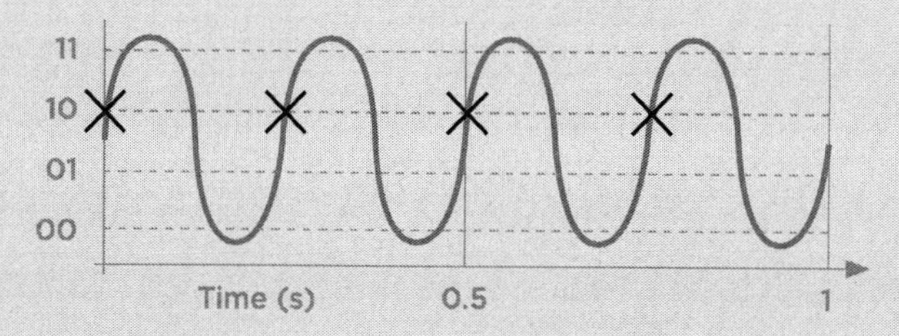


**1 mark for each correct cross to indicate a digital sample**

**Crosses should all be in line with the original cross at 10, at the same point in the wave cycle [max. 3 marks]**

ii. 10, 10, 10, 10 (1)

iii. **AO3 (3 marks)/AO4 (3 marks)**

1 mark is awarded for each point/process (AO3 maximum 3) with a further mark for an explanation of the point (AO4 maximum 3)

| AO3 | AO4 |
|---|---|
| The sample rate needs to be higher | Because the waveform peaks and troughs are not represented/accurate |
| 4Hz is the same frequency as the wave | It doesn't satisfy Nyquist's Theorem, so the sampled wave is not an accurate representation of the original |
| Sample rate should be at least twice the highest frequency | A sample rate higher than 8Hz would be a more appropriate sample rate to ensure that the wave peaks and troughs are captured |

iv. Quantisation error/quantisation distortion (1)

At 8 bits the quantisation distortion would be perceived as hiss (1)

Accept answers greater than 4 bits (1)

**[max. 2 marks]**

v. Unnecessarily high sample rate (1)

Would take up lots of disk space (1)

No audible difference (1)

Beyond limits of human hearing (1)

**[max. 2 marks]**

## Question 11

### Drum machines and matrix editors

***a.** Acceptable answers:

| Part of Kit | Role |
|---|---|
| **Kick** | Four-to-the-floor pattern/every crotchet beat (1) |
| **Snare/clap** | Crotchet beats 2 and 4/backbeat and a fill at the end (1) |
| **Hi-hat** | Alternating closed/open hi-hats except last beat, which has four semiquaver open hi-hats (1) |
| **Shaker** | Playing on semiquaver beats throughout (1) |
| **Crash** | Single hit at the start of the cycle/first semiquaver of beat 1 (1) |

**[max. 5 marks]**

***b.** Acceptable answers:

- 'Swing' turned up to 60% to give swung rhythms
- Velocities of the shaker part have been edited to emphasise the first semiquaver beat

**[max. 2 marks]**

***c.** Acceptable answers:

- Quantise (1) with 1/16 resolution (1)
- Percentage/iterative quantise (1)
- Groove templates (1)

**[max. 3 marks]**

# SECTION B

## *Question 12

### Recording vocals

**Total for AS Level: 16 marks – AO3 4 marks, AO4 12 marks**
**Total for A Level: 20 marks – AO3 5 marks, AO4 15 marks**

**Marking instructions**
Markers must apply the descriptors in line with the general marking guidance and the qualities outlined in the levels-based mark scheme below.

**Responses that demonstrate only AO3 without any AO4 should be awarded marks as follows:**

**AS Level:**

- Level 1 AO3 performance: 1 mark
- Level 2 AO3 performance: 2 marks
- Level 3 AO3 performance: 3 marks
- Level 4 AO3 performance: 4 marks.

**A Level:**

- Level 1 AO3 performance: 1 mark
- Level 2 AO3 performance: 2 marks
- Level 3 AO3 performance: 3 marks
- Level 4 AO3 performance: 4 marks
- Level 5 AO3 performance: 5 marks.

> Content shown below is for AS and A Level. Content specific to A Level only is shown in italics.

**Indicative content guidance**

The indicative content below is not prescriptive and candidates are not required to include all of it. Other relevant material not suggested below must also be credited.

Relevant points may include:

| AO3 | AO4 |
|---|---|
| Large diaphragm condenser | Large diaphragm condenser: low noise/good signal-to-noise ratio/ *relatively fast transient response (small diaphragm condenser would have a faster transient response)* |
| Close mic recording | Appropriate for a close mic recording. If the song was quieter, it might be more appropriate to move the singer closer to the microphone to capture even more dynamic and frequency detail. If the microphone was further away, more reverb could be captured, although the room is acoustically treated. This means that reverb is likely to be added after the recording, during mixing. This is often better than natural reverb as the amount/type/ specific parameters can be altered in the mix |
| Using pop shield/ suspension mount | **Pop shield:** avoids plosive sounds. It disperses the air to avoid sudden and large movements on the diaphragm, which would result in a 'pop' sound. This sound is difficult and sometimes impossible to remove/significantly improve during mixing.<br><br>**Suspension mount:** avoids sound of rumble picked up from the stand/ movement in the room; would be beneficial to attach lead to stand to avoid weighing the microphone down |
| Placed so that the pop shield is 10-15cm away from mic and the singer is then 10–15cm away from pop shield | Proximity effect when closer to (directional) microphone might be used as a creative effect. This would increase the low frequency content of the captured signal |
| *Singer is on-axis to the mic, with mic level with singer's mouth* | *On axis positioning in front of microphone – ensures all frequencies are captured. An off-axis mic placement would mean that the high frequency content would not be captured so well, giving a slightly duller sound. Capture will be unfocused if off-axis, especially if the vocalist moves while singing, but could be used to limit HF content if this was desired* |

| | |
|---|---|
| Headphone monitoring | Monitoring via headphones to reduce spill. Can end up with issues from other instruments and click tracks, especially if the vocal is performed quietly. It is important to ensure that the headphones aren't too loud. Closed-back headphones are appropriate because they spill less into the room |
| Background noise should be kept to a minimum | The room is acoustically treated and reverb would be minimal. It might be too dry; the engineer could add reverb to the monitor mix to make the vocalist feel more comfortable and helps with vocal tuning |

**AS Level: Levels based mark scheme:**

| Level | Mark | Descriptor |
|---|---|---|
| | 0 | ■ No rewardable material. |
| Level 1 | 1–4 | ■ Demonstrates limited knowledge and understanding of production techniques/technology used, some of which may be inaccurate or irrelevant (AO3)<br>■ Shows limited analysis and deconstruction of production techniques/ technology used with unsuccessful attempts at chains of reasoning (AO4)<br>■ Makes limited evaluative and/or critical judgements about the production techniques/technology used (AO4)<br>■ Makes an unsupported or generic conclusion, drawn from an arqument that is unbalanced or lacks coherence (AO4 ) |
| Level 2 | 5–8 | ■ Demonstrates knowledge and understanding of production techniques/ technology used, which are occasionally relevant but may include some inaccuracies (AO3)<br>■ Shows some analysis and deconstruction of production techniques/ technology used with simplistic chains of reasoning (AO4)<br>■ Makes some evaluative and/or critical judgements about the production techniques/technology used (AO4)<br>■ Comes to a conclusion partially supported by an unbalanced arqument with limited coherence (AO4) |
| Level 3 | 9–12 | ■ Demonstrates clear knowledge and understanding of production techniques/ technology used, which are mostly relevant and accurate (AO3)<br>■ Shows clear analysis and deconstruction of production techniques/ technology used with competent chains of reasoning (AO4)<br>■ Makes clear evaluative and critical judgements about the production techniques/technology used (AO4)<br>■ Comes to a conclusion generally supported by an argument that may be unbalanced or partially coherent (AO4) |
| Level 4 | 13–16 | ■ Demonstrates detailed knowledge and understanding of production techniques/technology used, which are relevant and accurate (AO3)<br>■ Shows detailed and accurate analysis and deconstruction of production techniques/technology used, with logical chains of reasoning on occasion (AO4)<br>■ Makes detailed and valid evaluative and critical judgements about the production techniques/technology used (AO4)<br>■ Comes to a conclusion, largely supported by a balanced argument (AO4) |

**A Level: Levels based mark scheme:**

| Level | Mark | Descriptor |
|---|---|---|
| | 0 | ■ No rewardable material. |
| Level 1 | 1–4 | ■ Demonstrates limited knowledge and understanding of production techniques/technology used, some of which may be misunderstood or confused (AO3)<br>■ Shows limited analysis and deconstruction of production techniques/ technology used with little attempt at chains of reasoning (AO4)<br>■ Makes limited evaluative and/or critical judgements about the production techniques/technology used (AO4)<br>■ Makes an unsupported or generic conclusion, drawn from an argument that is unbalanced or lacks coherence. (AO4) |
| Level 2 | 5–8 | ■ Demonstrates knowledge and understanding of production techniques/ technology used, which are occasionally relevant but may include some inaccuracies (AO3)<br>■ Shows some analysis and deconstruction of production techniques/ technology used with simplistic chains of reasoning (AO4)<br>■ Makes some evaluative and/or critical judgements about the production techniques/technology used (AO4)<br>■ Comes to a conclusion partially supported by an unbalanced argument with limited coherence. (AO4) |
| Level 3 | 9–12 | ■ Demonstrates clear knowledge and understanding of production techniques/technology used, which are mostly relevant and accurate (AO3)<br>■ Shows clear analysis and deconstruction of production techniques/ technology used with competent chains of reasoning (AO4)<br>■ Makes clear evaluative and critical judgements about the production techniques/technology used (AO4)<br>■ Comes to a conclusion generally supported by an argument that may be unbalanced or partially coherent. (AO4) |
| Level 4 | 13–16 | ■ Demonstrates detailed knowledge and understanding of production techniques/technology used, which are relevant and accurate (AO3)<br>■ Shows detailed and accurate analysis and deconstruction of production techniques/technology used, with logical chains of reasoning on occasion (AO4)<br>■ Makes detailed and valid evaluative and critical judgements about the production techniques/technology used (AO4)<br>■ Comes to a conclusion, largely supported by a balanced argument. (AO4) |
| Level 5 | 17–20 | ■ Demonstrates sophisticated and accurate knowledge and understanding of production techniques/technology used throughout (AO3)<br>■ Shows sophisticated and accurate analysis throughout, and deconstructs production techniques/technology used with logical chains of reasoning throughout (AO4)<br>■ Makes sophisticated and valid evaluative and critical judgements about the production techniques/technology used (AO4)<br>■ Comes to a rational, substantiated conclusion, fully supported by a balanced argument that is drawn together coherently. (AO4) |

## *Question 13

### Compression

**Total for AS Level: 16 marks – AO3 4 marks, AO4 12 marks**
**Total for A Level: 20 marks – AO3 5 marks, AO4 15 marks**

**Marking instructions**
Markers must apply the descriptors in line with the general marking guidance and the qualities outlined in the levels-based mark scheme below.

**Responses that demonstrate only AO3 without any AO4 should be awarded marks as follows:**

**AS Level:**

- Level 1 AO3 performance: 1 mark
- Level 2 AO3 performance: 2 marks
- Level 3 AO3 performance: 3 marks
- Level 4 AO3 performance: 4 marks.

**A Level:**

- Level 1 AO3 performance: 1 mark
- Level 2 AO3 performance: 2 marks
- Level 3 AO3 performance: 3 marks
- Level 4 AO3 performance: 4 marks
- Level 5 AO3 performance: 5 marks.

**Content shown below is for AS and A Level. Content specific to A Level only is shown in italics.**

**Indicative content guidance**
The indicative content below is not prescriptive and candidates are not required to include all of it. Other relevant material not suggested below must also be credited.

Relevant points may include:

| AO3 | AO4 |
|---|---|
| The compressor is being used to control the dynamic range of the vocal part/push down the peaks/make the overall volume more even | A vocal part would require more compression when combined with electronic parts with a narrow dynamic range. The vocal part would naturally have a wider dynamic range than the electronic parts so compression would help the vocal to cut through the mix and maintain the intelligibility of the words |
| Low threshold value means there is likely to be a lot of compression<br><br>Ratio is set at 5:1. This is the input volume compared to the output volume | A low threshold has been set because there are quiet phrases in the vocal part. The compressor is being used to add a lot of compression to increase the volume of these quiet sounds. If set incorrectly, this would create a ducking effect/be overcompressed. The input gain is adding about 2dB, meaning that the signal going into the compressor is probably slightly quiet. The make-up gain is used after compression to compensate for the compressor reducing the gain/level. It is set at around 2dB, which might not be enough given the low threshold. The ratio might need to be set higher; in electronic dance music heavy compression is often used, and 5:1 is not very heavy |

| | |
|---|---|
| *The attack is the time taken for the compressor to reduce the gain/start compressing and the release is the time taken for the compressor to stop working (after the signal falls below the threshold)* | *The fast attack is appropriate as it means it will prevent transients being too loud/because of the high amount of gain reduction. A fast release means that the volume will be consistently sustained across each word that is compressed. However, a fast release will also mean that the compressed vocal will duck/pump. A longer release time might make the sound more natural* |
| *Knee is the bend in the response curve near the threshold* | *Soft knee will make the vocal sound more natural, as the compression will be applied more gradually. This will reduce the audible change from uncompressed to compressed/ gradual onset of compression (around the threshold).* *If the vocal needs a significant amount of compression, the hard knee setting would make the compressor act more aggressively when the signal goes above the threshold* |
| There is a limiter function | The limiter is switched on but the threshold is quite high so is likely to control wayward peaks as opposed to 'brick walling'. This will give a natural sounding vocal but will prevent the odd peak slipping through the compressor. However, if there are lots of loud peaks, the threshold may be set too high and would benefit from being lower. Soft clipping is selected; this recreates the sound of analogue equipment and is often desirable when creating a natural vocal sound |

**The AS Level and A Level levels based assessment grids are given on pages 73-74.**

## **Question 14** (A Level only)

### Synthesisers

**AO3 (5 marks)/AO4 (15 marks)**

**Marking instructions**
Markers must apply the descriptors in line with the general marking guidance and the qualities outlined in the levels-based mark scheme below.

**Responses that demonstrate only AO3 without any AO4 should be awarded marks as follows:**

- Level 1 AO3 performance: 1 mark
- Level 2 AO3 performance: 2 marks
- Level 3 AO3 performance: 3 marks
- Level 4 AO3 performance: 4 marks
- Level 5 AO3 performance: 5 marks.

**Indicative content guidance**
The indicative content below is not prescriptive and candidates are not required to include all of it. Other relevant material not suggested below must also be credited.

Relevant points may include:

| AO3 | AO4 |
|---|---|
| The synthesiser is a digital reproduction of an analogue synthesiser (Roland Juno 60) | Since this is an emulation, it is designed to recreate the 'vintage' sound of a hardware synthesiser, including unwanted characteristics. This means that it would be easier to use, for example, multiple instances/ alter settings after recording if the lead synthesiser is not suitable once recorded, or for layering multiple sounds to create a denser timbre |
| DCO is a digitally controlled **oscillator.** There is also a sub-oscillator; these are often tuned an octave below the main oscillator | Digitally controlled oscillators stay in tune better than voltage controlled oscillators and are more stable; analogue VCOs would often drift in pitch and require retuning. It is important that the lead synthesiser sound is in tune, but sometimes musicians prefer the unpredictability/sound/ warmth of vintage analogue devices. The sub-oscillator is turned up to nearly maximum volume. This would add a square wave to the sound of the main oscillator. Sub-oscillators are often tuned an octave down, so the lead synthesiser notes would play in octaves |
| ADSR refers to the four **envelope** stages: attack (A) is the time to reach a note's maximum; decay (D) is the time to fall to the sustain level; sustain (S) is the level at which the note remains while a note is held; release (R) is the amount of time taken to return to zero<br><br>There is a **low pass filter** which removes high frequencies | The envelope is set to a long attack, long decay with a low sustain level and quick release. The low pass filter is routed via the envelope, which means the sound would start muffled, become brighter, and then decay to muffled again. The slow attack is not very suitable for a lead synth. There is a switch on the filter to invert the envelope. This means that you could use the synthesiser to create a bright sound that becomes muffled. This would mean that the cut off frequency would start at the maximum and would make it more suitable because a sound that is brighter at the start will make the note cut through in the mix, increasing its effectiveness as a lead part. However, the remainder of the note might not cut through as well if it is low pass filtered, as it will sound more muffled, so will lack sustain. A higher overall cut off frequency value would also help the lead synth part to cut through the mix. Resonance is turned up to about half, which would increase the volume of the frequencies around the cut off. This would emphasise the sound and make it more suitable for a lead synthesiser<br><br>The VCA is not routed to the envelope - it is in gate mode, meaning the note will simply switch on and off. This means that the sound will not hold after the note is pressed; this would be good for a detached, staccato lead synthesiser sound, but would not be as good for a lyrical synthesiser line with lots of held notes |
| **High pass filter**<br>The synthesiser also includes a high pass filter, which removes low frequencies | A static high pass filter is being used to remove low frequencies; for a high lead synthesiser, this would mean that low frequencies do not muddy the mix. Electro tracks often use layers of synthesisers so, if a separate synthesiser bass is used, this would ensure clarity to the mix |
| **LFO** stands for low frequency oscillator | An LFO is being used to control the oscillator. This would give a vibrato effect, which could add movement to a lead synthesiser sound. The LFO is synced to crotchet triplets. The LFO sync is a benefit of using a plugin. This could be set in time with the track, or a faster vibrato might be more effective |
| The chorus effect is switched on; there are two different types on the synthesiser | Chorus would make the lead synthesiser sound as if there are a number of different voices/thicker, adding weight to the sound in the mix. Chorus could also give the sound some stereo image, which would help to provide some movement/interest in the stereo field |

**Levels based mark scheme:**

| Level | Mark | Descriptor |
|---|---|---|
| | 0 | ■ No rewardable material. |
| **Level 1** | **1–4** | ■ Demonstrates limited knowledge and understanding of production techniques/technology used, some of which may be misunderstood or confused (AO3)<br>■ Shows limited analysis and deconstruction of production techniques/technology used with little attempt at chains of reasoning (AO4)<br>■ Makes limited evaluative and/or critical judgements about the production techniques/technology used (AO4)<br>■ Makes an unsupported or generic conclusion, drawn from an argument that is unbalanced or lacks coherence. (AO4) |
| **Level 2** | **5–8** | ■ Demonstrates knowledge and understanding of production techniques/technology used, which are occasionally relevant but may include some inaccuracies (AO3)<br>■ Shows some analysis and deconstruction of production techniques/technology used with simplistic chains of reasoning (AO4)<br>■ Makes some evaluative and/or critical judgements about the production techniques/technology used (AO4)<br>■ Comes to a conclusion partially supported by an unbalanced argument with limited coherence. (AO4) |
| **Level 3** | **9–12** | ■ Demonstrates clear knowledge and understanding of production techniques/technology used, which are mostly relevant and accurate (AO3)<br>■ Shows clear analysis and deconstruction of production techniques/technology used with competent chains of reasoning (AO4)<br>■ Makes clear evaluative and critical judgements about the production techniques/technology used (AO4)<br>■ Comes to a conclusion generally supported by an argument that may be unbalanced or partially coherent. (AO4) |
| **Level 4** | **13–16** | ■ Demonstrates detailed knowledge and understanding of production techniques/technology used, which are relevant and accurate (AO3)<br>■ Shows detailed and accurate analysis and deconstruction of production techniques/technology used, with logical chains of reasoning on occasion (AO4)<br>■ Makes detailed and valid evaluative and critical judgements about the production techniques/technology used (AO4)<br>■ Comes to a conclusion, largely supported by a balanced argument. (AO4) |
| **Level 5** | **17–20** | ■ Demonstrates sophisticated and accurate knowledge and understanding of production techniques/technology used throughout (AO3)<br>■ Shows sophisticated and accurate analysis throughout, and deconstructs production techniques/technology used with logical chains of reasoning throughout (AO4)<br>■ Makes sophisticated and valid evaluative and critical judgements about the production techniques/technology used (AO4)<br>■ Comes to a rational, substantiated conclusion, fully supported by a balanced argument that is drawn together coherently. (AO4) |

## Mechanical copyrights

**Vienna**
Ure/Currie/Allen/Cann
Universal Music Publishing Limited

**In My Life**
McCartney/Lennon
Sony/ATV Music Publishing (UK) Limited

**On The Sunny Side Of The Street**
McHugh/Fields
EMI Music Publishing Ltd/Shapiro Bernstein & Co Limited

**Runaway (U&I)**
Karlsson/Dennis/Eklow/Koitzsch/Rundberg/Karlsson
Universal Music Publishing Limited/Imagem Music/Kobalt Music Publishing Ltd/BMG Rights Management (UK) Limited

**Levels**
Bergling/James/Woods/Kirkland/Pournouri
EMI Music Publishing Ltd/Sony/ATV Music Publishing (UK) Limited

**Levels (Skrillex Remix)**
Bergling/James/Woods/Kirkland/Pournouri/Moore
EMI Music Publishing Ltd/Sony/ATV Music Publishing (UK) Limited/Kobalt Music Publishing Ltd

**Purple Haze**
Hendrix
Universal/MCA Music Limited

**Ornithology**
Harris/Parker
Universal Music Publishing Limited

**Don't Dream It's Over**
Finn
Kobalt Music Publishing Ltd

**Oxygene Part II**
Jarre
BMG Rights Management (UK) Limited

**Angel**
Vowles/Del Naja/Andy/Marshall
Universal/Island Music Limited/Universal Music Publishing MGB Limited

**Bang Bang**
Bono
Edward Kassner Music Co Ltd

**Shot You Down**
Bono/Franks/Dinsdale
Edward Kassner Music Co Ltd
EMI Music Publishing Ltd

**One More Time**
Moore/Christo/Bangalter
BMG Rights Management (UK) Limited/Imagem London Limited

**Another Brick In The Wall (Part 2)**
Waters
BMG Rights Management (UK) Limited

**Proper Education**
Waters
BMG Rights Management (UK) Limited

## Picture credits

Page 15, page 42, page 46: Shutterstock

Screenshots: James Reevell

Drawn diagrams: Phil Gambrill

Letts

# AS

VISUAL
REVISION
GUIDE

# SUCCESS

## MATHEMATICS

Michael Jennings

# Contents

## Algebra and functions



## Coordinate geometry



## Sequences and series

## Trigonometry



## Differentiation



## Integration

# Indices and surds

- **Indices are sometimes called powers or exponents.**

EXAMPLE

$a^3 = a \times a \times a$

power or index (the 3), base (the a)

**Roots such as $\sqrt{2}$, $\sqrt{3}$, $\sqrt{5}$, $\sqrt[3]{6}$, etc. are sometimes known as surds. They are infinite, non-recurring decimals and so cannot be written exactly as decimals. For this reason, we often leave them as roots.**

## Laws of indices

- $a^m \times a^n = a^{m+n}$
- $a^m \div a^n = a^{m-n}$
- $(a^m)^n = a^{mn}$
- $(ab)^n = a^n b^n$
- $a^1 = a$
- $a^0 = 1$

**EXAMINER'S TOP TIP**
**Familiarity and flexibility with indices and their laws is crucial.**

These laws can be used to simplify expressions which involve the same base.

EXAMPLE

$$4x^3 \times 3x^2 = 4 \times x^3 \times 3 \times x^2 = 4 \times 3 \times x^3 \times x^2 = 12x^5$$

NOTE $4x^3 \times 3y^2$ can only be simplified to $12x^3y^2$.

## Different types of power

### Negative powers

A negative power is the reciprocal of the corresponding positive power. $a^{-n} = \frac{1}{a^n}$

EXAMPLES

$$3^{-2} = \frac{1}{3^2} = \frac{1}{9} \qquad x^{-1} = \frac{1}{x^1} = \frac{1}{x} \qquad \left(\frac{3}{4}\right)^{-2} = \frac{1}{\left(\frac{3}{4}\right)^2} = \frac{1}{\frac{9}{16}} = \frac{16}{9}$$

A quicker method for the third example is to invert the fraction first. $\left(\frac{3}{4}\right)^{-2} = \left(\frac{4}{3}\right)^2 = \frac{16}{9}$

### Fractional powers

These involve roots.

$$a^{\frac{1}{2}} = \sqrt{a} \qquad a^{\frac{1}{3}} = \sqrt[3]{a} \qquad a^{\frac{1}{4}} = \sqrt[4]{a}$$

cube root of $a$ — fourth root of $a$

EXAMPLES

$16^{\frac{1}{2}} = \sqrt{16} = 4$

NOTE Only the positive square root of 16. We need to write $-\sqrt{16}$ for the negative square root of 16.

To find $8^{\frac{2}{3}}$ we proceed as follows.

$$8^{\frac{2}{3}} = (8^{\frac{1}{3}})^2 = \sqrt[3]{8}^{\,2} = 2^2 = 4 \text{ or } 8^{\frac{2}{3}} = (8^2)^{\frac{1}{3}} = \sqrt[3]{64} = 4$$

In general, $a^{\frac{m}{n}} = (\sqrt[n]{a})^m$ or $\sqrt[n]{a^m}$

Find the value of $\left(\frac{27}{8}\right)^{-\frac{2}{3}}$

$$\left(\frac{27}{8}\right)^{-\frac{2}{3}} = \left(\frac{8}{27}\right)^{\frac{2}{3}} = \left(\sqrt[3]{\frac{8}{27}}\right)^2 = \left(\frac{2}{3}\right)^2 = \frac{4}{9}$$

For a negative power, flip the fraction first.

# Laws of surds

- $\sqrt{(a \times b)} = \sqrt{a} \times \sqrt{b}$
- $\sqrt{\left(\frac{a}{b}\right)} = \frac{\sqrt{a}}{\sqrt{b}}$

**EXAMINER'S TOP TIP**
If you are not sure of an algebraic result, put some numbers in and see if it works. If it does, it's probably right, if it doesn't, it's definitely wrong!

**EXAMPLES**

$\sqrt{8} = \sqrt{4 \times 2} = \sqrt{4} \times \sqrt{2} = 2\sqrt{2}$

$\sqrt{\frac{3}{4}} = \frac{\sqrt{3}}{\sqrt{4}} = \frac{\sqrt{3}}{2}$

$\sqrt{2} \times \sqrt{2} = \sqrt{2 \times 2} = \sqrt{4} = 2$ (This result is not surprising if you think about it!)

$3\sqrt{3} \times 4\sqrt{3} = 3 \times \sqrt{3} \times 4 \times \sqrt{3} = 3 \times 4 \times \sqrt{3} \times \sqrt{3} = 12 \times \sqrt{3 \times 3} = 12 \times \sqrt{9} = 12 \times 3 = 36$

NOTE $\sqrt{a \pm b} \neq \sqrt{a} \pm \sqrt{b}$

**EXAMPLES**

$\sqrt{(4 + 9)} \neq \sqrt{4} + \sqrt{9}$ LHS $= \sqrt{13}$ RHS $= 2 + 3 = 5$

**A common mistake** is to say $\sqrt{x^2+y^2} = x + y$

We can manipulate surds using the above laws, when appropriate, and also the **usual algebraic rules**.

**EXAMPLES**

1. Evaluate $(\sqrt{2} + 3\sqrt{3})^2$ Compare with $(x + 3y)^2$
   $= (\sqrt{2} + 3\sqrt{3})(\sqrt{2} + 3\sqrt{3}) = \sqrt{2}\sqrt{2} + 3\sqrt{3}\sqrt{2} + 3\sqrt{3}\sqrt{2} + 3\sqrt{3} \times 3\sqrt{3} = 2 + 6\sqrt{6} + 27 = 29 + 6\sqrt{6}$
2. Write $\sqrt{63}$ as the simplest possible surd. $\sqrt{63} = \sqrt{(9 \times 7)} = \sqrt{9}\sqrt{7} = 3\sqrt{7}$
3. Express $6\sqrt{5}$ as a single square root. $6\sqrt{5} = \sqrt{36}\,\sqrt{5} = \sqrt{(36 \times 5)} = \sqrt{180}$
4. Simplify $\sqrt{50} + \sqrt{8} + \sqrt{2} - 2\sqrt{18}$
   $\sqrt{50} + \sqrt{8} + \sqrt{2} - 2\sqrt{18} = 5\sqrt{2} + 2\sqrt{2} + \sqrt{2} - 2 \times 3\sqrt{2} = (5 + 2 + 1 - 6)\sqrt{2} = 2\sqrt{2}$

# Rationalising the denominator of a fraction

We do not usually write surds in the denominator of a fraction when this can be avoided. This is called **rationalising the denominator**.

**EXAMPLES**

Rationalise the denominator of these.

(a) $\frac{1}{\sqrt{2}}$ (b) $\frac{1}{3 - \sqrt{2}}$ (c) $\frac{2}{\sqrt{6} + 2}$

(a) Multiply top and bottom by $\sqrt{2}$

$$\frac{1}{\sqrt{2}} \times \frac{\sqrt{2}}{\sqrt{2}} = \frac{\sqrt{2}}{2}$$

(b) Multiply top and bottom by the denominator with the sign changed.

$$\frac{1}{3 - \sqrt{2}} \times \frac{3 + \sqrt{2}}{3 + \sqrt{2}} = \frac{3 + \sqrt{2}}{9 - 3\sqrt{2} + 3\sqrt{2} - 2} = \frac{3 + \sqrt{2}}{7}$$

(c) $$\frac{2}{\sqrt{6} + \sqrt{2}} \times \frac{\sqrt{6} - \sqrt{2}}{\sqrt{6} - \sqrt{2}} = \frac{2\sqrt{6} - 2\sqrt{2}}{6 - 2} = \frac{2\sqrt{6} - 2\sqrt{2}}{4} = \frac{\sqrt{6} - \sqrt{2}}{2}$$

# Quick test

**1** ***Find the values of:*** *(a)* $27^{-\frac{2}{3}}$ *(b)* $\left(\frac{4}{9}\right)^{-\frac{1}{2}}$ *(c)* $\left(\frac{27}{8}\right)^{-\frac{4}{3}}$ *(d)* $\frac{4^{-\frac{3}{2}}}{8^{-\frac{2}{3}}}$

**2** ***Simplify:*** *(a)* $\frac{x^{-\frac{2}{3}}x^{\frac{1}{4}}}{x^{\frac{1}{6}}}$ *(b)* $(xy^2)^p\sqrt{x^q}$ *(c)* $\frac{x^{-\frac{2}{3}}y^{-\frac{1}{3}}}{(x^4y^2)^{\frac{-1}{6}}}$

**3** ***Simplify:*** *(a)* $\sqrt{75} + 2\sqrt{12} - \sqrt{27}$ *(b)* $\sqrt{24} - 3\sqrt{6} - \sqrt{216}$

**4** ***Express each in the form*** $a + b\sqrt{c}$: *(a)* $(1 + \sqrt{2})(3 - 2\sqrt{2})$ *(b)* $\frac{\sqrt{5} + 1}{\sqrt{5} - 1}$ *(c)* $\sqrt{\left(\frac{1}{2}\right)} + \sqrt{\left(\frac{1}{4}\right)} + \sqrt{\left(\frac{1}{8}\right)}$

1. (a) $\frac{1}{9}$ (b) $\frac{3}{2}$ (c) $\frac{16}{81}$ (d) $\frac{1}{2}$ 2. (a) $x^{-\frac{7}{12}}$ (b) $x^{(p+\frac{1}{2}q)}y^{2p}$ (c) 1 3. (a) $6\sqrt{3}$ (b) $-7\sqrt{6}$ 4. (a) $-1 + \sqrt{2}$ (b) $\frac{3}{2} + \frac{1}{2}\sqrt{5}$ (c) $\frac{1}{2} + \frac{3}{4}\sqrt{2}$

# Quadratic equations 1 – factorisation and completing the square

- **An equation of the form $ax^2 + bx + c = 0$, where $a$, $b$ and $c$ are any numbers, $a \neq 0$, is called a quadratic equation or, simply, a quadratic.**

**The highest power of $x$ in an equation is called its degree. The degree of an equation is also the maximum number of solutions or roots that the equation can have. Quadratic equations have degree 2. Quadratics can therefore have two, one or no solutions.**

## Collecting terms

The first thing to do when solving a quadratic is to collect all the terms on one side of the equation so that we have zero on the other side.

EXAMPLES

| | | |
|---|---|---|
| $x^2 = 4x + 1$ | becomes | $x^2 - 4x - 1 = 0$ |
| $5 - x^2 = 3x$ | becomes | $x^2 + 3x - 5 = 0$ |
| $2x - 8 - x^2 = 0$ | becomes | $x^2 - 2x + 8 = 0$ |
| $\frac{4}{x} - x = 3$ | becomes | $4 - x^2 = 3x$ becomes $x^2 + 3x - 4 = 0$ |

**EXAMINER'S TOP TIP**
When solving a quadratic equation, always arrange the equation so that you have a positive number of $x^2$ terms.

## Methods for solving quadratic equations

### 1 Factorisation

This is usually the easiest method.

The equation $ax^2 + bx + c = 0$ will factorise if $b^2 - 4ac$ is a perfect square.

EXAMPLE

$x^2 + 4x + 3 = 0$ — $b^2 - 4ac = 4^2 - (4 \times 1 \times 3) = 4$, a perfect square. The equation does factorise.

$(x + 3)(x + 1) = 0$ — We now use a simple, but very important, basic property of numbers.
If $a \times b = 0$, then either $a = 0$ *or* $b = 0$

so, $x + 3 = 0$ *or* $x + 1 = 0$

i.e. $x = -3$ *or* $x = -1$

Check your answers by substituting your values of $x$ back into the equation.
$(-3)^2 + (4 \times -3) + 3 = 9 - 12 + 3 = 0$ and $(-1)^2 + (4 \times -1) + 3 = 1 - 4 + 3 = 0$

**EXAMINER'S TOP TIP**
Completing the square has other applications, apart from solving quadratics, so it must be learned.

### 2 Completing the square

This method will always work although it is quite difficult.

EXAMPLE

Solve $2x^2 - 4x + 1 = 0$ — $b^2 - 4ac = (-4)^2 - (4 \times 2 \times 1) = 18 - 8 = 8$, which is *not* a perfect square. The equation does *not* factorise.

$x^2 - 2x + \frac{1}{2} = 0$ — Divide the equation by two to give a coefficient of 1 for $x^2$ term.

$x^2 - 2x = -\frac{1}{2}$ — Move the constant term to the other side of the equation.
Add a number to the LHS to make it a perfect square.
The number you need is $\left(\frac{\text{number of } x\text{s}}{2}\right)^2$ i.e. $\left(\frac{-2}{2}\right)^2 = 1$.

$x^2 - 2x + 1 = -\frac{1}{2} + 1$ — The number must be added to both sides to keep the equation balanced.

$x^2 - 2x + 1 = \frac{1}{2}$

$(x - 1)^2 = \frac{1}{2}$ — This number will always be half of the number of $x$s on the previous line.

**Completing the square continued**

| | |
|---|---|
| $(x - 1) = \pm\sqrt{\frac{1}{2}}$ | There are two square roots. |
| $x = 1 \pm \sqrt{\frac{1}{2}}$ | |
| $x = 1 + \sqrt{\frac{1}{2}}$ | *or* $1 - \sqrt{\frac{1}{2}}$ |
| $= 1.71$ (3 s.f.) | *or* $0.293$ (3 s.f.) |

# Finding the factors for factorisation

The actual factorisation process can be done either by **inspection** or by this longer method.

To factorise $ax^2 + bx + c = 0$

- Check to see if $b^2 - 4ac$ is a perfect square. If it is, the equation factorises.
- Find two whole numbers, $p$ and $q$, such that $pq = ac$ and $p + q = b$

Use the first equation to find possible values of $p$ and $q$, then *check* to see if they satisfy the second equation.

- Use $p$ and $q$ to factorise the equation.

**EXAMPLE**

Solve $2x^2 + 7x = 15$ — Make equation equal to 0

$2x^2 + 7x - 15 = 0$ — $b^2 - 4ac = 7^2 - (4 \times 2 \times -15) = 49 + 120 = 169 = 13^2$ so equation factorises.

Find $p$ and $q$, such that $p \times q = 2 \times -15 = -30$ *and* $p + q = 7$

Write down possible pairs of factors of $-30$

| | | |
|---|---|---|
| $1 \times -30$ | *but* | $1 + -30 \neq 7$ |
| $2 \times -15$ | *but* | $2 + -15 \neq 7$ |
| $3 \times -10$ | *but* | $3 + -10 \neq 7$ |
| $-3 \times 10$ | *and* | $-3 + 10 = 7$ |

$p = -3$ and $q = 10$ (or other way round)

Split the $x$ term using $p$ and $q$.

| | | |
|---|---|---|
| $2x^2 - 3x + 10x - 15 = 0$ | *or* | $2x^2 + 10x - 3x - 15 = 0$ |
| $x(2x - 3) + 5(2x - 3) = 0$ | *or* | $2x(x + 5) - 3(x + 5) = 0$ |
| $(x + 5)(2x - 3) = 0$ | *or* | $(2x - 3)(x + 5) = 0$ |
| $x = -5$ | *or* | $x = \frac{3}{2}$ |
| | *or* | $x = \frac{3}{2}$ *or* $x = -5$ |

**NOTE** Once we have found the values for $p$ and $q$, the solutions to the equation will always be $x = \frac{-p}{a}$ *or* $\frac{-q}{a}$

In the example, $x = -\frac{(-3)}{2} = \frac{3}{2}$ *or* $x = -\frac{10}{2} = -5$

# Quick test

**1** ***Solve each of these quadratic equations using factorisation.***

***(a)*** $2x^2 = 5x$ ***(b)*** $x^2 = 9x - 20$ ***(c)*** $6x^2 - 5x - 6 = 0$ ***(d)*** $11x + 3 - 4x^2 = 0$

**2** ***Solve each of these quadratic equations by completing the square. Leave your answers in <u>exact</u> form.***

***(a)*** $x^2 + 8x + 6 = 0$ ***(b)*** $2x^2 - 4x - 1 = 0$ ***(c)*** $4x - 3x^2 + 2 = 0$

1. (a) $x = 0$ or $x = \frac{5}{2}$ (b) $x = 4$ or $x = 5$ (c) $x = \frac{3}{2}$ or $x = -\frac{2}{3}$ (d) $x = 3$ or $x = -\frac{1}{4}$ 2. (a) $x = -4 \pm \sqrt{10}$ (b) $x = 1 \pm \sqrt{\frac{3}{2}}$ (c) $x = \frac{2 \pm \sqrt{10}}{3}$

# Quadratic equations 2 – the quadratic formula

- **The quadratic formula will always work and is the easiest way of solving a quadratic which does not factorise.**

**If $ax^2 + bx + c = 0$, then**

$$x = \frac{-b \pm \sqrt{b^2 - 4ac}}{2a}$$

**where $a$, $b$ and $c$ can be any numbers, except $a$ cannot be a zero.**

**EXAMINER'S TOP TIP**
You need to learn this formula

EXAMPLE

**Solve $2x^2 = 6x + 3$**

$2x^2 - 6x - 3 = 0$

$a = 2, b = -6, c = -3$

$$x = \frac{-(-6) \pm \sqrt{(-6)^2 - 4 \times 2 \times (-3)}}{2 \times 2}$$

**EXAMINER'S TOP TIP**
This subtraction must be done last

$$x = \frac{6 \pm \sqrt{36 - -24}}{4}$$

$$x = \frac{6 \pm \sqrt{60}}{4}$$

$$x = \frac{6 + \sqrt{60}}{4} \quad \text{or} \quad x = \frac{6 - \sqrt{60}}{4}$$

$x = 3.44$ *or* $x = -0.436$ (3 s.f.)

## Deriving the formula

The formula is derived by completing the square.

$$ax^2 + bx + c = 0$$

$$x^2 + \frac{b}{a}x + \frac{c}{a} = 0$$ Divide through by $a$ first.

$$x^2 + \frac{b}{a}x = -\frac{c}{a}$$ Transfer the constant term to the other side.

$$x^2 + \frac{b}{a}x + \left(\frac{b}{2a}\right)^2 = -\frac{c}{a} + \left(\frac{b}{2a}\right)^2$$ This is the completing the square step.

$$\left(x + \frac{b}{2a}\right)^2 = \frac{b^2}{4a^2} - \frac{c}{a}$$ Swapping the terms round.

$$\left(x + \frac{b}{2a}\right)^2 = \frac{b^2 - 4ac}{4a^2}$$ Use a common denominator.

$$\left(x + \frac{b}{2a}\right) = \pm\sqrt{\frac{b^2 - 4ac}{4a^2}} = \pm\frac{\sqrt{b^2 - 4ac}}{2a}$$ Two square roots!

$$x = \frac{-b \pm \sqrt{b^2 - 4ac}}{2a}$$

## Solving quadratic equations

### Mixed worked examples

**1** Solve $2x^2 - 3x = 0$ — If the number term is missing always use factorisation.

$2x^2 - 3x = 0 \Rightarrow x(2x - 3) = 0 \quad \Rightarrow \quad x = 0$ *or* $2x - 3 = 0 \Rightarrow x = \frac{3}{2}$

**2** Solve $x^2 = x$

$x^2 - x = 0 \Rightarrow x(x - 1) = 0 \quad \Rightarrow \quad x = 0$ *or* $x - 1 = 0 \Rightarrow x = 1$

**3** Solve $2x^2 - 9 = 0$ — If there is no $x$ term in the equation, use this method.

$2x^2 - 9 = 0$

$2x^2 = 9$

$x^2 = \frac{9}{2}$

$x = \pm\sqrt{\frac{9}{2}}$ — Two square roots.

$x = \pm 2.12$ (3 s.f.)

# Solving quadratic equations *continued*

**4** Solve $2x^2 + 3x = 2$

$\Rightarrow 2x^2 + 3x - 2 = 0$

$b^2 - 4ac = 3^2 - 4 \times 2 \times (-2) = 9 - (-16) = 25$, a perfect square. It will factorise.
We need $p$ and $q$ such that $pq = 2 \times -2 = -4$ *and* $p + q = 3$
Use $pq = -4$ to find possible values of $p$ and $q$

$1 \times -4 = -4$ *but* $1 + (-4) \neq 3$

$-1 \times 4 = -4$ *and* $-1 + 4 = 3$

$p = -1, q = 4$

We could write down the answers using $x = -\frac{p}{a}$ *or* $x = -\frac{q}{a}$, but it is better to show working.

$2x^2 - x + 4x - 2 = 0$

$\Rightarrow x(2x - 1) + 2(2x - 1) = 0$

$\Rightarrow (x + 2)(2x - 1) = 0$

$x = -2$ *or* $x = \frac{1}{2}$

You may well be able to get this more quickly using inspection!

**5** Solve $x^2 + 3x - 1 = 0$

$b^2 - 4ac = 3^2 - 4 \times 1 \times (-1) = 9 - -4 = 13$.
This is not a perfect square, so use formula, $a = 1$, $b = 3$, $c = -1$.

**NOTE** We use the value of $b^2 - 4ac$ found above in the formula.

$x = \frac{-3 \pm \sqrt{13}}{2 \times 1}$

$x = \frac{-3 \pm \sqrt{13}}{2}$

$x = \frac{-3 + \sqrt{13}}{2} \approx 0.303$ (3 s.f.) *or* $x = \frac{-3 - \sqrt{13}}{2} \approx -3.30$ (3 s.f.)

Sometimes the equation may not, at first sight, appear to be a quadratic.

**EXAMPLES**

**6** Solve $4x + \frac{7}{x} = 29$

Multiply through by $x$ to clear the fraction.

$4x^2 + 7 = 29x$

$4x^2 - 29x + 7 = 0$

$(4x - 1)(x - 7) = 0$

$x = \frac{1}{4}$ *or* $x = 7$

Here is a harder example.

**7** Solve $\frac{2}{x} + \frac{2}{x + 1} = 3$

To add two fractions, we need a common denominator. The product of the two denominators will always be a possible common denominator.

$\frac{2(x + 1) + 2x}{x(x + 1)} = 3$

$4x + 2 = 3x(x + 1)$

$0 = 3x^2 - x - 2$

$0 = (3x + 2)(x - 1)$

$x = -\frac{2}{3}$ *or* $x = 1$

## Quick test

**1** ***Solve each of these quadratic equations using the formula. Give your answers to 2 decimal places.***

**(a)** $2x^2 + 6x + 3 = 0$ **(b)** $3x^2 + x = 3$ **(c)** $3 + 4x - 2x^2 = 0$ **(d)** $x^2 - 3x - 2 = 0$

**2** ***Solve each of these equations using an appropriate method. Give your answers to 2 decimal places when necessary.***

**(a)** $2x^2 = 7x$ **(b)** $16 = \frac{1}{x^2}$ **(c)** $3x^2 - 48 = 0$ **(d)** $10x = 1 + \frac{3}{x}$ **(e)** $2x + 2 = \frac{7}{x} - 1$ **(f)** $\frac{3}{x - 1} + \frac{3}{x + 1} = 4$

1. (a) $x = -0.63$ or $x = -2.37$ (b) $x = 0.85$ or $x = -1.18$ (c) $x = -0.58$ or $x = 2.58$ (d) $x = 3.56$ or $x = -0.56$
2. (a) $x = 0$ or $x = \frac{7}{2}$ (b) $x = \pm\frac{1}{4}$ (c) $x = \pm 4$ (d) $x = -\frac{1}{2}$ or $x = \frac{3}{5}$ (e) $x = -2.77$ or $x = 1.27$ (f) $x = -\frac{1}{2}$ or $x = 2$

# Quadratic inequalities / functions

- **An inequality which can be put in the form $ax^2 + bx + c > 0$ or similar is called a quadratic inequality.**

## Solving a quadratic inequality

Find the **critical values of $x$**. These are the values of $x$ which **make the expression equal to zero** (the **solutions of the corresponding quadratic equation**).

Mark the critical values on a number line. They will divide the number line up into three pieces if there are two distinct solutions, or two pieces if there are two equal solutions.

Test a value of $x$ in any of the parts of the number line to see whether it satisfies the inequality.
If it does, that part of the number line is in the solution set for the inequality.
If it doesn't, that part of the number line is not in the solution set.
The parts of the number line that satisfy the inequality will **alternate**, i.e. we get

*or*

✗ ✓ ✗
CV CV

**EXAMINER'S TOP TIP**
Always test $x = 0$, if available, to see if it satisfies the inequality.

**EXAMPLE** Solve $x^2 > x + 6$

$x^2 - x - 6 > 0$

$x^2 - x - 6 = 0$ This will give the critical values.

$(x - 3)(x + 2) = 0$

$x = 3$ *or* $x = -2$ These are the critical values.

Test $x = 0$ in the original inequality.

$0^2 > 0 + 6$ $x = 0$ does not satisfy the inequality.

$x > 3$ *or* $x < -2$ The solution set is shown below.

NOTE Circles on a number line show that the critical values are not included in the solution set.

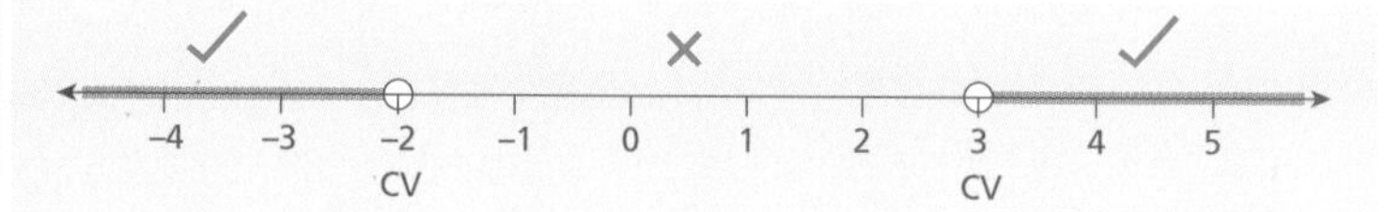


## Quadratic functions

When a variable, $y$, is related by some rule or formula to another variable, $x$, we say that **$y$ is a function of $x$**.
If the highest power of $x$ in the formula is 1, $y$ is a **linear function of $x$**. (The word **linear** is used because if we plotted a graph of $y$ against $x$ we would obtain a **straight line**.)
If the highest power of $x$ in the formula is 2, $y$ is a **quadratic function of $x$**.

## Graph of a quadratic function

The simplest examples are $y = x^2$ and $y = -x^2$.

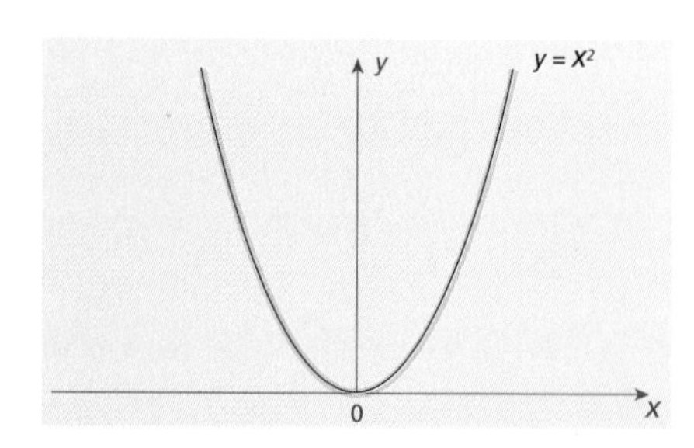


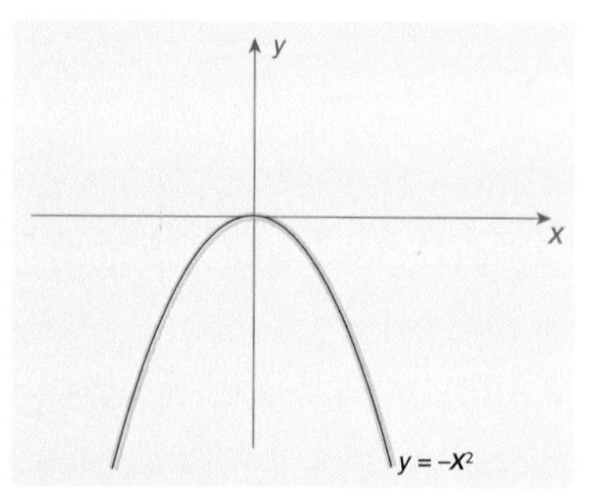


Both graphs are parabolas. They are symmetrical about the $y$-axis. The graph of any quadratic function, $y = ax^2 + bx + c$ is a parabola. There are six possibilities.

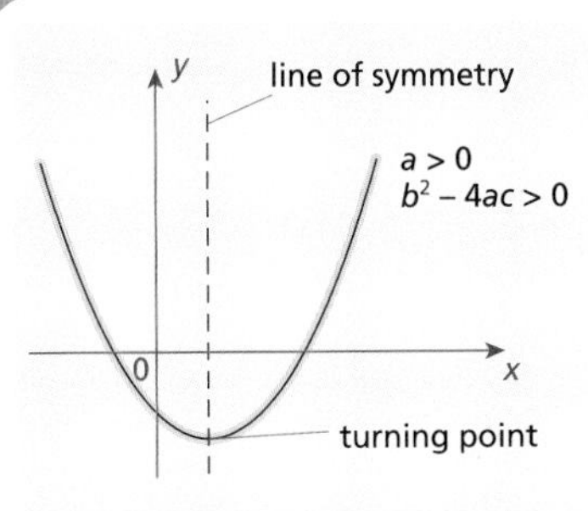


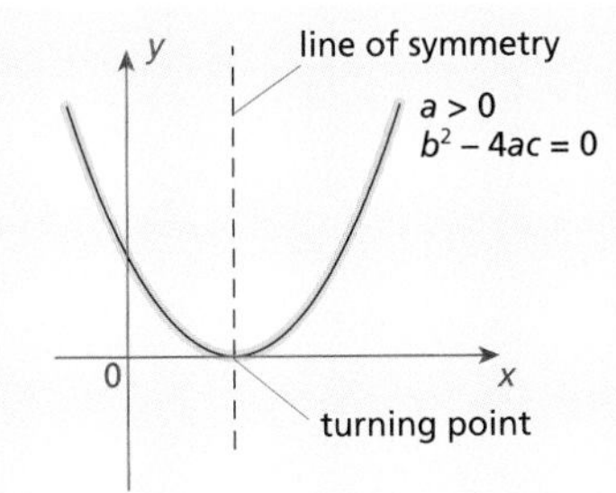


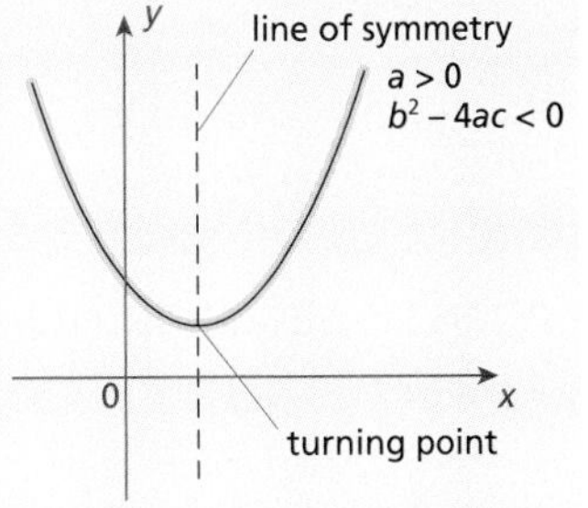


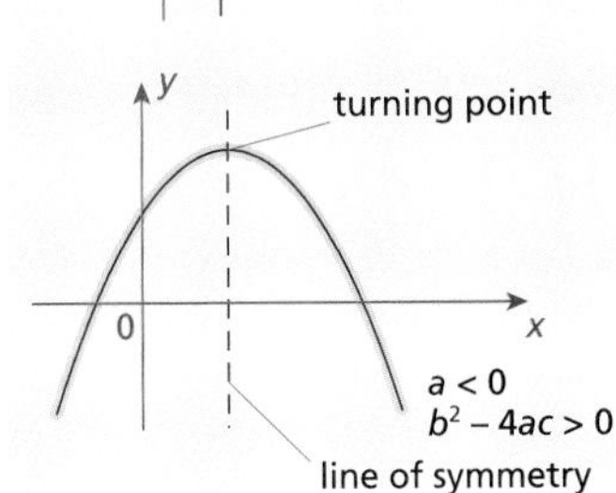


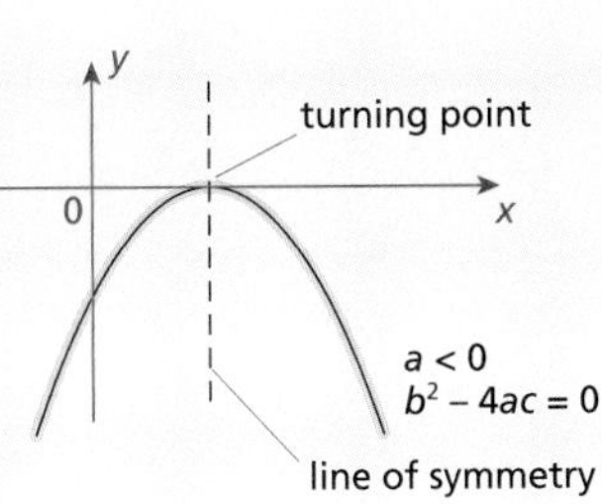


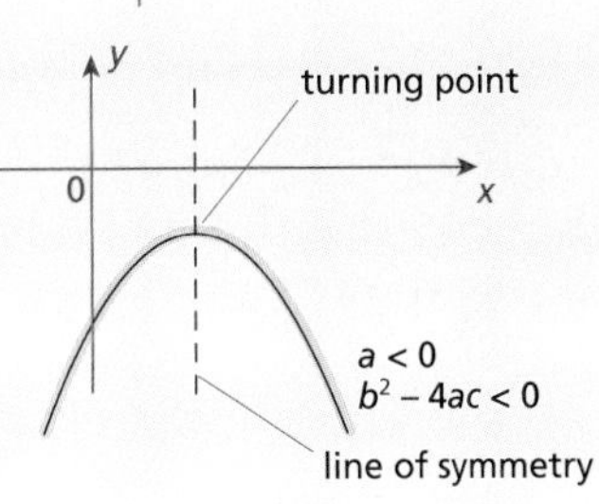


In all cases, the equation of the line of symmetry of the graph is $x = \frac{-b}{2a}$.
$b^2 - 4ac$ is called the **discriminant** because it allows us to discriminate between the various cases.

# Using the discriminant

The discriminant tells us how many times the graph $y = ax^2 + bx + c$ crosses the $x$-axis. It tells us how many solutions the equation $ax^2 + bx + c = 0$ has.

If $b^2 - 4ac > 0$, there are two distinct solutions.
If $b^2 - 4ac = 0$, there is one repeated solution.
If $b^2 - 4ac < 0$, there are no solutions.

**EXAMINER'S TOP TIP**
**When dealing with quadratic functions, the value of the discriminant gives us a lot of information about the function.**

**EXAMPLE**

Sketch the curves with these equations.

(a) $y = x^2 - x - 6$
$a = 1, b = -1, c = -6$ NOTE $a > 0$
$b^2 - 4ac = (-1)^2 - 4 \times 1 \times (-6)$
$= 1 + 24 = 25$
Perfect square so equation factorises.
$y = (x - 3)(x + 2)$ by inspection
Put $y = 0$ to find $x$-axis intercepts.
$x = 3$ and $x = -2$ Line of symmetry $x = \frac{1}{2}$
Put $x = 0$ to find $y$-axis intercept,
$y = -6$

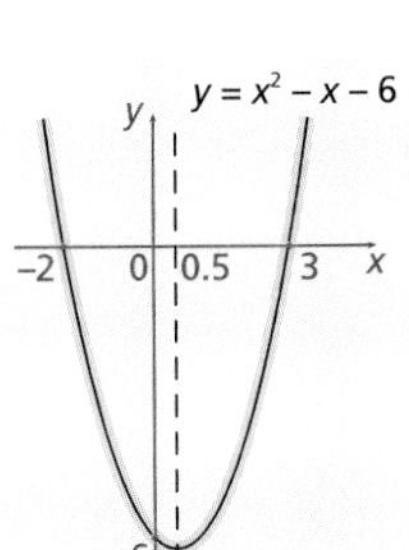


(b) $y = 4x - x^2 - 5$
$a = -1, b = 4, c = -5$ NOTE $a < 0$
$b^2 - 4ac = 4^2 - 4 \times (-1) \times (-5)$
$= 16 - 20 = -4 < 0$
This graph does not cross $x$-axis.
Put $x = 0$,
Graph crosses $y$-axis at $y = -5$
Line of symmetry $x = \frac{-b}{2a} = \frac{-4}{-2} = 2$
Put $x = 2$, $y = 8 - 4 - 5 = -1$

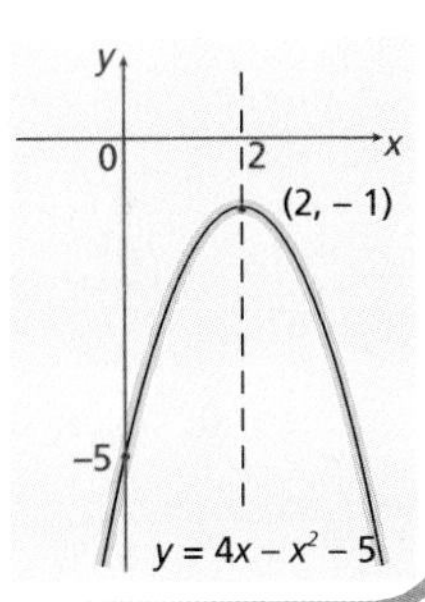


# Quick test

**1** ***Solve these inequalities.***

***(a)*** $x^2 + x > 12$ ***(b)*** $x^2 - 9 \le 0$ ***(c)*** $2x^2 + x < 6$ ***(d)*** $(x - 1) \le (x - 1)^2$

**2** ***Sketch these. Give the coordinates of the turning point and any points where the graph cuts the axes.***

***(a)*** $y = x^2 - 6x + 9$ ***(b)*** $y = 5x^2 - 15x$ ***(c)*** $y = 25 - x^2$ ***(d)*** $y = -5 - 4x - x^2$

1. (a) $x < -4$ or $x > 3$ (b) $-3 \le x \le 3$ (c) $-2 < x < \frac{3}{2}$ (d) $x \le 1$ or $x \ge 2$

2. (a)

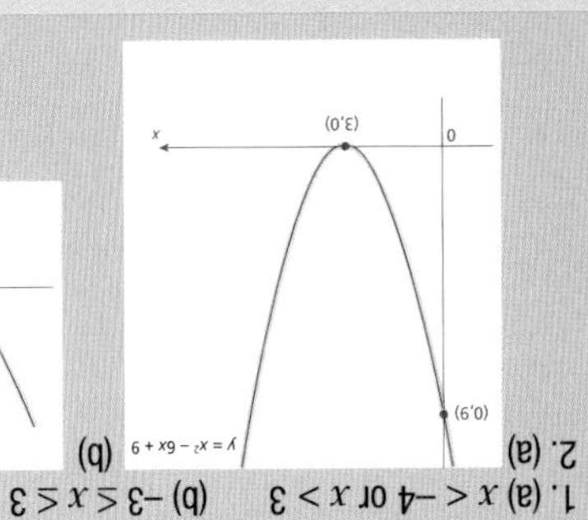

(b)

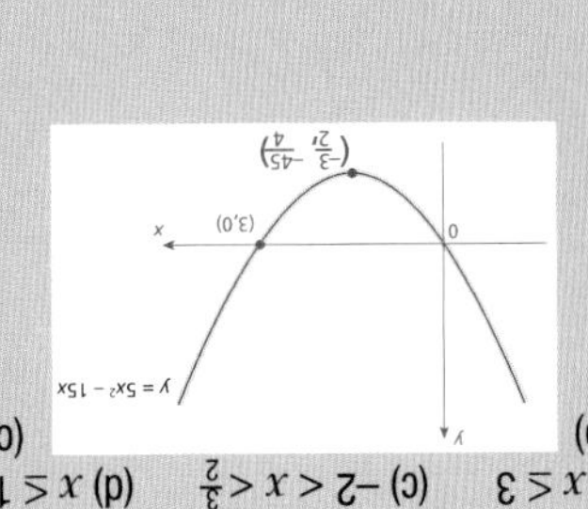

(c)

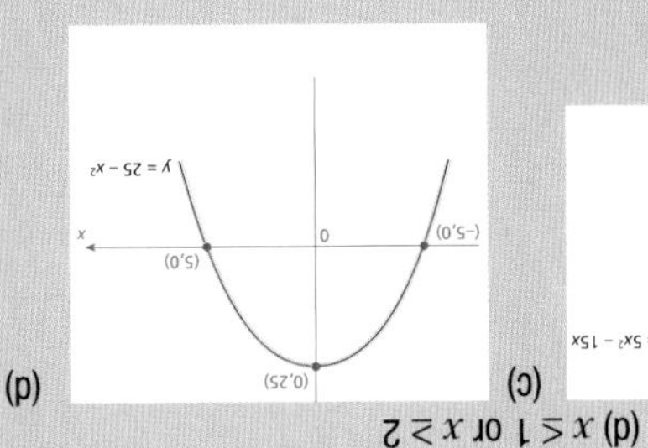

(d)

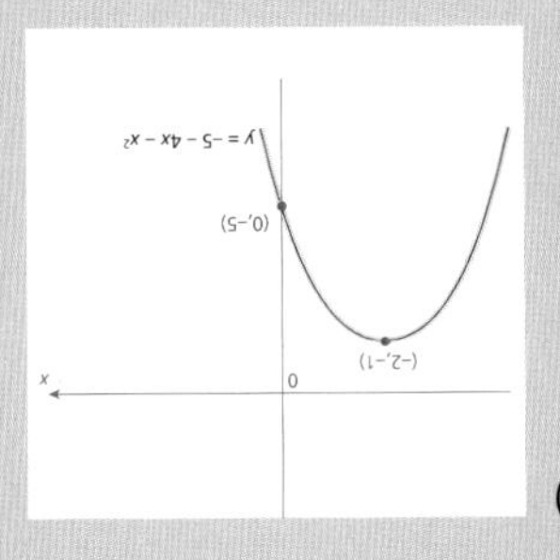

# Applications of completing the square

**Completing the square can be used to:**

- **find the maximum or minimum value of a quadratic expression**
- **help sketch a quadratic graph**

## Finding the minimum or maximum value of a quadratic expression

EXAMPLE

Find the minimum value of $x^2 - 8x + 18$.
At what value of $x$ does it occur?

We need to complete the square, i.e. add a number to $x^2 - 8x$ to give a perfect square (see page 11).

In this case, the number is $\left(\frac{8}{2}\right)^2 = 16$

$x^2 - 8x + \mathbf{16} - \mathbf{16} + 18$

**Add** and **then subtract** to **keep the expression the same!**

$= x^2 - 8x + \mathbf{16} - \mathbf{16} + 18$
$= (x - 4)^2 - 16 + 18$
$= (x - 4)^2 + 2$

**EXAMINER'S TOP TIP**
**Check this is correct by multiplying it out and checking that it is the same as the expression that you started with!**

Since $(x - 4)^2 \geq 0$ for all values of $x$, the whole expression must be $\geq 2$. Its **minimum value** is 2 when $(x - 4)^2 = 0$, i.e. when $x = 4$

EXAMPLE

Find the maximum value of $2x - x^2 + 5$.
At what value of $x$ does it occur?

We 'take out' the negative sign from the $x^2$ and $x$ terms only:
$2x - x^2 + 5 = -(x^2 - 2x) + 5$

We complete the square of the expression **inside the bracket**.

$-(x^2 - 2x + \mathbf{1}) + \mathbf{1} + 5 = -(x - 1)^2 + 6$

NOTE To balance the books, we must **add** 1 here.

$-(x - 1)^2 + 6 = 6 - (x - 1)^2$

Since $(x - 1)^2 \geq 0$, the expression will be $\leq 6$

i.e. $2x - x^2 + 5 \geq 6$

The **maximum value** is 6 when $(x - 1)^2 = 0$, i.e. when $x = 1$

## Sketching a quadratic graph

EXAMPLE

Sketch $y = x^2 - 8x + 18$
$y = (x - 4)^2 + 2$ from above.
The **minimum value** is 2 when $(x - 4)^2 = 0$, i.e. when $x = 4$

The graph will be

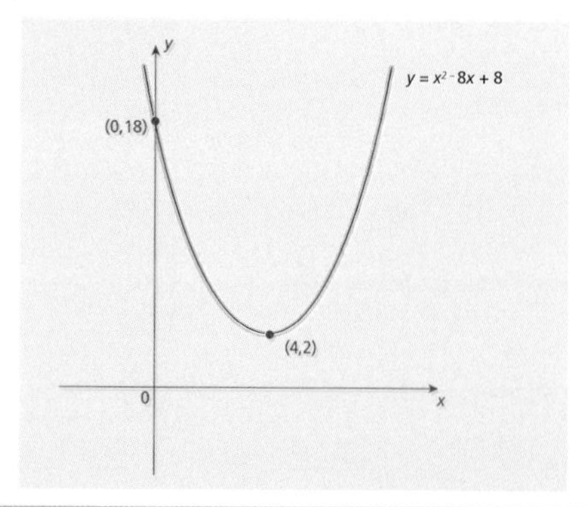


EXAMPLE

Sketch $2x - x^2 + 5$
$y = 6 - (x - 1)^2$ from above.
The **maximum value** is 6 when $(x - 1)^2 = 0$, i.e. when $x = 1$

The graph will be

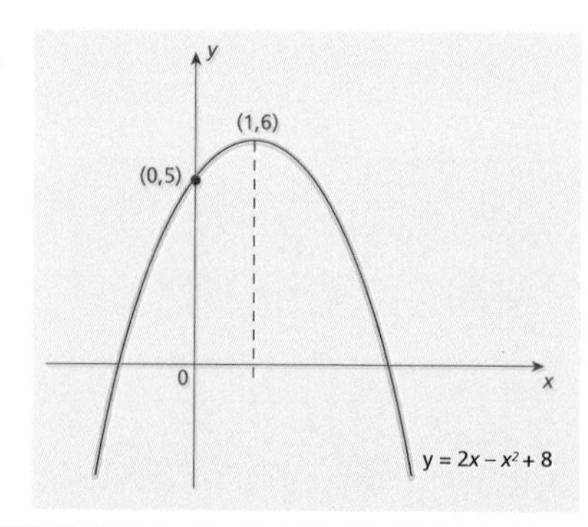

# Further examples of completing the square

In all cases, if we square the bracket and simplify, we must get the **same expression** that we had originally. All we are doing is writing the original expression in a **different form**.

$x^2 - 12x = x^2 - 12x + \mathbf{36} - \mathbf{36}$
$\quad = (x - 6)^2 - 36$

**NOTE** In every case we **add** a number to complete the square, and **then subtract the same number** to balance the books.

$x^2 + x = x^2 + x + \mathbf{\frac{1}{4}} - \mathbf{\frac{1}{4}}$
$\quad = \left(x + \frac{1}{2}\right)^2 - \frac{1}{4}$

$x^2 - 10x - 5 = x^2 - 10x + \mathbf{25} - \mathbf{25} - 5$
$\quad = (x - 5)^2 - 30$

$6 - x - x^2 = -x^2 - x + 6 = -(x^2 + x) + 6$
$= -\left(x^2 + x + \mathbf{\frac{1}{4}}\right) + \mathbf{\frac{1}{4}} + 6$
$= -\left(x + \frac{1}{2}\right)^2 + 6\frac{1}{4}$
$= 6\frac{1}{4} - \left(x + \frac{1}{2}\right)^2$

Because of the – sign at the front, we have actually **subtracted $\frac{1}{4}$** so we **add $\frac{1}{4}$** to balance the books.

$2x^2 - 12x + 7 = 2(x^2 - 6x) + 7$
$\quad = 2(x^2 - 6x + \mathbf{9}) - \mathbf{18} + 7$
$\quad = 2(x - 3)^2 - 11$

Because of the 2 at the front, we have actually **added 18**, so we **subtract 18** to balance the books.

## Quick test

**1** *Complete the square for each of the following.*

*(a) $x^2 + 8x$ (b) $x^2 + 2x - 15$ (c) $2x^2 + 16x + 5$ (d) $2x^2 - 10x$ (e) $6 + 4x - x^2$ (f) $3 - 2x - x^2$*

**2** *Use your answers to write down the maximum or minimum value of the expressions in question 1 and the values of $x$ for which they occur. Sketch the graphs.*

1.(a) $(x + 4)^2 - 16$ (b) $(x + 1)^2 - 16$ (c) $2(x + 4)^2 - 27$ (d) $2(x - \frac{5}{2})^2 - \frac{25}{2}$ (e) $10 - (x - 2)^2$ (f) $4 - (x + 1)^2$

2.(a) Minimum value is –16 when $x = -4$

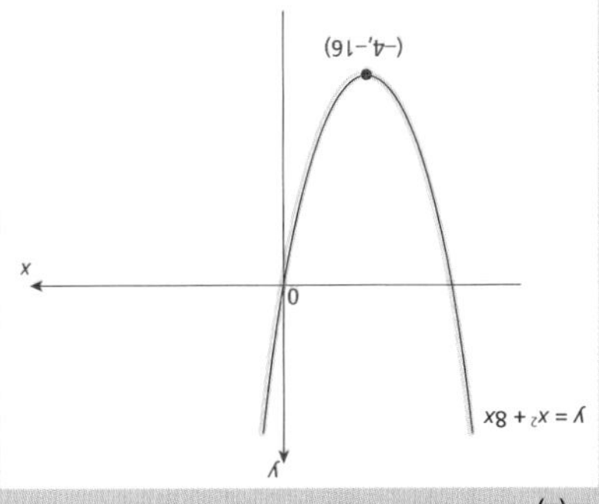


(c) Minimum value is –27 when $x = -4$

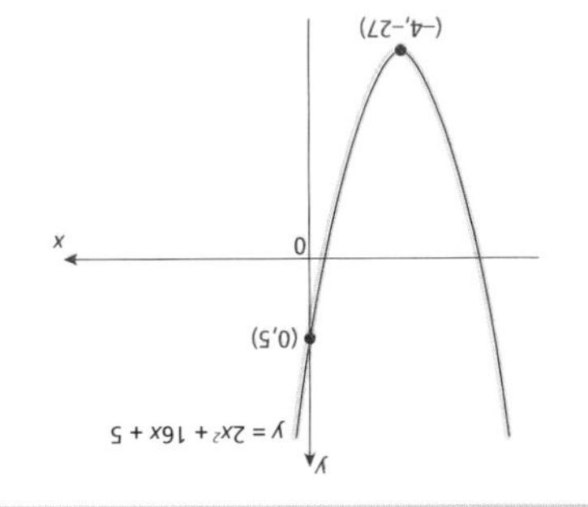


(e) Maximum value is 10 when $x = 2$

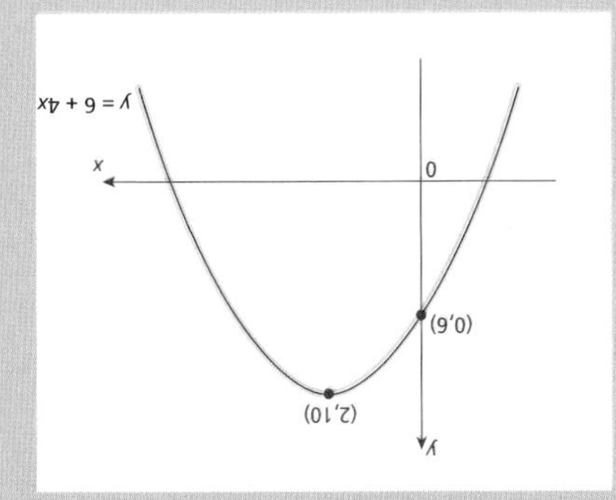


(b) Minimum value is –16 when $x = -1$

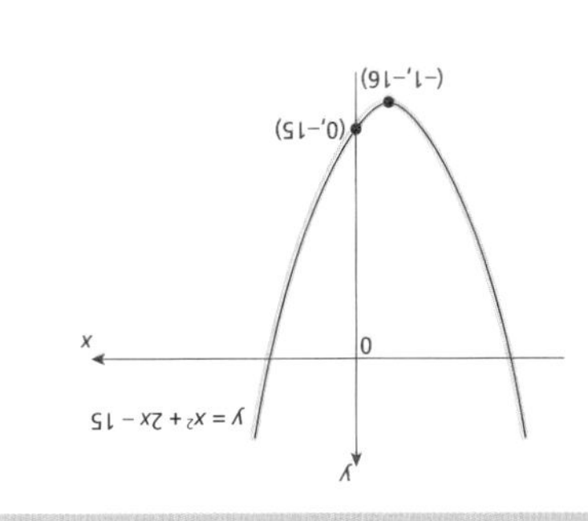


(d) Minimum value is $-\frac{25}{2}$ when $x = \frac{5}{2}$

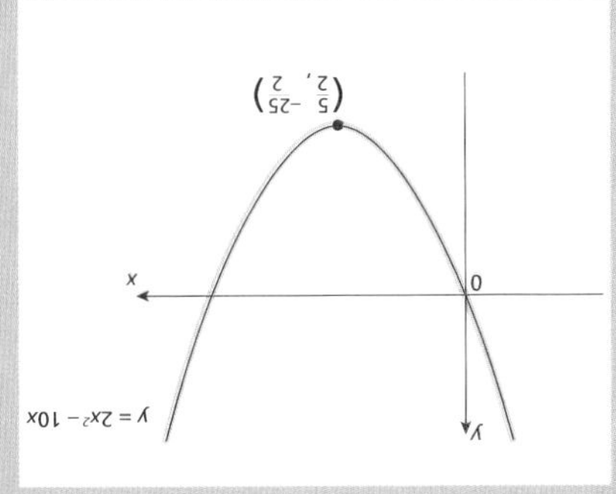


(f) Maximum value is 4 when $x = -1$

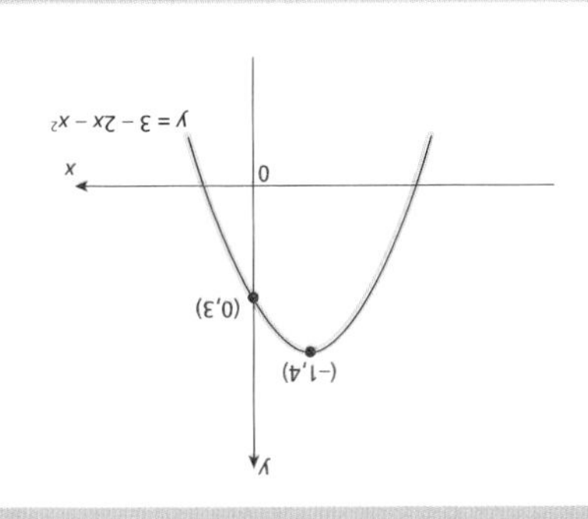

# Simultaneous equations

- **Simultaneous equations are equations which are satisfied at the same time. You must be able to solve two such equations when one is linear and the other is quadratic.**

## Solving simultaneous equations

**EXAMINER'S TOP TIP**

**We always substitute from the linear equation into the quadratic equation. Choose carefully which variable you substitute for. Sometimes one is much easier than the other.**

### Using the substitution method

EXAMPLE $x + y = 7$

$x^2 + y^2 = 25$

|  |  |
|---|---|
| Make $x$ or $y$ the subject of the linear equation | $y = 7 - x$ |
| Substitute for $x$ or $y$ in the quadratic equation | $x^2 + (7 - x)^2 = 25$ |
| Write quadratic in form $ax^2 + bx + c = 0$ | $2x^2 - 14x + 24 = 0$<br>$x^2 - 7x + 12 = 0$ |
| Solve quadratic for $x$ or $y$ | $(x - 3)(x - 4) = 0$<br>$x = 3$ *or* $x = 4$ |
| Use linear equation to find corresponding $x$ or $y$ values | $y = 4$ *or* $y = 3$ |
| State solutions | $x = 3, y = 4$ *or* $x = 4, y = 3$ |

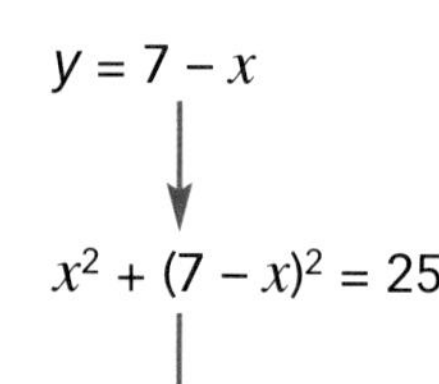

## Graphical interpretation of simultaneous linear and quadratic equations

When solving a linear and quadratic equation simultaneously, graphically we are finding the **coordinates of the point(s) of intersection of a straight line and a curve**.

In the example above, the curve is a circle, centre (0, 0), radius 5. The line intersects the circle at the two points (3, 4) and (4, 3).

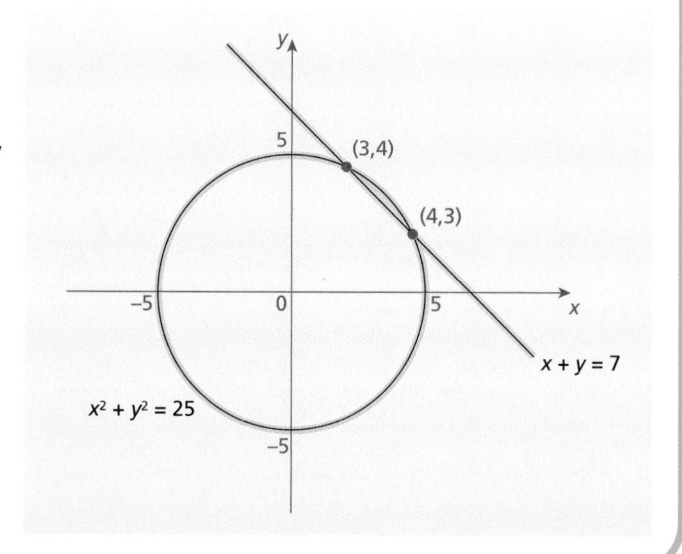

## Further examples

Solve $x + 2y = 1$
$y^2 + xy = 4$

Here, it is much easier to find $x$ in terms of $y$: $x = 1 - 2y$

$$y^2 + (1 - 2y)y = 4$$
$$y^2 + y - 2y^2 = 4$$
$$y^2 - y + 4 = 0$$

The discriminant, $b^2 - 4ac = (-1)^2 - (4 \times 1 \times 4) = 1 - 16 = -15 < 0$
Since the discriminant $< 0$, the equation has *no* solutions. Graphically, this means that **the straight line, $x + 2y = 1$ does not intersect the curve**, $y^2 + xy = 4$.

Solve $x^2 + 3x + 5y = 20$
$x + 3y = 1$

Even though it involves fractions, eliminating $y$ is easier as we only have to substitute once.

$$y = \frac{1 - x}{3}$$
$$x^2 + 3x + 5\left(\frac{1 - x}{3}\right) = 20$$
$$3x^2 + 9x + 5 - 5x = 60$$
$$3x^2 + 4x - 55 = 0$$
$$(3x - 11)(x + 5) = 0$$

$$y = \frac{1 - \frac{11}{3}}{3} = -\frac{8}{9} \quad \textit{or} \quad y = \frac{1 - -5}{3} = 2$$

$$\textit{So, } x = \frac{11}{3},\ y = \frac{-8}{9} \quad \textit{or} \quad x = -5,\ y = 2$$

Solve $x - 2y = 7$
$x^2 + 4y^2 = 37$

Here, we find $x$ in terms of $y$: $x = 2y + 7$

$$(2y + 7)^2 + 4y^2 = 37$$
$$4y^2 + 28y + 49 + 4y^2 = 37$$
$$8y^2 + 28y + 12 = 0$$
$$2y^2 + 7y + 3 = 0$$
$$(2y + 1)(y + 3) = 0$$
$$y = -\frac{1}{2} \quad \textit{or} \quad y = -3$$
$$x = 6 \quad \textit{or} \quad x = 1$$
$$\textit{So, } x = 6,\ y = -\frac{1}{2} \quad \textit{or} \quad x = 1,\ y = -3$$

## Quick test

***Solve these simultaneous equations.***

**1** $2x + y = 1$
$x^2 + y^2 = 1$

**2** $y - x = 2$
$2x^2 + 3xy + y^2 = 8$

**3** $y = x^2 + 3$
$y = 4x$

**4** $u - v = 3$
$u^2 + v^2 = 89$

1. $x = 0, y = 1$ or $x = \frac{4}{5}, y = -\frac{3}{5}$ 2. $x = -2, y = 0$ or $x = \frac{1}{3}, y = \frac{7}{3}$ 3. $x = 3, y = 12$ or $x = 1, y = 4$ 4. $u = 8, v = 5$ or $u = -5, v = -8$

# Polynomials 1
## – definitions and the four basic operations

- **A polynomial is an algebraic expression which is the sum of a number of terms.**

EXAMPLE

$$x^3 - 2x^2 + 4$$

**terms** (each of $x^3$, $-2x^2$, $4$)

**powers must be positive whole numbers or zero**

**number in front of each term is called its coefficient**

**constant term as it has no $x$s**

## Degree of a polynomial

The **highest power of** $x$ in a polynomial is called its **degree**. The **general form** of a polynomial of **degree $n$** is

$$a_n x^n + a_{n-1} x^{n-1} + \ldots + a_2 x^2 + a_1 x + a_0 \text{ where } a_n \neq 0$$

**NOTE** Some, or even all, of the other coefficients could be zero.

## Notation

We use P($x$), Q($x$), R($x$), f($x$), etc. to denote a polynomial in $x$

EXAMPLES

$P(x) = 2x^3 - x + 1$

$Q(y) = 3y^2 + 2y - 4$

$f(t) = t - 1$

## Adding, subtracting and multiplying

We can **add, subtract and multiply** two polynomials in the **same variable**.

EXAMPLES

$P(x) = 2x^2 + 3x - 1 \qquad Q(x) = x^3 + 5x + 3$

$P(x) + Q(x) = 2x^2 + 3x - 1 + x^3 + 5x + 3 = x^3 + 2x^2 + 8x + 2$

$P(x) - Q(x) = 2x^2 + 3x - 1 - (x^3 + 5x + 3)$ The brackets are very important when subtracting.

$= 2x^2 + 3x - 1 - x^3 - 5x - 3$

$= -x^3 + 2x^2 - 2x - 4$

$P(x).\,Q(x) = (2x^2 + 3x - 1)(x^3 + 5x + 3)$

$= 2x^2(x^3 + 5x + 3) + 3x(x^3 + 5x + 3) - 1(x^3 + 5x + 3)$

$= 2x^5 + 10x^3 + 6x^2 + 3x^4 + 15x^2 + 9x - x^3 - 5x - 3$

$= 2x^5 + 3x^4 + 9x^3 + 21x^2 + 4x - 3$

# Dividing polynomials

**NOTE** For AS, you only need to be able to divide by $(x - a)$ or $(x + a)$ where a is a positive whole number.

**EXAMPLE**

Divide $2x^3 - 3x^2 + 5x + 4$ by $(x - 2)$

$$
\begin{array}{r|l}
 & 2x^2 + x + 7 \\
x - 2 & 2x^3 - 3x^2 + 5x + 4 \\
 & 2x^3 - 4x^2 \\
 & \quad x^2 + 5x \\
 & \quad x^2 - 2x \\
 & \qquad 7x + 4 \\
 & \qquad 7x - 14 \\
 & \qquad\quad 18
\end{array}
$$

$x$ goes into $2x^3$, $2x^2$ times.

This is $2x^2(x - 2)$. Now subtract.

$x$ goes into $x^2$, $x$ times.

$x$ goes into $7x$, 7 times.

This is $7(x - 2)$. Now subtract.

This is the remainder.

So, $\dfrac{2x^3 - 3x^2 + 5x + 4}{x - 2} = 2x^2 + x + 7 \quad \text{r } 18$

*or,* $\dfrac{2x^3 - 3x^2 + 5x + 4}{x - 2} = 2x^2 + x + 7 + \dfrac{18}{x - 2}$

*Compare this with* $\dfrac{59}{7} = 8 \text{ r } 3$ *or* $\dfrac{59}{7} = 8 + \dfrac{3}{7}$

**EXAMINER'S TOP TIP**

**When dividing, you must ensure that your working is aligned in columns.**

**EXAMPLE**

$$\frac{3x^3 - 4x + 1}{x + 3}$$

$$
\begin{array}{r|l}
 & 3x^2 - 9x + 23 \\
x + 3 & 3x^3 + 0x^2 - 4x + 1 \\
 & 3x^3 + 9x^2 \\
 & \quad -9x^2 - 4x \\
 & \quad -9x^2 - 27x \\
 & \qquad 23x + 1 \\
 & \qquad 23x + 69 \\
 & \qquad\quad -68
\end{array}
$$

**NOTE** There is no $x^2$ term in the polynomial that we are dividing. However, when we carry out the division, we must put in $0.x^2$ to keep the columns correct.

This is the remainder.

$$\frac{3x^3 - 4x + 1}{x + 3} = 3x^2 - 9x + 23 - \frac{68}{x + 3}$$

This is sometimes called a quotient. This is the answer.

By multiplying through by $(x + 3)$ this result can also be written as $3x^3 - 4x + 1 = (x + 3)(3x^2 - 9x + 23) - 68$

For an algebraic division

$$\frac{3x^3 - 4x + 1}{x + 3} = 3x^2 - 9x + 23 \quad \text{r} - 68$$

$$\frac{3x^3 - 4x + 1}{x + 3} = 3x^2 - 9x + 23 - \frac{68}{x + 3}$$

$$3x^3 - 4x + 1 = (x + 3)(3x^2 - 9x + 23) - 68$$

These are all equivalent.

## Quick test

**1** ***If*** $P(x) = 3x^3 - 2x - 6$ ***and*** $Q(x) = 2x^2 - 3x + 1$***, find these:*** **(a)** $P(x) + Q(x)$ **(b)** $P(x) - Q(x)$ **(c)** $P(x).Q(x)$

**2** ***Find these:***

**(a)** $\dfrac{2x^3 - 3x^2 - 3x + 2}{x - 2}$ **(b)** $\dfrac{2x^3 - 11x^2 + 12x - 35}{x - 5}$ **(c)** $\dfrac{x^4 + 2x^2 - 3x + 1}{x + 1}$ **(d)** $\dfrac{x^4 - 2}{x - 1}$

***In each case check your answers by putting in a simple value of x***

1. (a) $3x^3 + 2x^2 - 5x - 5$ (b) $3x^3 - 2x^2 + x - 7$ (c) $6x^5 - 9x^4 - x^3 - 6x^2 + 16x - 6$
2. (a) $2x^2 + x - 1$ (no remainder) (b) $2x^2 - x + 7$ (no remainder) (c) $x^3 - x^2 + 3x - 6$ r 7 (d) $x^3 + x^2 + x + 1$ r $-1$

# Polynomials 2 – the Factor Theorem

- **Just as numbers can be split into factors, polynomials can also be split into factors. This is called factorisation and is an important skill.** Compare these.

EXAMPLE

$42 = 7 \times 6$

**7 and 6 are factors of 42. However, we can factorise 6 into 3 and 2.**

**So, $42 = 7 \times 6 = 7 \times 3 \times 2$**

**7, 2 and 3 are all prime numbers, so 42 is now completely factorised.**

EXAMPLE

$x^3 - 7x - 6 = (x + 1)(x^2 - x - 6)$

**$(x + 1)$ and $(x^2 - x - 6)$ are factors of $x^3 - 7x - 6$**
**However, we can factorise $x^2 - x - 6$**

$x^2 - x - 6 = (x - 3)(x + 2)$

**So, $x^3 - 7x - 6 = (x + 1)(x - 3)(x + 2)$**

**The polynomial is now completely factorised.**

## Common factors

If the polynomial has no constant term (number) then we can take out a common factor from each term.

EXAMPLE

$2x^3 - 4x^2 + 6x = 2x(x^2 - 2x + 3)$

Quadratic cannot be factorised as $b^2 - 4ac = (-2)^2 - (4 \times 1 \times 3) = 4 - 12 = -8$ is *not* a perfect square.

EXAMPLE

$x^5 - 2x^3 = x^3(x^2 - 2)$

Quadratic cannot be factorised.

## The Factor Theorem

NOTE For AS Mathematics, you will be expected to be able to factorise any quadratic polynomial (using the method(s) outlined on page 6) and certain cubic polynomials (where the highest power in $x$ is 3) using the Factor Theorem.

When solving quadratic equations by factorisation (see page 6) it is easy to find the values of $x$ which satisfy the equation once we have the factors.

EXAMPLE

$x^2 - 2x - 3 = 0$

$(x - 3)(x + 1) = 0$ $\quad x = 3$ *or* $x = -1$

We can use this idea in reverse to find factors.
If $x = 3$ and $x = -1$ are solutions, then $(x - 3)$ and $(x + 1)$ must be factors.

EXAMPLE

$P(x) = x^2 - 2x - 3$

$P(3) = 3^2 - (2 \times 3) - 3 = 0 \Rightarrow (x - 3)$ is a factor of $P(x)$.

$P(-1) = -1^2 - (2 \times -1) - 3 = 1 + 2 - 3 = 0 \Rightarrow (x + 1)$ is a factor of $P(x)$.

NOTE $P(2) = 2^2 - (2 \times 2) - 3 = 4 - 4 - 3 \neq 0$ *so* $(x - 2)$ is not a factor of $P(x)$.

EXAMPLE

$2x^2 - 3x - 2 = 0$

$(2x + 1)(x - 2) = 0$

$x = -\frac{1}{2}$ *or* $x = 2$.

Turning this around, we can say that since $x = -\frac{1}{2}$ and $x = 2$ are solutions, $(2x + 1)$ and $(x - 2)$ must be factors.

**The Factor Theorem**
If $P(x)$ is a polynomial and $P(a) = 0$, then $(x - a)$ must be a factor of $P(x)$.
← *a* is some number

**EXAMINER'S TOP TIP**
**This is a very important result and needs to be learned.**

# Further examples

> **EXAMINER'S TOP TIP**
> Always clear the fractions in factors.

EXAMPLES

$P(x)$ is a polynomial.
If $P(3) = 0$, $P(-2) = 0$ and $P\left(\frac{1}{2}\right) = 0$, then $(x - 3)$, $(x + 2)$ and $\left(x - \frac{1}{2}\right)$ are factors of $P(x)$.

In this last case we can multiply by 2 to clear the fraction, i.e. $(2x - 1)$ is a factor of $P(x)$.

If $P-\left(\frac{1}{3}\right) = 0$ and $P\left(-\frac{3}{4}\right) = 0$, then $\left(x + \frac{1}{3}\right)$ and $\left(x + \frac{3}{4}\right)$ are factors of $P(x)$,
i.e. $(3x + 1)$ and $(4x + 3)$ are factors of $P(x)$.

# Factorising a cubic polynomial

EXAMPLE

Factorise $x^3 + x^2 - 4x - 4$
Let $P(x) = x^3 + x^2 - 4x - 4$
$P(1) = 1^3 + 1^2 - 4 - 4 = -6 \neq 0$

This is an important step and will help you present your solution clearly. We start by searching for a value of $x$ (usually a small positive or negative whole number) which makes $P(x) = 0$.

$P(-1) = (-1)^3 + (-1)^2 - 4 \times -1 - 4 = -1 + 1 - 4 + 4 = 0$ By Factor Theorem, $(x + 1)$ is factor of $P(x)$.
So, $P(x) = (x + 1)Q(x)$ where $Q(x)$ is another polynomial.

There are two ways of finding $Q(x)$

**1** Since $P(x) = (x + 1)Q(x)$, $\frac{P(x)}{x + 1} = Q(x)$

$$\begin{array}{r} x^2 - 4 \\ x + 1\,\overline{)\,x^3 + x^2 - 4x - 4} \\ \underline{x^3 + x^2 \qquad\qquad} \\ 0 \quad 0 - 4x - 4 \\ \underline{-4x - 4} \\ 0 \quad 0 \end{array}$$

$x^2 - 4$ ← This is $Q(x)$.

$P(x) = (x + 1)(x^2 - 4)$
We must now factorise $x^2 - 4$ if possible.

$x^2 - 4 = x^2 - 2^2$, a difference of two squares

$= (x + 2)(x - 2)$

So, $P(x) = (x + 1)(x + 2)(x - 2)$

**2** We can find $Q(x)$ by inspection.

$$x^3 + x^2 - 4x - 4 = (x + 1)(x^2 - 4)$$

The first term must be $x^2$ to give $x^3$ when multiplied out.
The constant term must be $-4$ to give $-4$ when multiplied out.

To find the missing middle $x$ term, we focus on the $x^2$ terms on either side of the equation.
On LHS we have one $x^2$ term.

To obtain $x^2$ terms on RHS we combine as follows.

$$(x + 1)(x^2 - 4)$$

The missing term must be $0.x^2$ as we already have $1 \times x^2$ which balances LHS.
Then proceed as before to give $P(x) = (x + 1)(x + 2)(x - 2)$
**Check answer** by **putting small value of $x$ on both sides**.

$x = 1$
LHS $= 1^3 + 1^2 - 4 \times -1 - 4 = 1 + 1 - 4 - 4 = -6$
RHS $= (1 + 1)(1 + 2)(1 - 2) = 2 \times 3 \times -1 = -6$

> **EXAMINER'S TOP TIP**
> This is called a difference of two squares. It has a well-known factorisation: $a^2 - b^2 = (a + b)(a - b)$. Learn this!

# Quick test

***Factorise the following:***

**1** $2x^3 - 3x^2 - 11x + 6$ **2** $3x^3 - 8x^2 - 17x + 14$ **3** $4x^3 - 20x^2 + 13x + 12$ **4** $x^3 + 2x^2 - x - 2$

1. $(x - 3)(2x - 1)(x + 2)$ 2. $(3x - 2)(x^2 - 2x - 7)$ 3. $(2x - 3)(2x + 1)(x - 4)$ 4. $(x - 1)(x + 1)(x + 2)$

# Polynomials 3 – the Remainder Theorem

- There is a quick way to find the remainder in a polynomial division without having to perform the division.

EXAMPLE

$$\frac{2x^3 - 3x^2 + 5x + 4}{x - 2} = 2x^2 + x + 7 \quad \text{r } 18$$

If we did not know what the remainder was and we hadn't done the division to get the answer A($x$), then

$$\frac{2x^3 - 3x^2 + 5x + 4}{x - 2} = \text{A}(x) \quad \text{r R}$$

i.e. $\frac{2x^3 - 3x^2 + 5x + 4}{x - 2} = \text{A}(x) + \frac{\text{R}}{x - 2}$

i.e. $2x^3 - 3x^2 + 5x + 4 = (x - 2)\text{A}(x) + \text{R}$

We can find R without knowing A($x$) by putting $x = 2$ on both sides.

$$(2 \times 2^3) - (3 \times 2^2) + (5 \times 2) + 4 = (2 - 2)\text{A}(2) + \text{R}$$

Since this is 0, $0 \times \text{A}(2) = 0$ no matter what A(2) is so,

$$16 - 12 + 10 + 4 = 0 + \text{R}$$
$$18 = \text{R}$$

Hence, the remainder, when P($x$) is divided by ($x$ – 2), is given by P(2).

## The Remainder Theorem

**The Remainder Theorem**

The remainder when a polynomial P($x$) is divided by ($x - a$) is P($a$).

EXAMINER'S TOP TIP
This is an important result and should be learned.

NOTE If the division is by ($x + a$), then the remainder is P($-a$).

If the division is by ($ax + b$), then the remainder is $\text{P}\left(-\frac{b}{a}\right)$.

To determine the value of $x$ which needs to be substituted in, equate the bracket, by which you are dividing, to zero, and solve for $x$.

# Examples using the Remainder Theorem

**1** Find the remainder when $3x^3 + 7x^2 + 2x + 1$ is divided by $(x - 2)$.
Let $P(x) = 3x^3 + 7x^2 + 2x + 1$
Then remainder $= P(2) = (3 \times 2^3) + (7 \times 2^2) + (2 \times 2) + 1 = 24 + 28 + 4 + 1 = 57$

**2** Find the remainder when $2x^3 + 4x^2 - 6x + 1$ is divided by $(2x - 1)$.
Let $P(x) = 2x^3 + 4x^2 - 6x + 1$
Then remainder $= P(\frac{1}{2})$ (To find this value, put $2x - 1 = 0 \Rightarrow x = \frac{1}{2}$)
$P(\frac{1}{2}) = (2 \times (\frac{1}{2})^3) + (4 \times (\frac{1}{2})^2) - (6 \times (\frac{1}{2})) + 1 = \frac{2}{8} + \frac{4}{4} - 3 + 1 = -\frac{3}{4}$

**3** Find the remainder when $x^4 + 3x - 1$ is divided by $(3x + 2)$.
Let $P(x) = x^4 + 3x - 1$
Then remainder $= P(-\frac{2}{3})$ $(3x + 2 = 0 \Rightarrow x = -\frac{2}{3})$
$P(-\frac{2}{3}) = (-\frac{2}{3})^4 + 3(-\frac{2}{3}) - 1 = \frac{16}{81} - 2 - 1 = -3 + \frac{16}{81} = -\frac{227}{81}$

**4** When $x^3 + ax^2 + 3x - 1$ is divided by $(x + 2)$, the remainder is 1. Find the value of $a$.
Let $f(x) = x^3 + ax^2 + 3x - 1$ $(x + 2 = 0 \Rightarrow x = -2)$
Remainder $f(-2) = (-2)^3 + a(-2)^2 + 3(-2) - 1 = 1$
$-8 + 4a - 6 - 1 = 1$
$4a - 15 = 1$
$4a = 16, a = 4$

**5** When divided by $x + 1$, the polynomial $ax^3 + bx^2 - 13x + 6$ leaves a remainder of 18. Given that $2x - 1$ is a factor of the polynomial, find the values of $a$ and $b$.

Let $P(x) = ax^3 + bx^2 - 13x + 6$ $(x + 1 = 0 \Rightarrow x = -1)$
$P(-1) = a(-1)^3 + b(-1)^2 + 13 + 6 = 18$
$= -a + b + 13 + 6 = 18$
$-1 = -a + b$ [1]

Using the Factor Theorem, $2x - 1 = 0 \Rightarrow x = \frac{1}{2}$, so $P(\frac{1}{2}) = 0$
$a(\frac{1}{2})^3 + b(\frac{1}{2})^2 - 13(\frac{1}{2}) + 6 = 0$
$\frac{1}{8}a + \frac{1}{4}b - 6\frac{1}{2} + 6 = 0$ Multiply by 8 to clear fractions.
$a + 2b = 4$ [2]
$-a + b = -1$ [1] [2] + [1]
$3b = 3, b = 1$ so $a = 2$

**EXAMINER'S TOP TIP**
If there are 2 unknowns to find, set up 2 simultaneous equations using the two facts given in the question, and solve them.

# Quick test

**1** *Find the remainder when P$x$ is divided by Q($x$).*
(a) $P(x) = 3x^3 + 2x^2 - 6x + 1$, $Q(x) = x - 2$ (b) $P(x) = 2x^3 + 3x^2 - 7x - 14$, $Q(x) = x + 5$
(c) $P(x) = 4x^4 + 2x^2 - x - 7$, $Q(x) = 2x - 1$ (d) $P(x) = 4x^3 + 6x^2 + 3x + 2$, $Q(x) = 2x + 3$

**2** *When divided by $2x - 3$, the polynomial $4x^3 - ax^2 - 2x - 7$ leaves a remainder of 8. Find the value of the constant a.*

**3** *The polynomial $ax^3 + x^2 + bx - 4$ leaves a remainder of –6 when divided by $x - 1$ and also has $x - 2$ as a factor. Find the values of a and b.*

1. (a) 21 (b) −154 (c) $-6\frac{3}{4}$ (d) $-2\frac{1}{2}$ 2. −2 3. $a = 1, b = -4$

# Polynomials 4 – identities

- **An identity is true for all values of $x$. We often use ≡ to indicate an identity.**
  **Look at these:**
  **$2x + 1 = 5$**
  **$3(x + 2) - 4 = 3x + 2$**

**The first is an equation and is only true for certain values of $x$.**
**$x = 2$ is the solution of this equation.**
**The second is an identity: what is on the RHS is identical to what is on LHS after simplification.**

## Solving identities

To find unknown constant(s) in an identity we can use one, or both, of these techniques.

1. **Substitute** one or more values for $x$ to produce one or more equations.
2. **Equate coefficients** of one or more terms on each side.

**EXAMINER'S TOP TIP**
Although you need to learn both methods for solving identities, the substitution method is usually much easier.

EXAMPLE

Find the constants A and B such that $A(x + 2) + B(x + 1) \equiv x$

**Substitution**

An identity is true for all values of $x$ so we can put in any value for $x$.
If possible, use values of $x$ to make the working easy by eliminating one of the unknowns in each case.

Put $x = -2$: $A(-2 + 2) + B(-2 + 1) = -2$
$A \times 0 - B = -2$     $B = 2$
Put $x = -1$: $A(-1 + 2) + B(-1 + 1) = -1$
$A + B \times 0 = -1$     $A = -1$

**Equating coefficients**

Multiply out the LHS and collect terms.
$Ax + 2A + Bx + B \equiv x$
$x(A + B) + 2A + B \equiv x$
LHS **must be identical** to RHS.
$A + B = 1$     Equating coefficients of $x$
$2A + B = 0$     Equating constant terms.

Solving simultaneous equations gives
$A = -1$ and $B = 2$ as before.

Sometimes a combination of the two methods is needed:

EXAMPLE

Find the values of A, B and C such that
$A(x^2 + 4) + (x - 2)(Bx + C) \equiv 7x^2 - x + 14$
Put $x = 2$: $A(2^2 + 4) + (2 - 2)(2B + C) = (7 \times 2^2) - 2 + 14$
$8A + 0 = 28 - 2 + 14 = 40$     $A = 5$
Put $x = 0$: $A(0^2 + 4) + (0 - 2)(B \times 0 + C) = 7 \times 0^2 - 0 + 14$
$4A - 2C = 14$
$20 - 2C = 14$
$2C = 6$     $C = 3$

Equate coefficients of $x^2$ to find B.
$A + B = 7$     $B = 2$
We could also find B by substituting another value for $x$

Put $x = 1$: $A(1^2 + 4) + (1 - 2)(B \times 1 + C) = (7 \times 1^2) - 1 + 14$
$5A - B - C = 7 - 1 + 14 = 20$
$25 - B - 3 = 20$     $B = 2$

# Evaluating a polynomial

You can evaluate a polynomial for a particular value of $x$.

Suppose $P(x) = 2x^3 + 3x - 4$

Then $P(1) = (2 \times 1^3) + (3 \times 1) - 4 = 2 + 3 - 4 = 1$

$P(2) = (2 \times 2^3) + (3 \times 2) - 4 = 16 + 6 - 4 = 18$

$P(-3) = (2 \times (-3)^3) + (3 \times (-3)) - 4 = -54 - 9 - 4 = -67$

# Checking your answers by evaluating polynominals

EXAMPLE

Suppose $P(x) = 2x^2 + 5x - 3$ and $Q(x) = x^3 + x^2 - 2$

Then
$$\begin{aligned} P(x)Q(x) &= (2x^2 + 5x - 3)(x^3 + x^2 - 2) \\ &= 2x^2 (x^3 + x^2 - 2) + 5x(x^3 + x^2 - 2) - 3(x^3 + x^2 - 2) \\ &= 2x^5 + 7x^4 + 2x^3 - 7x^2 - 10x + 6 \end{aligned}$$

It is very easy to make a mistake when carrying out this process so a simple check is very useful.

$P(1) = 2 + 5 - 3 = 4$ $\quad Q(1) = 1 + 1 - 2 = 0$ $\quad$ So, $P(1)Q(1) = 4 \times 0 = 0$

Put $x = 1$ in $P(x)Q(x) = 2x^5 + 7x^4 + 2x^3 - 7x^2 - 10x + 6$ and check that you also get 0

$1 + 7 + 2 - 7 - 10 + 6 = 0$

EXAMPLE

$$\frac{2x^3 - 3x^2 + 5x + 4}{x - 2} = 2x^2 + x + 7 + \frac{18}{x - 2}$$

To **check** this answer we can put in a simple $x$ value like $x = 1$

$\text{LHS} = \frac{2 - 3 + 5 + 4}{1 - 2} = \frac{8}{-1} = -8$ $\qquad$ $\text{RHS} = 2 + 1 + 7 + \frac{18}{1 - 2} = 10 - 18 = -8$

Any $x$ value except $x = 2$ will work as a check here!
(Why won't $x = 2$ work?)

**EXAMINER'S TOP TIP**

**You can check answers when processing polynomials by substituting in a simple value for $x$ (such as $x = 1$) and ensuring that your answers tally. If they don't, it's definitely wrong, if they do, it's probably right.**

# Quick test

***Find the values of the constants A, B and C.***

1. $A(x + 2) + B(x - 1) \equiv 6x + 3$
2. $A(x + 3) + B(x + 2) \equiv 4x + 9$
3. $(Ax + B)(x + 1) + C(x^2 + 3) \equiv x - 3$
4. $4x^2 - 12x + 25 \equiv A(x + B)^2 + C$

1. $A = B = 3$ 2. $A = 1, B = 3$ 3. $A = 1, B = 0, C = -1$ 4. $A = 4, B = -\frac{3}{2}, C = 16$

# Exponentials and logarithms 1 – graphs and log laws

- A function of the form $2^x$, $3^{-2x}$, $10^{x+1}$, etc. is called an exponential function because $x$ appears as a power or exponent.

The logarithm of a number to a certain base is the power of the base that is required to give the number.

**EXAMINER'S TOP TIP**
Before starting this section, revise the section on indices (page 4).

EXAMPLE

We know that $2^3 = 8$. This relationship can be expressed using logarithm notation. We write

$$\log_2 8 = 3$$

This number is called the base of the logarithm.

## Graphs of exponential functions of form $a^x$

$y = 2^x$ has this graph.

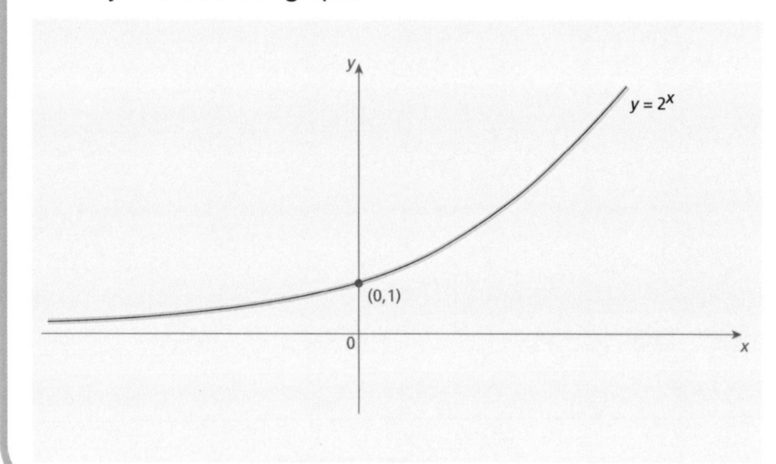


There are a number of key points.

- $2^0 = 1$ so the graph passes through (0, 1)
- The graph is asymptotic to the $x$-axis.
- $2^x > 0$ for all values of $x$

A graph of this type is sometimes called an exponential growth curve.

## Logarithms

EXAMPLES

Find $\log_{10}100$ — To find this, you need to find the power of 10 that will give 100. Since $10^2 = 100$,

$\log_{10}100 = 2$

$\log_4 16 = 2$ $\quad \log_3 27 = 3$ $\quad \log_2 2 = 1$ $\quad \log_5 1 = 0$

### Negative logarithms

EXAMPLES

Find $\log_3\left(\frac{1}{3}\right)$ — To find this, you need to find the power of 3 that will give $\frac{1}{3}$. Since $3^{-1} = \frac{1}{3}$,

$\log_3\left(\frac{1}{3}\right) = -1$

$\log_4\left(\frac{1}{16}\right) = -2$ $\quad \log_{10}\left(\frac{1}{1000}\right) = -3$ $\quad \log_5\left(\frac{1}{5}\right) = -1$

## Using graphs

All the Examples we have looked at so far give logarithms which are integers. Many logarithms are not whole numbers.

**EXAMPLE**

Find $\log_2 5$

To find this, you need to find the power of 2 that will give 5.
$2^2 = 4$ and $2^3 = 8$, so the answer is somewhere between 2 and 3, probably closer to 2.
You could find an approximate answer by using the graph of $y = 2^x$

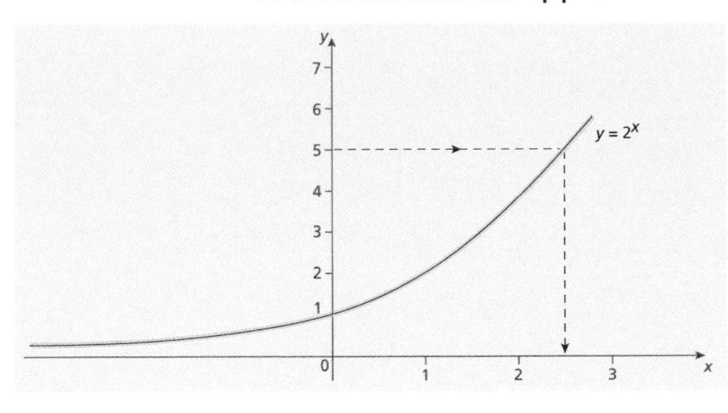


This gives approximately 2.3 (the actual answer is 2.3219280…)
**Finding logarithms, base 2, is equivalent to using the graph of $y = 2^x$ in reverse, from the $y$-axis to the $x$-axis.**

NOTE This means that **we cannot take the logarithm of a negative number or zero.** It also means that **the logarithm of any number between 0 and 1 will be negative.**

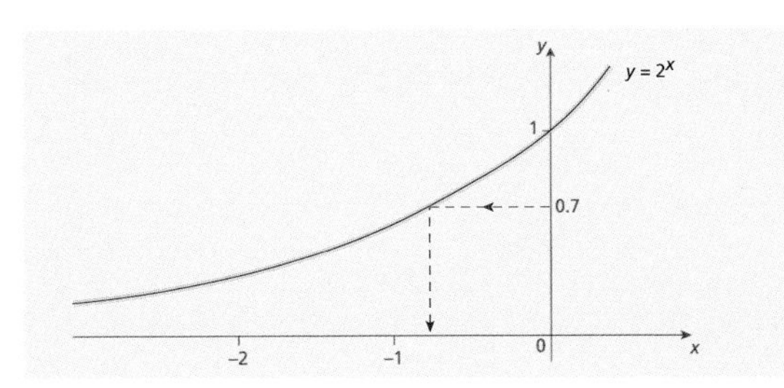


**EXAMPLE**

Find $\log_2 0.7$

This gives approximately –0.514…
The graph method will only give us **approximate** answers.

## Laws of logarithms

These are the laws of logarithms.

These are the same as the 3 laws of indices, just written in a different form. For these laws to apply, **all logarithms** must be to **the same base**.

- $\log_a xy = \log_a x + \log_a y$
- $\log_a (x/y) = \log_a x - \log_a y$
- $\log_a x^k = k\log_a x$

Special case: $\log_a \left(\frac{1}{x}\right) = \log_a x^{-1} = -\log_a x$

- $\log_a a = 1$ ($a^1 = a$)
- $\log_a 1 = 0$ ($a^0 = 1$)

**EXAMINER'S TOP TIP**
You need to be flexible and confident in the use of these laws in both directions, i.e. from left to right and right to left.

**EXAMPLES**

Simplify $\log_a 5 + 2\log_a 3 - \log_a 6$

$\log_a 5 + 2\log_a 3 - \log_a 6 = \log_a 5 + \log_a 3^2 - \log_a 6$

$(\log_a 5 + \log_a 9) - \log_a 6 = \log_a (5 \times 9) - \log_a 6$

$= \log_a \frac{45}{6} = \log_a \frac{15}{2}$

## Quick test

**1 Find the exact value of $x$.**

(a) $\log_x 36 = \frac{1}{2}$ (Hint: so $x^{\frac{1}{2}} = 36$) (b) $\log_x 9 = -2$ (c) $\log_x 125 = 3$

**2 Write these as a single logarithm.**

(a) $2\log_a 3 - 3\log_a 2 + 4\log_a 1$ (b) $\log_a 5 + (\frac{1}{2})\log_a 16 - \log_a 2$ (c) $5\log_a a + (\frac{1}{3})\log_a 27 + \log_a 2$

**3 Express these in terms of $\log_a$, $\log_a y$ and $\log_a z$**

(a) $\log_a \frac{x}{yz}$ (b) $\log_a \frac{x^2y^3}{z^4}$ (c) $\log_a \sqrt{(xyz)}$ (d) $\log_a \frac{xy}{\sqrt{(z^3)}}$ (e) $\log_a \sqrt{\frac{x}{y}}$

1. (a) 1296 (b) $\frac{1}{3}$ (c) 5 2. (a) $\log_a \frac{9}{8}$ (b) $\log_a 10$ (c) $\log_a 6a^5$ 3. (a) $\log_a x - \log_a y - \log_a z$ (b) $2\log_a x + 3\log_a y - 4\log_a z$ (c) $\frac{1}{2}\log_a x + \frac{1}{2}\log_a y + \frac{1}{2}\log_a z$ (d) $\log_a x + \log_a y - \frac{3}{2}\log_a z$ (e) $\frac{1}{2}\log_a x - \frac{1}{2}\log_a y$

# Exponentials and logarithms 2

## – solving equations of form $a^x = b$

$$a^x = b$$
$$\log_{10} a^x = \log_{10} b$$
$$x \log_{10} a = \log_{10} b$$
$$x = \frac{\log_{10} b}{\log_{10} a}$$

EXAMPLE

**Find $x$ to 3 d.p. if $2^x = 5$.**

**Since $2^2 = 4$ and $2^3 = 8$, $x$ is clearly between 2 and 3 and, on page 24, we found an approximate answer using the graph of $y = 2^x$.**

**Exact answer is $x = \frac{\log_{10} 5}{\log_{10} 2}$.**

**Using the log button on a calculator, $x = 2.322$ (3 d.p.).**

## Further examples

**1** Solve $3^{x+2} = 30$

$$\log_{10}(3^{x+2}) = \log_{10} 30$$
$$(x+2)\log_{10} 3 = \log_{10} 30$$
$$x + 2 = \frac{\log_{10} 30}{\log_{10} 3}$$
$$x = \frac{\log_{10} 30}{\log_{10} 3} - 2 = 1.096 \text{ (3 d.p.)}$$

*or*

$$3^{(x+2)} = 30$$
$$3^x \times 3^2 = 30$$
$$9 \times 3^x = 30$$
$$3^x = \frac{30}{9} = \frac{10}{3}$$

Take logs base 10

$$\log_{10} 3^x = \log_{10} \frac{10}{3}$$
$$x \log_{10} 3 = \log_{10} \frac{10}{3}$$
$$x = \frac{\log_{10}\left(\frac{10}{3}\right)}{\log_{10} 3} = 1.096 \text{ (3 d.p.)}$$

**2** Solve $5^{(2x)} = 21$

$$\log_{10} 5^{2x} = \log_{10} 21$$
$$2x \log_{10} 5 = \log_{10} 21$$
$$2x = \frac{\log_{10} 21}{\log_{10} 5}$$
$$x = \frac{1}{2} \times \frac{\log_{10} 21}{\log_{10} 5} = 0.946 \text{ (3 d.p.)}$$

*or*

$$5^{(2x)} = 21$$
$$(5^x)^2 = 21$$
$$5^x = \sqrt{21}$$
$$\log_{10} 5^x = \log_{10}\sqrt{21}$$
$$x \log_{10} 5 = \log_{10}\sqrt{21}$$
$$x = \frac{\log_{10}\sqrt{21}}{\log_{10} 5} = 0.946 \text{ (3 d.p.)}$$

**EXAMINER'S TOP TIP**

**$\log_{10}(x \pm y) \neq \log_{10} x \pm \log_{10} y$**
**$\log_{10}(x \pm y)$ cannot be simplified (just as $\sqrt{(x \pm y)}$ cannot be simplified)**

**3** Solve $3^{(2x)} - 6 \times 3^x + 5 = 0$

NOTE Taking logs of both sides won't work here for 2 reasons.

**1** We can't take $\log_{10}0$

**2** We can't simplify the log of a sum or difference of terms.

The key point is spotting that $3^{(2x)} = (3^x)^2$.

$3^{(2x)} - 6 \times 3^x + 5 = 0 = (3^x)^2 - 6 \times 3^x + 5$

This is now a **quadratic** in $3^x$

Replace $3^x$ by $y$

$$y^2 - 6y + 5 = 0$$
$$(y - 5)(y - 1) = 0$$
$$y = 5 \text{ or } y = 1$$
$$3^x = 5 \text{ or } 3^x = 1$$

If $3^x = 1$, $x = 0$

$$3^x = 5$$
$$\log_{10}3^x = \log_{10}5$$
$$x = \frac{\log_{10}5}{\log_{10}3} = 1.465 \text{ (3 d.p.)}$$

# Finding logarithms to any base

Although we only have logarithms to base 10 on the calculator, this is enough to find the exact value of the logarithm of a number to **any base**.

**EXAMINER'S TOP TIP**

It's a good idea to see what size of answer to expect. $3^2 = 9$ and $3^3 = 27$, so the answer will be somewhere between 2 and 3

**EXAMPLE**

Find the value of $\log_3 16$ to 3 d.p.

$$\text{Let } x = \log_3 16$$

This means the same as $3^x = 16$

$$\log_{10}3^x = \log_{10}16$$
$$x \log_{10}3 = \log_{10}16$$
$$x = \frac{\log_{10}16}{\log_{10}3}$$

$$\log_3 16 = \frac{\log_{10}16}{\log_{10}3} = 2.524 \text{ (3 d.p.)}$$

Note the **form** of this answer.

$$\log_5 7 = \frac{\log_{10}7}{\log_{10}5} = 1.209 \text{ (3 d.p.)}$$

$$\log_3 20 = \frac{\log_{10}20}{\log_{10}3} = 2.727 \text{ (3 d.p.)}$$

In general: $\log_b a = \dfrac{\log_{10}a}{\log_{10}b}$

# Quick test

***1* *Solve these. Give answers to 3 s.f.*** *(a)* $3^x = 5$ *(b)* $2^{(x+1)} = 7$ *(c)* $4^{(2x)} = 10$

***2* *Find the value of these to 3 s.f.*** *(a)* $\log_4 12$ *(b)* $\log_6 3$ *(c)* $\log_9 13$ *(d)* $\log_8 7$

1. (a) 1.46 (b) 1.81 (c) 0.830 2. (a) 1.79 (b) 0.613 (c) 1.17 (d) 0.936

# Graphs and graph transformations

### Simple graphs of the form $y = x^n$

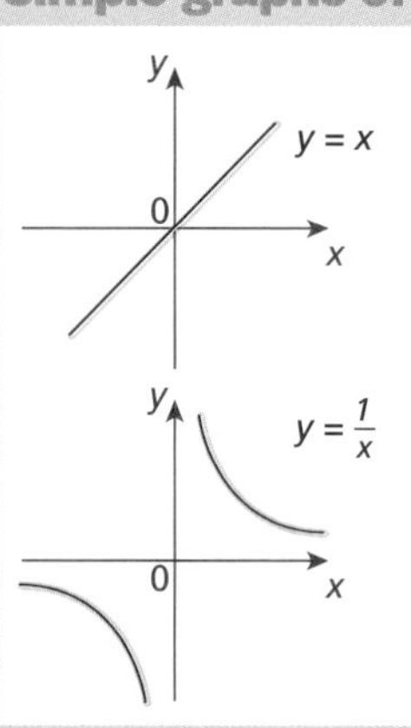


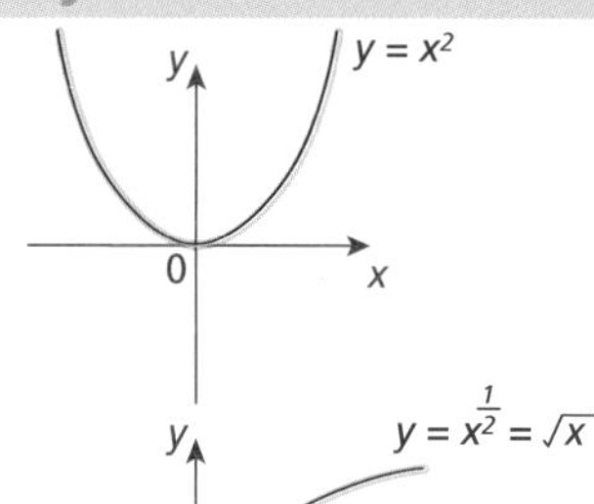


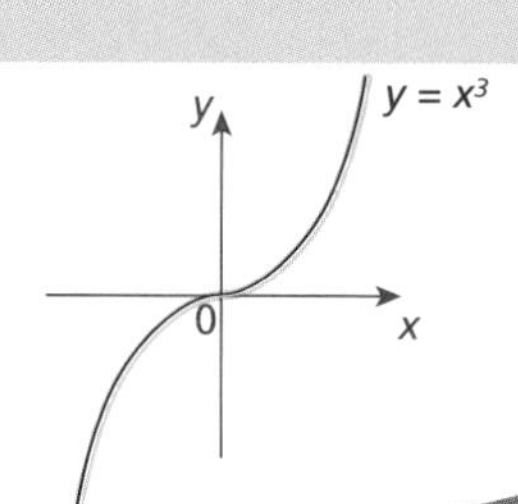


**EXAMINER'S TOP TIP**
You need to learn these as they are the building blocks for many other curves.

### Graph transformations

**Suppose we have the graph of some function, $y = f(x)$. What is the effect on the graph if we modify the equation slightly?**

- **Modifications outside the bracket have an effect in the *y*-direction that are what you would expect.**
- **Modifications inside the bracket have an effect in the *x*-direction that are the opposite of what you would expect.**

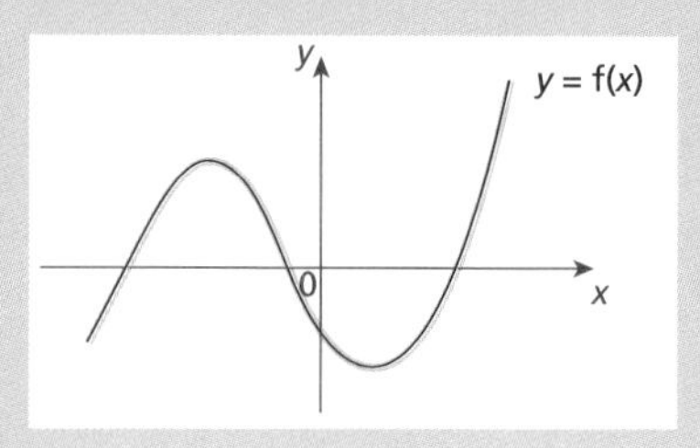


## Graph transformations outside the bracket

EXAMPLE

$y = f(x) + 2$ **adds 2 to the *y*-coordinate** of every point on the original graph. The graph is **shifted 2 units up in the *y*-direction**, shift with vector $\begin{pmatrix} 0 \\ 2 \end{pmatrix}$

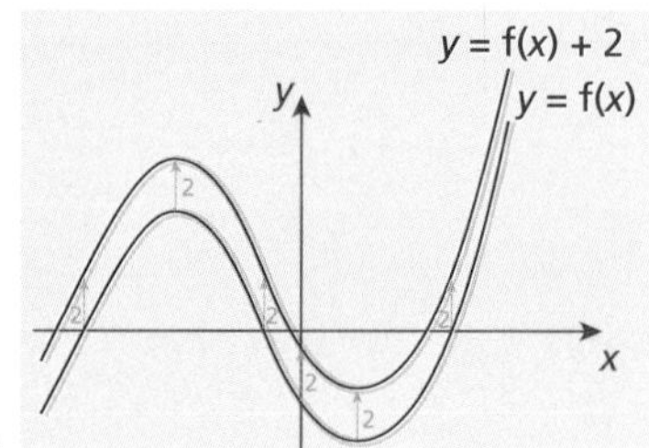


EXAMPLE

$y = 2f(x)$ **multiplies the *y*-coordinate** of every point on the original graph **by 2**. The graph is **stretched by a scale factor of 2 in the *y*-direction**.

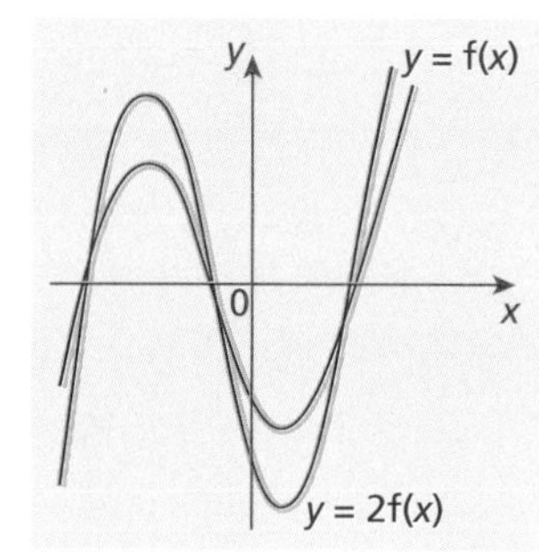


NOTE The **points on the *x*-axis stay the same**, since their *y*-coordinate is 0 and $2 \times 0 = 0$! All other points end up **twice as far from the *x*-axis as they were**.

**EXAMINER'S TOP TIP**
You need to learn the effects of these basic transformations – they are very useful for sketching more complicated graphs.

## Graph transformations inside the bracket

EXAMPLE

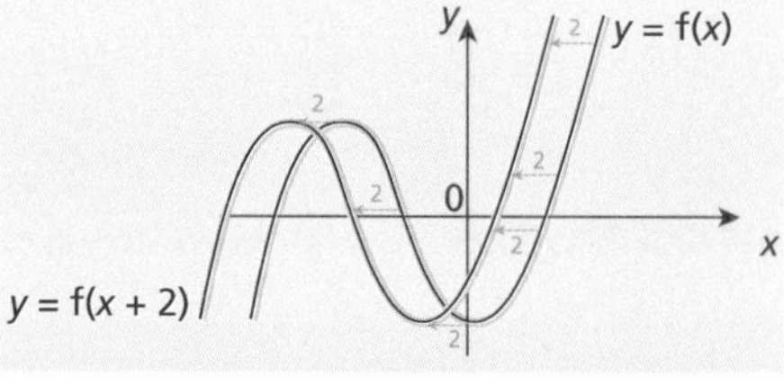


$y = f(x + 2)$ **subtracts 2 from the *x*-coordinate** of every point on the original graph. The graph is **shifted 2 units to the left in the *x*-direction**, shift with vector $\begin{pmatrix} -2 \\ 0 \end{pmatrix}$

EXAMPLE

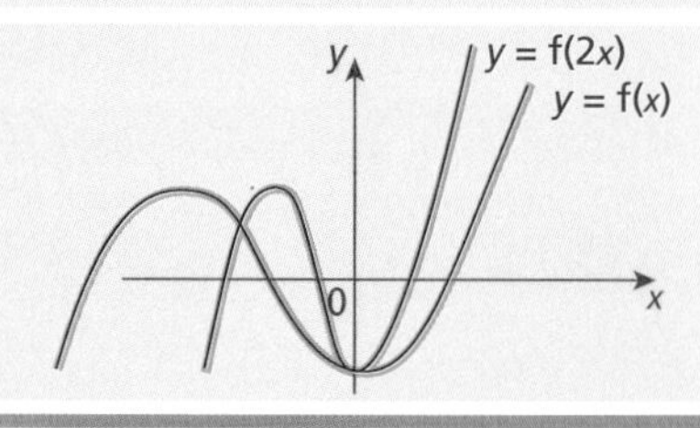


$y = f(2x)$ **multiplies the *x*-coordinate** of every point on the original graph by $\frac{1}{2}$. The graph is **stretched by a scale factor of $\frac{1}{2}$ in the *x*-direction**.

NOTE The **points on the *y*-axis stay the same**, since their *x*-coordinate is 0 and $2 \times 0 = 0$! All other points end up **half as far from the *y*-axis as they were**.

## Some special cases

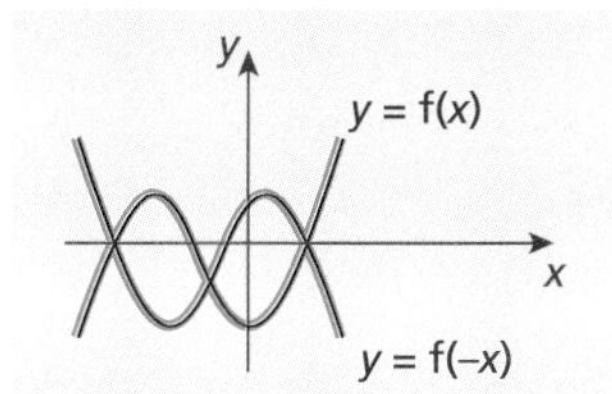


$y = -f(x)$ **multiplies the $y$-coordinate** of every point on the original graph by −1. The graph is **reflected in the $x$-axis**.

EXAMPLE

$y = f(-x)$ **multiplies the $x$-coordinate** of every point on the original graph **by $\frac{1}{-1}$ = −1**. The graph is **reflected in the $y$-axis**.

## Combinations of transformations

EXAMPLE Sketch $\mathbf{y} = \dfrac{1}{x+2} + 1$

We can build up the graph, starting with $y = f(x) = \dfrac{1}{x}$

**EXAMINER'S TOP TIP**
Ensure that you get the order of the transformations correct.

We want the graph of $y = f(x + 2) + 1$

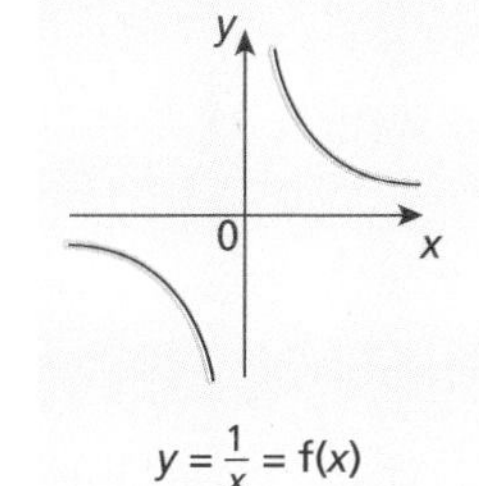


shift $\binom{-2}{0}$

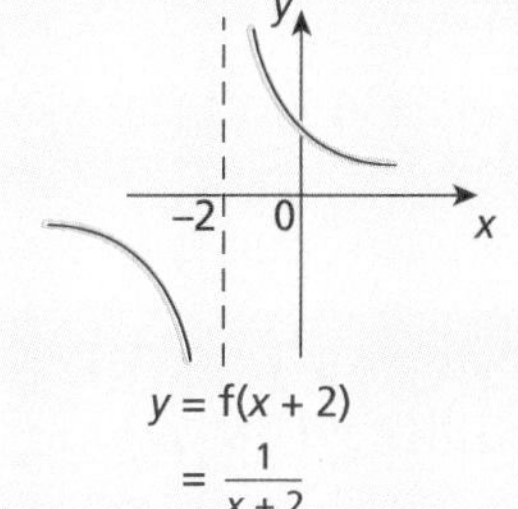


shift $\binom{0}{1}$

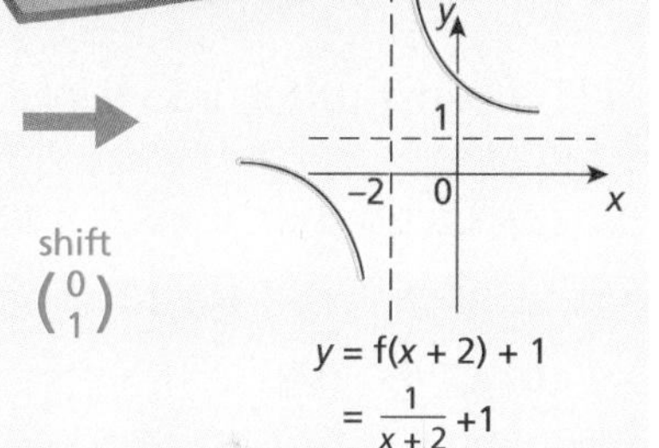


Overall transformation is shift $\begin{pmatrix}-2\\1\end{pmatrix}$

## Quick test

**1 Given that $f(x) = x^2$, sketch these graphs on separate diagrams.**

**(a) $y = f(x + 2)$ (b) $y = -f(x)$ (c) $y = 2 - f(x)$ (d) $y = 2f(x)$ (e) $y = f(2x)$ (f) $y = f(2 - x)$**

**2 Sketch these. (a) $y = \dfrac{-1}{x+1}$ (b) $y = (x - 2)^2 - 3$**

2.

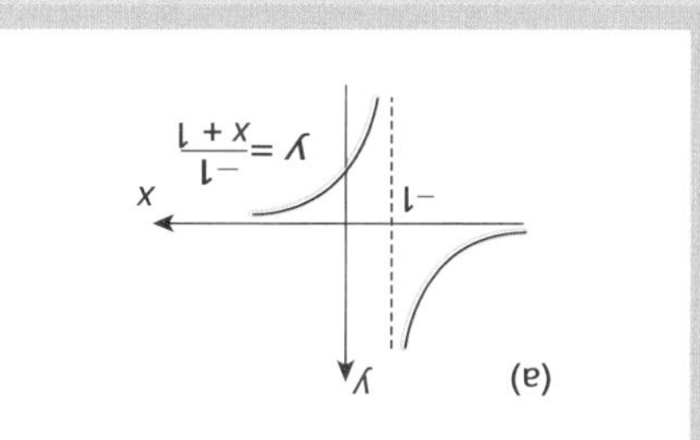


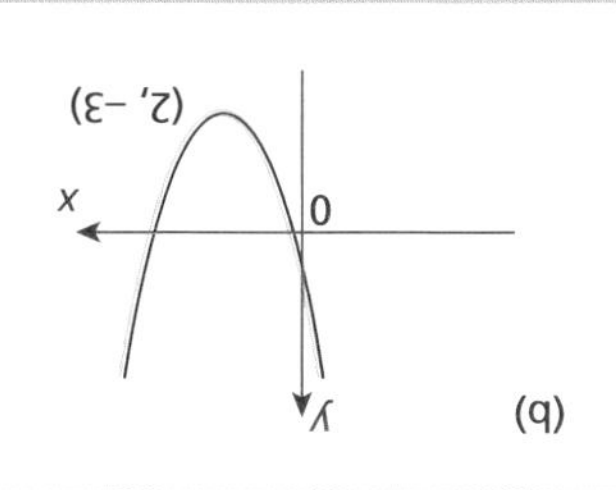


1.

(a) y = f(x + 2)

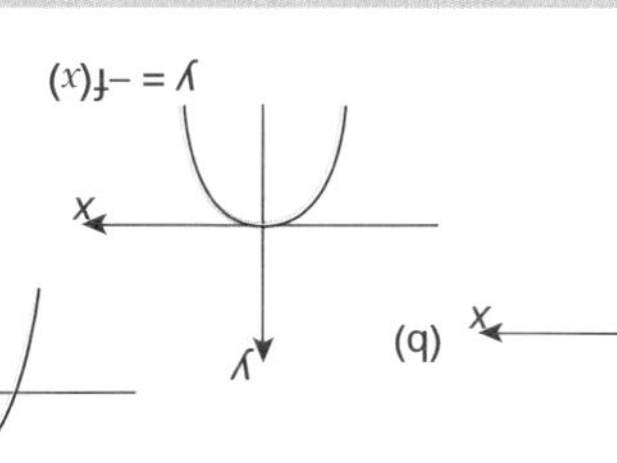


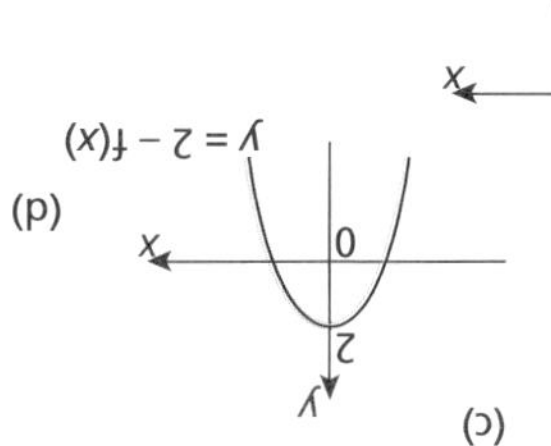


(d) y = 2f(x)

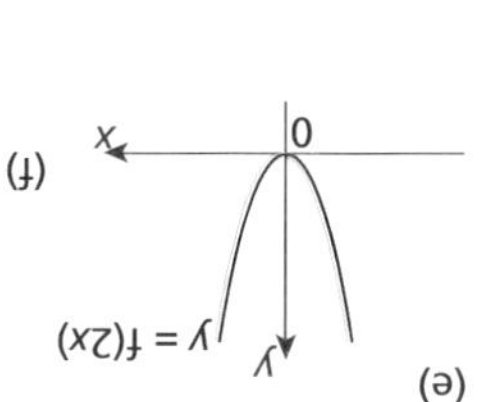


(f) y = f(2 − x)

## Exam-style questions

Use the questions to test your progress. Check your answers on page 94.

1 **(a)** Write $4^{(x+1)}$ as a power of 2. [1]
**(b)** Hence, or otherwise, solve the equation $4^{(x+1)} = 2^{(1-3x)}$. [1]

2 Express $2\sqrt{48} + \sqrt{75} - 5\sqrt{12}$ in the form $a\sqrt{b}$ where $a$ and $b$ are integers, and $b$ is as small as possible. [2]

3 $3x^2 + 12x + 5 = A(x + B)^2 + C$
**(a)** Find the values of A, B and C. [3]
**(b)** Hence, or otherwise, find the minimum value of $3x^2 + 12x + 5$. [2]
**(c)** Solve the equation $3x^2 + 12x + 5 = 0$, leaving your answers in surd form. [2]

4 **(a)** Find the roots of the equation $2(x + 1)(x - 4) = (x - 2)^2$ leaving your answers in surd form. [3]
**(b)** Hence find the set of values of $x$ for which $2(x + 1)(x - 4) - (x - 2)^2 > 0$. [3]

5 Solve the simultaneous equations $2x - y = -1$ $xy + y = 3$ [2]

6 The polynomial $f(x) \equiv 2x^3 + px^2 - x + q$ is exactly divisible by both $(x - 1)$ and $(x + 2)$.
**(a)** Find the values of $p$ and $q$. [2]
**(b)** Hence factorise $f(x)$ completely. [1]

7 **(a)** Show that $4^x = (2^x)^2$. [1]
**(b)** Hence solve the equation $5 \times (2^x) - 4^x = 4$. [2]

8 By substituting $y = x^{\frac{1}{2}}$ or otherwise, find the values of $x$ for which $4x + 8 = 33x^{\frac{1}{2}}$. [2]

9 **(a)** Given that $x = 27$, find, without using a calculator, the values of
**(i)** $x^{\frac{1}{3}}$ **(ii)** $x^{-\frac{2}{3}}$ **(iii)** $x^0$. [3]
**(b)** Given that $2^{2y-1} = \frac{1}{8}$, find the value of $y$. [1]

10 A new rectangular playground is to have its length, $x$ m, 5 m more than its width.
The perimeter of the playground is to be more than 32 m.
**(a)** Find a linear inequality in $x$. [1]
The area of the playground is to be less than 104 m$^2$.
**(b)** Find a quadratic inequality in $x$. [1]
**(c)** By solving your inequalities, find the set of possible values of $x$. [3]

**11** $f(x) = 12x^3 + Ax^2 + Bx - 2$
When $f(x)$ is divided by $(x - 1)$ and $(x + 1)$ the remainders are 15 and –3 respectively.
**(a)** Find the values of A and B. [2]
**(b)** Using your values of A and B, find the values of $x$ for which $f(x) = 0$. [2]

**12** The diagram shows the graph of $y = f(x)$.

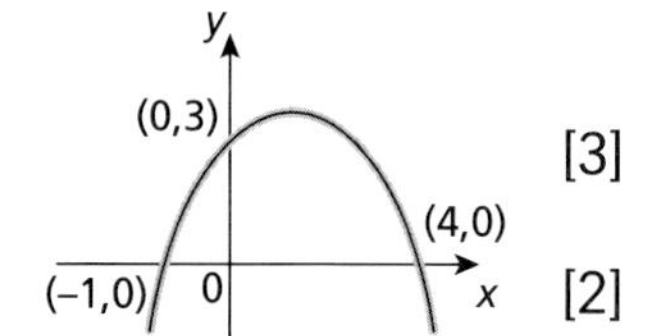


**(a)** Using separate diagrams, sketch the curves with these equations.
(i) $y = f(x - 1)$ (ii) $2y = -f(x)$ [3]
**(b)** On each sketch, write in the coordinates at which the curve meets the coordinate axes. [2]

**13** Solve for $x$ the equation $\frac{x-3}{x+1} = 2 - \frac{3}{x}$. [2]

**14** Solve these equations. Give your answers to 3 s.f.
**(a)** $2^{-x} = 6$ **(b)** $2^{2x} - 8(2^x) + 15 = 0$ [4]

**15** Given that $p = \log_{10}2$ and $q = \log_{10}3$, express these in terms of $p$ and $q$.
**(a)** $\log_{10}6$ **(b)** $\log_{10}4.5$ **(c)** $\log_{10}24$ **(d)** $\log_{10}648$ **(e)** $\log_2 3$ [5]

**16** By writing 1 as $\log_{10}10$, solve the equation
$\log_{10}(5x + 8) + \log_{10}(2x + 1) - 2\log_{10}(x + 1) = 1$. [3]

**17** Find the values of $x$ such that
$\log_{10}(x + 6) = 2\log_{10}(x - 6)$. [2]

**Total: /61**

# Straight lines

- **Any straight line has an equation of the form $ax + by + c = 0$, where $a$, $b$ and $c$ are three numbers.**

  **If we write the equation in the form $y = mx + c$, then $m$ is the gradient and $c$ is the intercept on the $y$-axis.**

  EXAMPLES

  **The line $y = 3$**

  **$y - 3 = 0$, so $a = 0$, $b = 1$, $c = -3$**

  **The line $x = -2$**

  **$x + 2 = 0$, so $a = 1$, $b = 0$, $c = 2$**

  **The line $y = 2x - 4$**

  **$2x - y - 4 = 0$,**

  **so $a = 2$, $b = -1$, $c = -4$**

**The equation of a straight line with gradient $m$, passing through a point $(x_1, y_1)$ is $y - y_1 = m(x - x_1)$**

EXAMPLE

**Find the equation of the line passing through (–1, 2) with gradient 3.**

$$y - 2 = 3(x - (-1)) = 3x + 3$$
$$3x - y + 5 = 0$$

**Check: $(3 \times -1) - 2 + 5 = 0$**

**EXAMINER'S TOP TIP**

**Check that the coordinates of the point on the line do satisfy the final version of the equation of the line.**

## Sketching straight lines

Usually the quickest way to sketch a given straight line is to find where it cuts the axes.

- Put $x = 0$ to find where it cuts the $y$-axis.
- Put $y = 0$ to find where it cuts the $x$-axis.

EXAMPLE

Sketch $2x - 3y + 6 = 0$

$x = 0, y = 2$

$y = 0, x = -3$

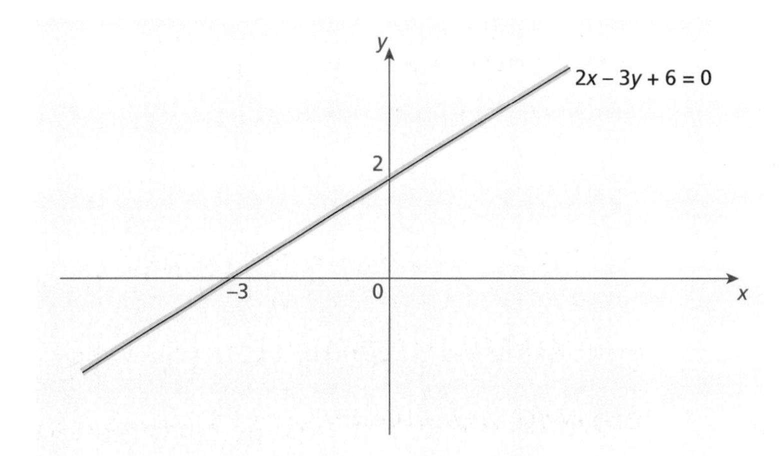

# Parallel and perpendicular lines

- **Parallel lines** have the **same** gradient.
- If $m_1$ and $m_2$ are the gradients of two perpendicular lines, then $m_1m_2 = -1$ *and* $m_2 = \frac{-1}{m_1}$

To find the gradient of a line which is **perpendicular** to a given line with a given gradient, **invert the gradient and change its sign**.

**EXAMPLES**

$m_1 = \frac{3}{4}, m_2 = -\frac{4}{3}$

$m_1 = -\frac{2}{5}, m_2 = \frac{5}{2}$

$m_1 = 3, m_2 = -\frac{1}{3}$

$m_1 = -1\frac{1}{2} = -\frac{3}{2}, m_2 = \frac{2}{3}$

**EXAMINER'S TOP TIP**
When working with gradients, always use top-heavy fractions.

**EXAMPLE**

Find the equation of the straight line that is perpendicular to $2x + 3y - 6 = 0$ and passes through (–2, 1).

Find the gradient of $2x + 3y - 6 = 0$

$3y = -2x + 6$

$y = -\frac{2}{3}x + 2$ — Gradient is $-\frac{2}{3}$

Gradient of perpendicular line is $\frac{3}{2}$ — Invert and change sign.

Equation of perpendicular line is $y - 1 = \frac{3}{2}(x - -2)$

$2y - 2 = 3(x - -2) = 3x + 6$

$2y - 3x - 8 = 0$

# Midpoint, gradient and length of straight line

- The midpoint of a line joining two given points $(x_1, y_1)$ and $(x_2, y_2)$ is

$$\left(\left(\frac{x_1 + x_2}{2}\right), \left(\frac{y_1 + y_2}{2}\right)\right)$$ (the average of the two points)

**EXAMINER'S TOP TIP**
Learn these results

- The gradient of a line joining two given points $(x_1, y_1)$ and $(x_2, y_2)$ is

$\frac{y_2 - y_1}{x_2 - x_1}$ *or* $\frac{y_1 - y_2}{x_1 - x_2}$ (**NOTE** The **order** must be the same on the **top** and the **bottom** of the fraction.)

- The length of the line joining two given points $A(x_1, y_1)$ and $B(x_2, y_2)$ is

$AB = \sqrt{(x_1 - x_2)^2 + (y_1 - y_2)^2}$

**EXAMPLE**

Find the equation of the perpendicular bisector of the line AB where A is (–2, 4) and B is (4, 0).

Midpoint of AB is $\left(\frac{-2 + 4}{2}, \frac{4 + 0}{2}\right) = (1, 2)$

Gradient of AB $= \frac{4 - 0}{-2 - 4} = \frac{4}{-6} = -\frac{2}{3}$

Gradient of perpendicular bisector $= \frac{3}{2}$

Equation of perpendicular bisector is $y - 2 = \frac{3}{2}(x - 1)$

$2y - 4 = 3x - 3$

$2y - 3x - 1 = 0$

# Quick test

1. ***Find the equation of the straight line that pass through (–1, 3) and is:***
   ***(a) parallel to the line $3x + 4y + 1 = 0$***
   ***(b) perpendicular to the line $3x + 4y + 1 = 0$***
2. ***Find the equation of the perpendicular bisector of the line AB where A is (–4, 8) and B is (0, –2)***
3. ***Find the point of intersection of the lines $5x + 7y + 29 = 0$ and $11x - 3y - 65 = 0$***

1. (a) $3x + 4y - 9 = 0$ (b) $3y - 4x - 13 = 0$ 2. $2x - 5y + 11 = 0$ 3. (4, –7)

# Circles

## The equation of a circle

**Consider a circle of radius $r$, centre C $(a, b)$**

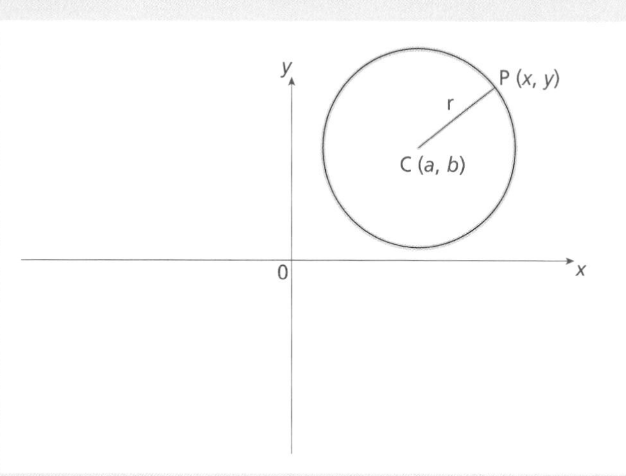


**Let P$(x, y)$ be any point on the circle.**

**CP = $r$**

**CP$^2$ = $r^2$**

$$(x - a)^2 + (y - b)^2 = r^2$$

**This is the equation of the circle.**

**EXAMINER'S TOP TIP**

**You need to learn this equation.**

EXAMPLES

**Find the equations of the circles with these centres and radii.**

**(a) Centre (0, 0), radius 2**

$(x - 0)^2 + (y - 0)^2 = 2^2$

$x^2 + y^2 = 4$

**(b) Centre (–1, 2), radius 2**

$(x - -1)^2 + (y - 2)^2 = 2^2$

$(x + 1)^2 + (y - 2)^2 = 4$

$x^2 + 2x + 1 + y^2 - 4y + 4 - 4 = 0$

$x^2 + y^2 + 2x - 4y + 1 = 0$

**(c) Centre (3, –4), radius 1**

$(x - 3)^2 + (y - -4)^2 = 1^2$

$(x - 3)^2 + (y + 4)^2 = 1$

$x^2 - 6x + 9 + y^2 + 8y + 16 - 1 = 0$

$x^2 + y^2 - 6x + 8y + 24 = 0$

## Finding the centre and radius of a circle

When the equation of a circle is multiplied out, it will take this form:
$x^2 + y^2 + 2gx + 2fy + c = 0$ where $g$, $f$ and $c$ are numbers.
The centre will be $(-g, -f)$ and the radius will be $\sqrt{g^2 + f^2 - c}$
Hence $g^2 + f^2 - c > 0$ otherwise the equation will not represent a circle.
If you are given the equation of a circle in this form, you need to be able to find the centre and radius, either by quoting the above results or by completing the square, as shown below.

EXAMPLES

Find the centre and radius of these circles:

(a) $x^2 + y^2 + 8x - 6y + 1 = 0$

(b) $2x^2 + 2y^2 - 12x - 3 = 0$

(a) $x^2 + y^2 + 8x - 6y + 1 = 0$

$x^2 + 8x + (\frac{8}{2})^2 + y^2 - 6y + (-\frac{6}{2})^2 = -1 + (\frac{8}{2})^2 + (-\frac{6}{2})^2$

$(x + 4)^2 + (y - 3)^2 = 24$

$(x - -4)^2 + (y - 3)^2 = (\sqrt{24})^2$

Centre is (–4, 3), radius is $\sqrt{24} = 2\sqrt{6}$

Complete the squares for $x$ and $y$ terms.
Keep the equation balanced!

(b) $2x^2 + 2y^2 - 12x - 3 = 0$

$x^2 + y^2 - 6x - \frac{3}{2} = 0$

$x^2 + -6x + (-\frac{6}{2})^2 + y^2 = \frac{3}{2} + (-\frac{6}{2})^2$

$(x - 3)^2 + y^2 = \frac{21}{2}$

Centre is (3, 0), radius is $\sqrt{\frac{21}{2}}$

Divide by 2 to get into standard format.
Complete the square for $x$; $y$ is already a square.

# Important circle properties

**1 The angle in a semicircle is a right angle.**

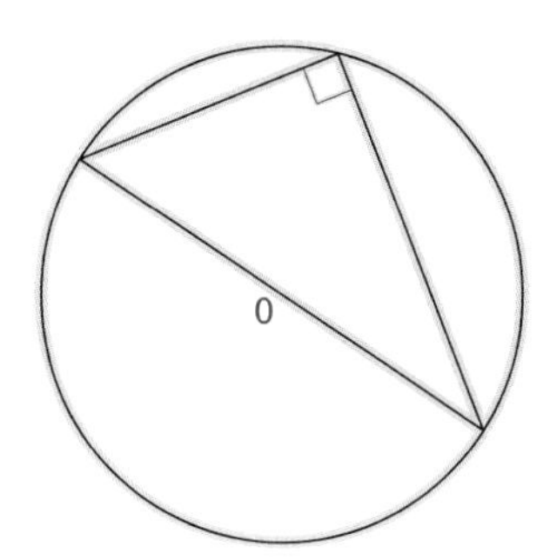


**2 The radius and tangent at P are perpendicular.**

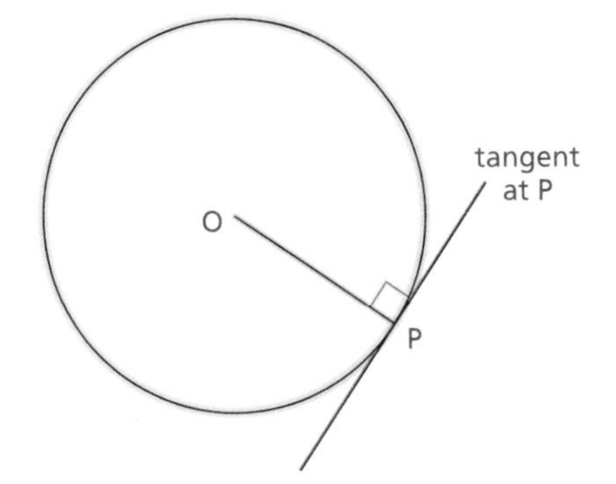


**3 A perpendicular from the centre to any chord bisects the chord.**

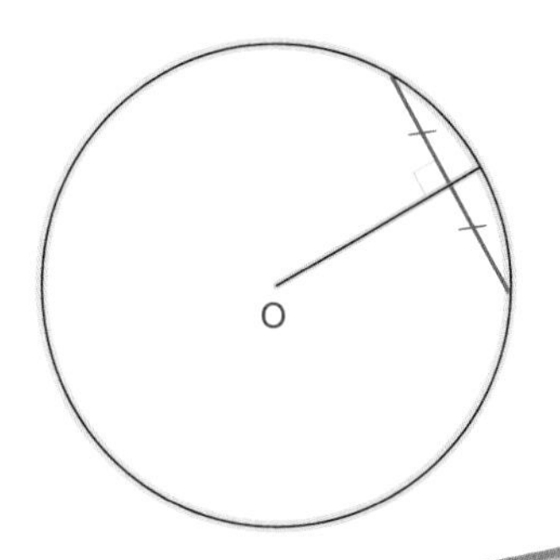


**EXAMINER'S TOP TIP**
**You will need to learn these as they may be tested.**

**EXAMPLE**

The ends of the diameter of a circle are the points A(2, –1) and B(–1, –5). Find the equation of the circle.
The centre of the circle will be the midpoint of AB.

$$\left(\left(\frac{2+-1}{2}\right), \left(\frac{-1+-5}{2}\right)\right) = \left(\frac{1}{2}, -3\right)$$

The radius of the circle will be <u>half</u> the length of AB.

$AB = \sqrt{(2--1)^2 + (-1--5)^2}$

$= \sqrt{3^2 + 4^2}$

$= \sqrt{25} = 5$, so radius is $\frac{5}{2}$

Equation of the circle is

$$(x - \tfrac{1}{2})^2 + (y - -3)^2 = (\tfrac{5}{2})^2$$

$$x^2 - x + \tfrac{1}{4} + y^2 + 6y + 9 = \frac{25}{4}$$

$$x^2 + y^2 - x + 6y + 3 = 0$$

**EXAMINER'S TOP TIP**
**In a question like this you can check your answer by ensuring that the coordinates of A and B satisfy your equation.**

Check:

A(2, –1) is on the circle.

$$2^2 + (-1)^2 - 2 + 6 \times (-1) + 3 = 4 + 1 - 2 - 6 + 3 = 0$$

B(–1, –5) is on the circle.

$$(-1)^2 + (-5)^2 - (-1) + 6 \times -5 + 3 = 1 + 25 + 1 - 30 + 3 = 0$$

# Quick test

**1** *Write down the equations of these circles. Simplify your answer in each case.*

*(a) centre (–1, 0), radius 2* *(b) centre (2, –4), radius 4* *(c) centre (0, 0), radius 1*

**2** *Find the centre and radius of each of these circles.*

*(a)* $x^2 + y^2 + 2x - 2y - 1 = 0$ *(b)* $x^2 + y^2 - 10y + 5 = 0$ *(c)* $2x^2 + 2y^2 - 8x + 12y - 3 = 0$

1. (a) $(x + 1)^2 + y^2 = 4$ $x^2 + y^2 + 2x - 3 = 0$
(b) $(x - 2)^2 + (y + 4)^2 = 16$ $x^2 + y^2 - 4x + 8y + 4 = 0$
(c) $x^2 + y^2 = 1$ $x^2 + y^2 - 1 = 0$
2. (a) centre (–1, 1), radius $\sqrt{3}$ (b) centre (0, 5), radius $\sqrt{20} = 2\sqrt{5}$ (c) centre (2, –3), radius $\sqrt{(\frac{29}{2})}$

# Exam-style questions

Use the questions to test your progress. Check your answers on page 94.

**1** The straight line $L_1$ passes through the points P and Q with coordinates (2, 2) and (6, 0) respectively.

**(a)** Find the equation for $L_1$. [2]

Another line $L_2$ passes through the point R with coordinates (–9, 0) and has a gradient of $\frac{1}{4}$.

**(b)** Find the equation for $L_2$. [2]

The lines $L_1$ and $L_2$ intersect at the point S.

**(c)** Find, to 2 d.p., the length of PS. [1]

**(d)** Calculate the area of $\Delta$ SRQ. [3]

**2** The graph shows part of the curve with equation $y = 16x - kx^2$, where $k$ is a constant. The points A and D have coordinates (0, 18) and (6, 15) respectively.

**(a)** Find the length of AD. Give your answer to 3 s.f. [2]

**(b)** The line L passes through the points A and D and intersects the curve at the points B and C, as shown in the diagram. Find the equation of L in the form $y = mx + c$, where $m$ and $c$ are constants. [3]

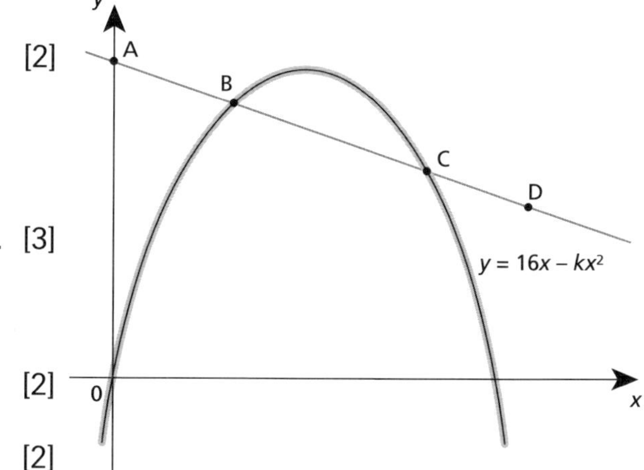


Point C has coordinates (4, 16).

**(c)** Show that $k = 3$. [2]

**(d)** Calculate the coordinates of B. [2]

**3** Solve the simultaneous equations

$$3x - y = 6$$
$$x^2 + xy - y^2 = 4$$ [2]

**4 (a)** Find an equation of the straight line passing through the points (–1, 5) and (4, –2), giving your answer in the form $ax + by + c = 0$, where $a$, $b$ and $c$ are integers. [2]

The line crosses the $x$-axis at P and the $y$-axis at Q. O is the origin.

**(b)** Find the area of $\Delta$ OPQ. [2]

**5** A circle has the equation $x^2 + y^2 - 16x - 12y + 96 = 0$.

**(a)** Find the coordinates of the centre. [2]

**(b)** Find the radius. [2]

**(c)** Find the least and greatest distances of the origin O from the circumference of the circle. [2]

**6** A circle has the equation $x^2 + y^2 - 10y = 0$.

**(a)** Find the coordinates of the centre. [2]

**(b)** Find the radius. [2]

**(c)** By solving simultaneously, show that the line with equation $4x - 3y + 40 = 0$ is a tangent to the circle. [3]

**7 (a)** Find an equation of the circle which has as its diameter the line joining the points P(3, 1) and Q(–2, 2). [3]

**(b)** Given that P and Q are opposite corners of a square, find the coordinates of the other two corners. [2]

**8** The line with equation $y = x + 2$ intersects the curve with equation $x^2 + y^2 = 12 - 2x$ at the points P and Q. The coordinates of P are both positive.

**(a)** Find the coordinates of P and Q. [2]

**(b)** Hence calculate the length of PQ. [1]

**9** The straight line through the points (1, 4) and (–3, –4) meets the axes at the points A and B. Find the area of the square that has AB as one of its sides. [2]

**10** The point P has coordinates (2, 5) and Q has coordinates (6, 1).

**(a)** Find the coordinates of M, the midpoint of PQ. [2]

**(b)** Show that the length of PM = $\sqrt{8}$. [1]

**(c)** Find the equation of the perpendicular bisector of PQ. [2]

The point R $(x, y)$ lies on the circle, centre M, and diameter PQ.

**(d)** Using the length of RM, write down an equation in $x$ and $y$. [1]

R lies on the perpendicular bisector of PQ.

**(e)** Find the two possible positions of R. [2]

**(f)** Find the equation of the tangent to the circle at point (6, 5). [2]

**Total: /47**

# Sequences

- A sequence is a list of numbers which follow a rule.
- The numbers in the sequence are sometimes called the terms of the sequence.

To define a sequence we usually write down a formula for the $n$th term (or general term).

We often use $u_1$ to denote the first term, $u_2$ to denote the second term, ... $u_n$ to denote the $n$th term.

EXAMPLE

Consider the sequence 5, 7, 9, 11, ... , $2n + 3$

1st term, $u_1$ — 2nd term, $u_2$ — general term, $u_n$

We can use the general term to write down any term in the sequence without having to write down all the previous terms.

$u_n = 2n + 3$, $u_{200} = (2 \times 200) + 3 = 403$

**EXAMINER'S TOP TIP**

Whatever sequence you have, it is usually a good idea to write down the first few terms, just to get a feel for what you are dealing with.

EXAMPLE

A sequence of numbers $u_1, u_2, \ldots$ is defined by $u_n = n^2 + 2n - 3$

(a) Write down the first three terms of the sequence.

(b) Which term is equal to 437?

(a) $u_1 = 1^2 + (2 \times 1) - 3 = 0$ $\quad u_2 = 2^2 + (2 \times 2) - 3 = 5$ $\quad u_3 = 3^2 + (2 \times 3) - 3 = 12$

(b) $n^2 + 2n - 3 = 437$

$n^2 + 2n - 440 = 0$

You may need to use the quadratic formula if you don't spot the factors.

$(n + 22)(n - 20) = 0$

$n = -22$ or $n = 20$

$n$ cannot be negative.

437 is the 20th term in the sequence.

# Iterative definition of a sequence

Iterate means to repeat.

We know that we can define the sequence 5, 7, 9, 11, ... by $u_n = 2n + 3$

Another way of defining a sequence is to:

- Give the first term, $u_1$
- Give a rule for finding a term from the previous term.

We can then keep repeating the rule to obtain the terms of the sequence.

For the sequence above,

$u_1 = 5$

$u_{n+1} = u_n + 2 \qquad n \geq 1$

$u_{n+1} = u_n + 2$: this is called the iteration formula

$n \geq 1$: this tells you what values of $n$ the formula applies to

$n = 1 \quad u_2 = u_1 + 2 = 5 + 2 = 7 \qquad n = 2 \quad u_3 = u_2 + 2 = 7 + 2 = 9$

$n = 3 \quad u_4 = u_3 + 2 = 9 + 2 = 11$

This gives 5, 7, 9, 11 ...

The disadvantage of this type of definition is that if we want the 200th term, we have to write down the previous 199 terms!

Sometimes the iteration formula may involve the previous two terms.

EXAMPLE

$u_1 = 1, u_2 = 1$

$u_{n+2} = u_n + u_{n+1}$

$n = 1 \quad u_3 = u_1 + u_2 = 1 + 1 = 2$

$n = 2 \quad u_4 = u_2 + u_3 = 1 + 2 = 3$

$n = 3 \quad u_5 = u_3 + u_4 = 2 + 3 = 5$

$n = 4 \quad u_6 = u_4 + u_5 = 3 + 5 = 8$

The sequence begins 1, 1, 2, 3, 5, 8, ... (This is the Fibonacci sequence.)

# The limit of a sequence

All the sequences so far have terms which get bigger. Sometimes, however, the terms of a sequence get closer and closer to some fixed number. The **sequence converges to a limit**.

EXAMPLE

$u_1 = 1 \quad u_{n+1} = \frac{1}{2}\left(u_n + \frac{2}{u_n}\right)$, $n \geq 1$ defines a sequence of numbers $u_1$, $u_2$, ...

(a) Write down the first four terms of the sequence.

(b) By putting $u_{n+1} = u_n$, find the limit of the sequence.

(a) $n = 1 \; u_2 = \frac{1}{2}\left(u_1 + \frac{2}{u_1}\right) = \frac{1}{2}\left(1 + \frac{2}{1}\right) = 1.5$

$n = 2 \; u_3 = \frac{1}{2}\left(u_2 + \frac{2}{u_2}\right) = \frac{1}{2}\left(1.5 + \frac{2}{1.5}\right) = 1.416\,6...$

$n = 3 \; u_3 = \frac{1}{2}\left(u_3 + \frac{2}{u_4}\right) = \frac{1}{2}\left(1.41 + \frac{2}{1.41}\right) = 1.414\,21...$

$n = 4 \; u_4 = \frac{1}{2}\left(u_4 + \frac{2}{u_4}\right) = \frac{1}{2}\left(1.414\,21 + \frac{2}{1.414\,21}\right) = 1.414\,21...$

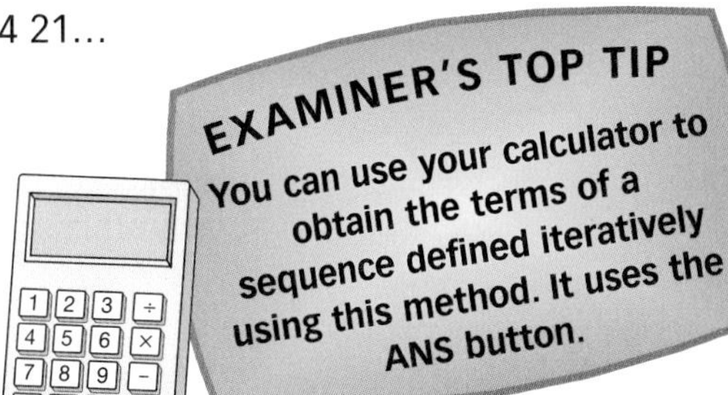


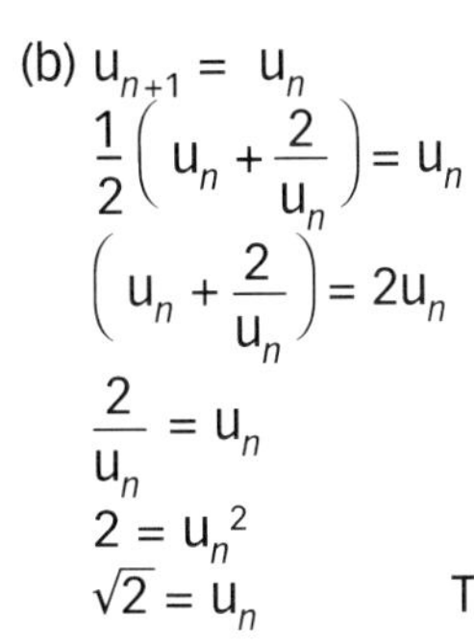

(b) $u_{n+1} = u_n$

$\frac{1}{2}\left(u_n + \frac{2}{u_n}\right) = u_n$

$\left(u_n + \frac{2}{u_n}\right) = 2u_n$

$\frac{2}{u_n} = u_n$

$2 = u_n^2$

$\sqrt{2} = u_n$ This tells us that the terms in the sequence are getting closer and closer to $\sqrt{2}$

Using a calculator to generate the terms of a sequence defined iteratively.
Press these buttons: 1 = ANS **then clear screen using C**.
Now enter the iteration formula, with $u_n$ replaced by ANS everywhere. In the example,

$\frac{1}{2}\left(\text{ANS} + \frac{2}{\text{ANS}}\right)$

If you press = you will generate the next term. Keep pressing = to produce more terms. Try it!

# Quick test

1 ***Write down the first three terms of the sequences whose nth terms are***
***(a) 4n + 1 (b) $2n^2 - 1$ (c) 2(n − 1).***

2 ***A sequence $u_1$, $u_2$, ... is defined by***
$u_n = \frac{1}{2}n(n + 1)$, $n \geq 1$.
***(a) Write down the first 3 terms.***
***(b) Find a formula for the difference between the nth and (n + 1)th terms.***
***(c) Which term of the sequence is 210?***

3 ***A sequence is defined by***
$u_1 = 1$
$u_{n+1} = 1 + \frac{1}{u_n}$, $n \geq 1$.
***Write down the first 6 terms of the sequence, giving your answers to 5 d.p.***

1. (a) 5, 9, 13 (b) 1, 7, 17 (c) 0, 2, 4 2. (a) 1, 3, 6 (b) $n + 1$ (c) 20th term 3. 1, 2, 1.5, 1.666 67, 1.6, 1.625

# Arithmetic series

- **An arithmetic series (or arithmetic progression) is a series in which each term is obtained from the previous term by adding on a fixed number. The fixed number is called the common difference and can be positive or negative.**

EXAMPLE

**2 + 5 + 8 + 11 + 14 + ... +32** This is an arithmetic series with common difference 3

**12 + 10 + 8 + 6 + 4 + 2 + 0 + ... + −14** This is an arithmetic series with common difference −2

**1 + 4 + 9 + 16 + 25** This is *not* an arithmetic series – there is no common difference!

## Using sigma notation

We have seen that a sequence consists of a set of terms $u_1, u_2, \ldots, u_n, \ldots$
If we write the **sum** of the first $n$ terms of the sequence $u_1 + u_2 + u_3 + \ldots + u_n$
we call this a **finite series** of $n$ terms.
To save time and space we can write this series using **sigma notation**. (The sigma sign is the capital Greek letter 's' for **sum**.)

This is the **upper** limit of the summation.

$$\sum_{r=1}^{r=n} u_r$$ ← This means take the **sum** of all terms $u_r$, starting at $r = 1$ and finishing at $r = n$

This is the **lower** limit of the summation.

EXAMPLE

Write out in full $\sum_{r=2}^{r=5}(2r-1)$.

$$\sum_{r=2}^{r=5}(2r-1) = (2\times 2-1) + (2\times 3-1) + (2\times 4-1) + (2\times 5-1) = 3+5+7+9 = 24$$

Write out in full $\sum_{r=3}^{r=6}(-1)^r r^2$.

$$\sum_{r=3}^{r=6}(-1)^r r^2 = (-1)^3\times 3^2 + (-1)^4\times 4^2 + (-1)^5\times 5^2 + (-1)^6\times 6^2$$
$$= -9 + 16 - 25 + 36 = 18$$

## The general arithmetic series

Suppose the first term is $a$ and the common difference is $d$. The series is

$a + (a + d) + (a + 2d) + (a + 3d) + \ldots$
1st 2nd 3rd 4th

The **nth term is $a + (n - 1)d$**

**EXAMINER'S TOP TIP**
**Learn the formula for the *n*th term.**

EXAMPLE

Suppose an arithmetic series has first term 20 and common difference − 2. Find

(a) 12th term (b) $n$th term.

(a) 12th term = $20 + (11 \times -2) = 20 - 22 = -2$

(b) $n$th term = $20 + (n-1)\times -2 = 20 - 2n + 2 = 22 - 2n$.

# The sum of an arithmetic series

EXAMPLE

Find the sum of the first 10 terms of the arithmetic series

$5 + 9 + 13 + \dots$

Common difference, $d$, = 4

10th term = $5 + (9 \times 4) = 5 + 36 = 41$

$S_{10} = 5 + 9 + 13 + \dots + 37 + 41$

and writing the terms in reverse order,

$S_{10} = 41 + 37 + 13 + \dots + 9 + 5$

$2S_{10} = 46 + 46 + 46 + \dots + 46 + 46$

$2S_{10} = 46 \times 10 = 460$

$S_{10} = 230$

**EXAMINER'S TOP TIP**

**You need to learn how to prove this result as you could be tested on it.**

# Proof of the general formula

Let $S_n = a + \dots\dots + (a + (n-1)d)$

and $S_n = (a + (n-1)d) + \dots\dots + a$ writing terms in reverse order

Adding

$2S_n = \{2a + (n-1)d\} + \dots\dots + \{2a + (n-1)d\}$

all $n$ terms are the same

$= n\{2a + (n-1)d\}$

$S_n = \frac{1}{2}n\{2a + (n-1)d\}$ Use this formula if you don't know the last term.

If we write the $n$th term (last term) as $\ell$, then

$S_n = n\left(\frac{a+l}{2}\right)$ i.e. number of terms × mean of first and last term. Use this formula if you are given the last term.

**EXAMPLES**

**1** Find the sum of the first 16 terms of the arithmetic series $4 + 2 + 0 + \dots$

Use $S_n = \frac{1}{2}n\{2a + (n-1)d\}$ with $n = 16$, $a = 4$, $d = -2$

$S_{16} = \frac{1}{2}16\{8 + (15 \times -2)\} = 8(8 - 30) = -176$

**2** Evaluate $\sum_{r=1}^{r=12}(1 - 3r)$.

First we need to check that we have an arithmetic series. Write down the first few terms and the last term.

$-2 + -5 + -8 + \dots + -35$ *It is an arithmetic series as the common difference is –3*

Use $S_{12} = 12 \times \left(\frac{-2 + -35}{2}\right)$ $\quad S_n = n\left(\frac{a+\ell}{2}\right)$

$= 6 \times (-37) = -222$

3 The 3rd and 7th terms of an arithmetic series are 9 and 19 respectively. Find the sum of the first 20 terms of the series.

$a + 2d = 9$ a is first term and d is common difference.

$a + 6d = 19$ Subtract top from bottom.

$4d = 10$

$d = \frac{5}{2}$, $a = 4$

Use $S_n = \frac{1}{2}n\{2a + (n-1)d\}$ with $n = 20$, $a = 4$, $d = \frac{5}{2}$

$S_{20} = \frac{1}{2}20\{8 + (19 \times \frac{5}{2})\} = 10 \times \frac{111}{2} = 555$

**EXAMINER'S TOP TIP**

**In problems where you don't know *a* or *d*, you will be given two pieces of information that allow you to set up two simultaneous equations which can then be solved to find a and/or *d*.**

# Quick test

**1** ***Evaluate these.***

***(a)*** $\sum_{r=1}^{32}(r - 3)$ ***(b)*** $\sum_{r=7}^{r=13}(3r - 2)$.

**2** ***The fifth and seventh terms of an arithmetic series are $\frac{1}{6}$ and $\frac{1}{2}$. Find the nth term and the sum of the first 18 terms.***

1. (a) 432 (b) 196 2. $n$th term $\frac{n-4}{6}$ Sum of first 18 terms is $16\frac{1}{2}$

# Geometric series

- **A series in which each term is obtained from the previous one by multiplying by some fixed number is called a geometric series (or geometric progression). The fixed number is called the common ratio and may be positive or negative, a fraction or a whole number.**

**EXAMPLES**

$2 + 4 + 8 + 16 + 32$ — **This is a geometric series with common ratio 2**

$4 - 2 + 1 - \frac{1}{2} + \frac{1}{4} - \frac{1}{8}$ — **This is a geometric series with common ratio $-\frac{1}{2}$**

$1 + 4 + 9 + 16 + 25$ — **This is *not* a geometric series.**

## The general geometric series

Suppose the first term is $a$ and the common ratio is $r$. The series is

| $a$ | + | $ar$ | + | $ar^2$ | + | $ar^3$ | + … |
|---|---|---|---|---|---|---|---|
| 1st | | 2nd | | 3rd | | 4th | |

The $n$th term is $ar^{n-1}$.

**EXAMPLE**

Suppose a geometric series has first term 20 and common difference $-\frac{1}{2}$.

(a) Find the 6th term.

(a) 6th term $= 20 \times (-\frac{1}{2})^5 = 20 \times (-\frac{1}{32}) = -\frac{5}{8}$

(b) Find the $n$th term.

(b) $n$th term $= 20 \times (-\frac{1}{2})^{n-1} = (-1)^{n-1} \times \frac{20}{2^{n-1}}$

## The sum of a geometric series

**Proof of the sum of a geometric series to $n$ terms**

Let $S_n = a + ar + ar^2 + \ldots + ar^{n-1}$

$rS_n = ar + ar^2 + \ldots + ar^{n-1} + ar^n$

$S_n - rS_n = a - ar^n$

$S_n(1 - r) = a(1 - r^n)$

$$S_n = \frac{a(1-r^n)}{(1-r)} = \frac{a(r^n-1)}{(r-1)}$$

Multiply by $r$ to move all terms along one place.
Subtract so that middle terms cancel.

**EXAMPLE**

Find the sum of the first 10 terms of the geometric series

$2 + 4 + 8 + 16 + \ldots$

$a = 2, r = 2, n = 10$

$S_n = \frac{2(2^{10}-1)}{(2-1)} = 2(2^{10} - 1) = 2 \times 1023 = 2046$

**EXAMINER'S TOP TIP**

Use $S_n = \frac{a(1-r^n)}{(1-r)}$ if $r < 1$

and $S_n = \frac{a(r^n-1)}{(r-1)}$ if $r > 1$

# A convergent geometric series

### The sum to infinity of a convergent geometric series

We have seen that the sum to $n$ terms of the geometric series with first term $a$ and common ratio $r$ is

$$S_n = \frac{a(1 - r^n)}{(1 - r)}$$

If $-1 < r < 1$, then $r^n \to 0$ as $n \to \infty$

$r^n$ tends to zero as $n$ gets bigger.

This means that

$$S_n \to \frac{a}{(1 - r)} \text{ as } n \to \infty$$

**EXAMINER'S TOP TIP**
You need to learn this result.

Sometimes we write $S_\infty = \dfrac{a}{(1 - r)}$, provided that $-1 < r < 1$,

and we say that the series converges, and has a sum to infinity.

**EXAMPLE**

Suppose we have a geometric series that starts

$$1 + \frac{1}{2} + \frac{1}{4} + \frac{1}{8} + \ldots$$

Here, $a = 1$ and $r = \frac{1}{2}$. Since $-1 < r < 1$, the series has a sum to infinity given by $\dfrac{a}{1 - r}$,

i.e. $S_\infty = \dfrac{1}{1 - \frac{1}{2}} = 2$

or, using sigma notation, $\displaystyle\sum_{r=0}^{r=\infty} \left(\frac{1}{2}\right)^r = 2.$

# Writing a recurring decimal as a fraction

### Using the sum to infinity of a geometric series

**EXAMPLE**

Suppose $S = 0.111\ldots.. = 0.\dot{1}$

Then $S = \dfrac{1}{10} + \dfrac{1}{100} + \dfrac{1}{1000} + \ldots$

This is a geometric series, $a = \dfrac{1}{10}$ $\quad r = \dfrac{1}{10}$

$$S = \frac{a}{1 - r} = \frac{\frac{1}{10}}{1 - \frac{1}{10}} = \frac{1}{10 - 1} = \frac{1}{9} \text{ so } 0.\dot{1} = \frac{1}{9}$$

**EXAMINER'S TOP TIP**
With this type of question, write things out in full to help you pick up the **pattern of the calculation**.

# Quick test

1. ***Find the sum of the first 12 terms of the geometric series $u_1 + u_2 + u_3 + \ldots + u_{12}$ when***
   ***(a) $u_1 = 3, u_2 = 6$ (b) $u_1 = 3, u_2 = 2$ (c) $u_1 = 3, u_2 = -2$.***
2. ***(a) Find the first 3 terms of a geometric series which has a 4th term of –3 and a 7th term of 81.***
   ***(b) Find also the sum of the first 12 terms of the series.***
3. ***Express the following recurring decimals as fractions using the sum to infinity of a geometric series:***
   ***(a) 0.999... (b) 0.161616... (Hint $\dfrac{16}{100} + \dfrac{16}{100\,000} + \ldots$)***

1. (a) 12 285 (b) 8.93 (c) 1.79 2. (a) $\frac{1}{9}, -\frac{1}{3}, +1$ (b) –14 762.2 3. (a) $\frac{1}{1} = 1$ (b) $\frac{16}{99}$

# Binomial series

- **Factorial notation**

**If $n$ is a non-negative integer, $n!$ ($n$ factorial) is defined as**

$$n! = n(n-1)(n-2)(n-3)\ldots 3 \times 2 \times 1 \text{ and } 0! = 1$$

EXAMPLES

**$3! = 3 \times 2 \times 1 = 6$** **$5! = 5 \times 4 \times 3 \times 2 \times 1 = 120$**

**A binomial expression is an expression which contains two terms.**

EXAMPLES

**$(1 + x)$ $(-2 + x^2)$ $(4x + y)$**

## Brackets containing a binomial expression

**Multiplying out or expanding a power of a bracket which contains a binomial expression**

$(a + b)^0 = 1$

$(a + b)^1 = a^1 + b^1$

$(a + b)^2 = a^2 + 2a^1b^1 + b^2$

$(a + b)^3 = a^3 + 3a^2b^1 + 3a^1b^2 + b^3$ The powers have all been put in to emphasise the pattern of the results.

There is a pattern here. Look at the $(a + b)^3$ result. We start with $a^3$ then, as the power of $a$ goes down, the power of $b$ goes up, until we get to $b^3$

The sum of the powers of each term is always 3

The numbers in front of the terms (**the binomial coefficients**) also follow a pattern.

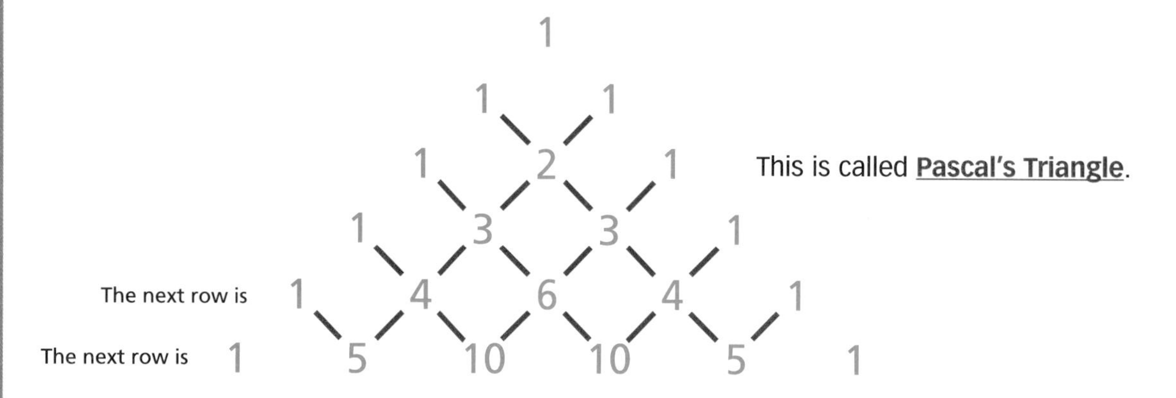


This is called **Pascal's Triangle**.

Apart from the 1s at either end, **each number is the sum of the 2 numbers above it in the previous row**.

$(a + b)^4 = a^4 + 4a^3b^1 + 6a^2b^2 + 4a^1b^3 + b^4$.

$(a + b)^5 = a^5 + 5a^4b^1 + 10a^3b^2 + 10a^2b^3 + 5a^1b^4 + b^5$.

NOTE

To obtain this result the basic way we would have to multiply out 5 brackets:

$(a + b)(a + b)(a + b)(a + b)(a + b)$, a very long-winded process!

Although we can **obtain the binomial coefficients from Pascal's Triangle**, this is very **inefficient** because we need to 'build up' the triangle until we get to the row we need.

## Binomial coefficients

If we **number the rows** of the triangle as follows:

| | | | |
|---|---|---|---|
| **1** | 0th | row corresponding to | $(a+b)^0$ |
| **1 1** | 1st | row corresponding to | $(a+b)^1$ |
| **1 2 1** | 2nd | row corresponding to | $(a+b)^2$ |
| **1 3 3 1** | 3rd | row corresponding to | $(a+b)^3$ |
| **1 4 6 4 1** | 4th | row corresponding to | $(a+b)^4$ |

and then number the individual entries in each row, beginning at 0 (corresponding to the coefficient of $b^0$), then the notation $\binom{n}{r}$ stands for the coefficient of the entry numbered $r$ in the row numbered $n$

$\binom{2}{1} = 2$; $\binom{4}{3} = 4$ ; $\binom{5}{2} = 10$ and $\binom{n}{r} = \frac{n!}{r!(n-r)!}$

NOTE $\binom{n}{o} = 1 \quad \binom{n}{n} = 1$

Sometimes the notation ${}^n_rC$ is used instead of $\binom{n}{r}$

**EXAMPLES**

$\binom{4}{3} = \frac{4!}{3!(4-3)!} = \frac{4 \times 3 \times 2 \times 1}{3 \times 2 \times 1 \times 1} = 4$; $\binom{5}{2} = \frac{5!}{2!(5-2)!} = \frac{5 \times 4 \times 3 \times 2 \times 1}{2 \times 1 \times 3 \times 2 \times 1} = 10$

**EXAMINER'S TOP TIP**
There is an alternative, quicker way of finding the value of a binomial coefficient.

## The Binomial Theorem

We can state this as follows.

$$(a+b)^n = a^n + \binom{n}{1}a^{n-1}b^1 + \binom{n}{2}a^{n-2}b^2 + \ldots + \binom{n}{r}a^{n-r}b^r + \ldots + \binom{n}{n-1}a^1b^{n-1} + b^n$$

where $\binom{n}{r} = \frac{n!}{r!(n-r)!}$ and ***n* is a positive integer**.

NOTE Binomial coefficients are symmetrical (look at Pascal's Triangle) $\binom{n}{r} = \binom{n}{n-r}$

**EXAMPLE**

Expand $(x - 2y)^3$ in ascending powers of $x$.

$(x - 2y)^3 = (x + (-2y))^3$

$= \binom{3}{0}x^3 + \binom{3}{1}x^2(-2y)^1 + \binom{3}{2}x^1(-2y)^2 + \binom{3}{3}(-2y)^3$ The brackets round $2y$ are **crucial** and **essential**.

$= x^3 - 6x^2y + 12y^2 - 8y^3$

Check: Binomial expansions are identities so are true for all values of $x$. To check an answer substitute a simple value of $x$ on both sides and check that you get the same answer. If you do, it's probably correct, if you don't, it's definitely wrong.

In the above put $x = 2$, $y = 1$ LHS: $(2-2)^3 = 0$ RHS; $8 - 24 + 24 - 8 = 0$

## Quick test

1. **Expand in ascending powers of x:** **(a)** $(3 - \frac{1}{2}x)^4$ **(b)** $(x + \frac{2}{x})^3$ **(c)** $(2x + 1)^4$.
2. **Find the term in $x^4$ in the expansion:** $(2 - x)^7$.
3. **Given that** $(\sqrt{3} - 2)^4 = a\sqrt{3} + b$, **find the values of a and b**

1. (a) $81 - 54x + \frac{27}{2}x^2 - \frac{3x^3}{2} + \frac{x^4}{16}$ (b) $\frac{8}{x^3} + \frac{12}{x} + 6x + x^3$ (c) $16x^4 + 32x^3 + 24x^2 + 8x + 1$

2. $\binom{7}{4}(-x)^4(2)^3 = \binom{7}{3}(-1)^2x^4 2^3 = \frac{7 \times 6 \times 5}{1 \times 2 \times 3} \times x^4 \times 8 = 280x^4$

3. $(\sqrt{3} + (-2))^4 = (\sqrt{3})^4 + 4(\sqrt{3})^3(-2)^1 + 6(\sqrt{3})^2(-2)^2 + 4(\sqrt{3})^1(-2)^3 + (-2)^4$
$= 9 - 24\sqrt{3} + 72 - 32\sqrt{3} + 16$
$= 97 - 56\sqrt{3}$ $a = -56$, $b = 97$

# Exam-style questions

Use the questions to test your progress. Check your answers on pages 94–95.

**1** A sequence $u_1, u_2, \ldots, u_n, \ldots$ is defined as follows:

$u_1 = 1, u_2 = -2$

$u_{n+2} = 2ku_{n+1} + 15u_n$, for $n \geq 1$ where $k$ is a constant.

**(a)** Find, in terms of $k$, an expression for $u_3$. [1]
**(b)** Hence find, in terms of $k$, an expression for $u_4$. [1]
**(c)** Given that $u_4 = -38$, find the possible values of $k$. [1]

**2** Given that $(1 + kx)^8 = 1 + 12x + px^2 + qx^3 + \ldots$ for all $x$.

**(a)** *(i)* find the value of $k$ [1]
*(ii)* find the value of $p$ [1]
*(iii)* find the value of $q$. [1]

**(b)** Using your values of $k$, $p$ and $q$, find the coefficient of the $x^3$ term in the expansion of $(1 - x)(1 + kx)^8$. [1]

**3** The sequence $u_1, u_2, \ldots, u_n, \ldots$ is defined as follows:

$u_1 = 2, u_{n+1} = \dfrac{n+1}{n} u_n$, for $n \geq 1$

**(a)** Find the values of $u_2$, $u_3$ and $u_4$. [3]
**(b)** Prove that $u_n = nu_1 = 2n$. [2]
**(c)** Find $\sum_{r=1}^{2N} u_r$. [1]

**4 (a)** A geometric series has first term 3 and common ratio 0.8.
Find the sum of the first 24 terms, giving your answer to 3 s.f. [2]

**(b)** An arithmetic series has general term $\frac{r}{2}$. Evaluate $\sum_{r=1}^{52} \frac{r}{2}$ [1]

**5** The sum of the first five terms of an arithmetic series is 60 and the sum of the first ten terms is 207.5.

**(a)** Find the first term and the common difference. [2]
**(b)** The sum of the first $n$ terms is 500. Find the value of $n$. [1]

6 **(a)** Expand $(2 + x)^4$ and $(2 - x)^4$ in ascending powers of $x$. [3]

**(b)** Using your answers, show that the equation $(2 + x)^4 - (2 - x)^4 = 80$ simplifies to the cubic equation $x^3 + 4x - 5 = 0$. [3]

**(c)** Show that 1 is a root of this equation. [2]

**(d)** Show that there are no other real roots. [2]

7 **(a)** Expand $(a + b)^4$. [1]

**(b)** Hence, or otherwise, simplify $x^4 + 4x^3(1 - x) + 6x^2(1 - x)^2 + 4x(1 - x)^3 + (1 - x)^4$. [3]

8 **(a)** Find the coefficient of $x^2$ in the expansion of $(3 - 2x)^5$. [2]

**(b)** Find the constant term in the expansion of $\left(x^2 - \frac{1}{x}\right)^6$. [2]

9 **(a)** Expand $\left(x - \frac{1}{x}\right)^3$. [1]

Given that $\left(x - \frac{1}{x}\right) = 3$.

**(b)** Show that $\left(x^3 - \frac{1}{x^3}\right) = 36$. [2]

**(c)** Expand $\left(x - \frac{1}{x}\right)^5$. [1]

**(d)** Hence find the value of $(x^5 - \frac{1}{x^5})$. [2]

10 Find the two values of $x$ for which 1, $x^2$ and $x$ are successive terms of an arithmetic series. [2]

11 The seventh term of an arithmetic series is 6 and the eighteenth term is 22.5. Find.

**(a)** the common difference [1]

**(b)** the first term of the series [1]

**(c)** Given also that the sum of the first *n* terms is 252, find the value of *n*. [1]

12 The coefficients of the $x$ and $x^2$ terms in the expansion of $(1 + kx)^n$ are 44 and 924 respectively.

**(a)** Find the values of the constants *k* and *n*. [2]

**(b)** Find the coefficient of $x^3$ in the expansion. [2]

**Total: /52**

# The sine rule and area of a triangle

- If we have a right-angled triangle then we can use the sine, cosine or tangent and Pythagoras to help us to solve problems.

  For a more general triangle which is not right-angled, we need to use:

  the sine rule and/or the cosine rule.

**NOTATION**

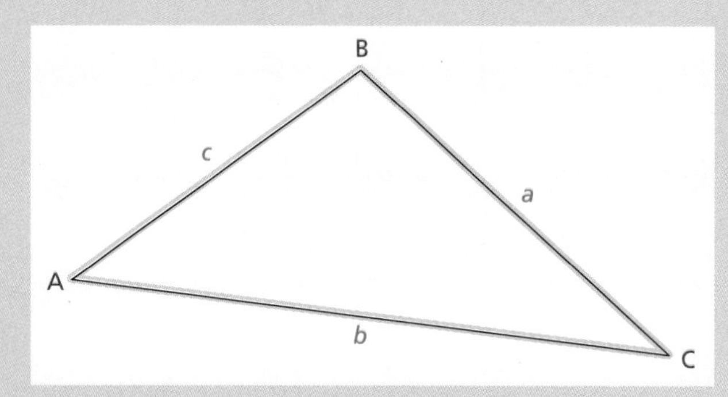


The triangle is always labelled as shown, with *a* the length of the side opposite angle *A*, etc.

## The sine rule

$$\frac{a}{\sin A} = \frac{b}{\sin B} = \frac{c}{\sin C} \quad or \quad \frac{\sin A}{a} = \frac{\sin B}{b} = \frac{\sin C}{c}$$

Use this version to find a **side**. Use this version to find an **angle**.

**EXAMINER'S TOP TIP**

**To use the sine rule you must have a side and an opposite angle plus another angle or side.**

NOTE The sine rule is true for all triangles but it should not be used for right-angled triangles.

## Finding unknown sides

**EXAMPLE**

Find, in cm to 3 s.f., the length of the side PQ of the triangle PQR in which ∠ PRQ = 62°, ∠ PQR = 47° and PR = 7cm.

Draw a sketch of the triangle. Although this doesn't need to be accurate, try to make the angles roughly the correct size, otherwise you could be misled.

We have a **side and an opposite angle**. Use the **sine rule**:

$$\frac{r}{\sin 62^\circ} = \frac{7}{\sin 47^\circ} \Rightarrow r = \frac{7\sin 62^\circ}{\sin 47^\circ} = 8.4509 = 8.45\text{cm (3 s.f.)}$$

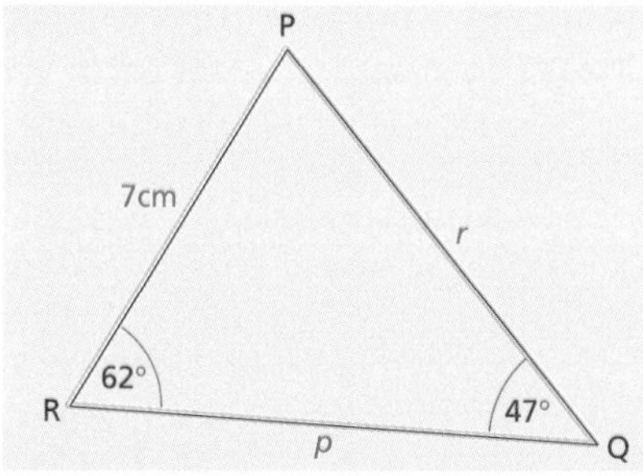


**EXAMPLE**

Find, in cm to 3 s.f., the length of the side PR of the triangle PQR in which QR = 6.4cm, ∠PRQ = 43° and ∠QPR = 71°.

Since we are trying to find *q*, we need Q = 180° – 71° – 43° = 66°

By **sine rule**:

$$\frac{q}{\sin 66^\circ} = \frac{6.4}{\sin 71^\circ} \Rightarrow q = \frac{6.4\sin 66^\circ}{\sin 71^\circ} = 6.18\text{cm (3 s.f.)}$$

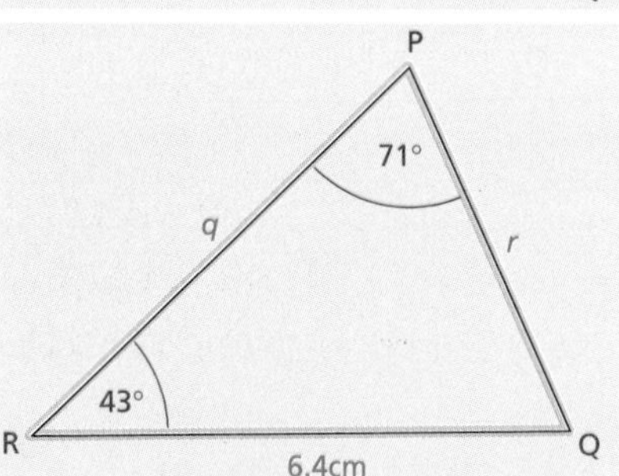

# Finding unknown angles

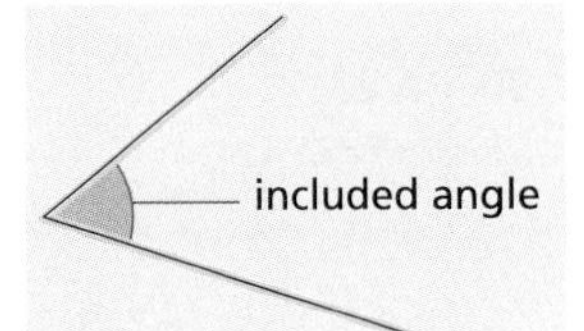


NOTE **Non-included angle** is one of the other two angles in the triangle.

If we are given **2 sides and a non-included angle**, *sometimes* there may be two possible triangles which fit the information.

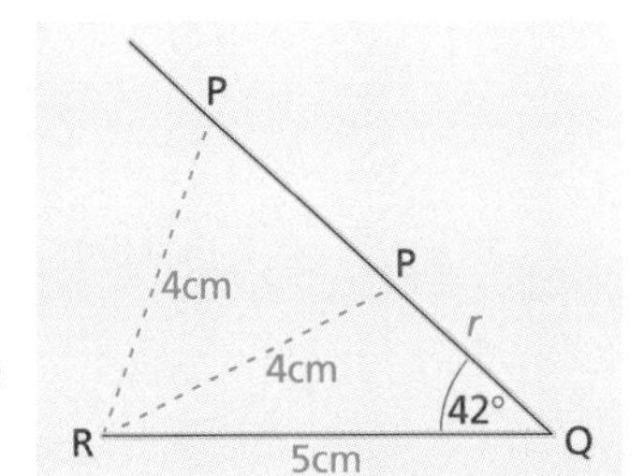


**EXAMPLE**

Find, in degrees to 1 d.p., the size of the angles ∠RPQ and ∠PRQ in the triangle PQR, where ∠PQR = 42° and PR = 4cm and QR = 5cm.

The sketch shows that there may be two possible triangles which fit the information.

**EXAMINER'S TOP TIP**
Always draw a sketch of the triangle.

$\frac{\sin P}{5} = \frac{\sin 42^\circ}{4}$ **Use this form of the sine rule as we are finding an angle.**

$\sin P = \frac{5\sin 42^\circ}{4} = 0.8364 \Rightarrow P = 56.76^\circ$ *or* $180^\circ - 56.76^\circ = 123.24^\circ$

The equation has two possible solutions in the range 0° to 180°

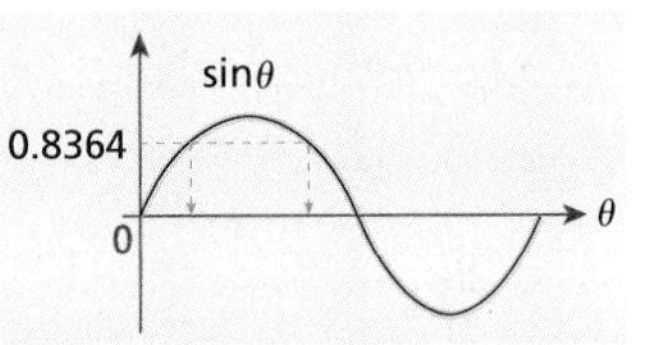


In this case, both values for P are possible since the given angle is 42°

$\angle PRQ = 180^\circ - 42^\circ - 56.76^\circ = 81.2^\circ$ (1 d.p) and $\angle RPQ = 56.8^\circ$ (1 d.p.) *or*

$\angle PRQ = 180^\circ - 42^\circ - 123.24^\circ = 14.8^\circ$ (1 d.p) and $\angle RPQ = 123.2^\circ$ (1 d.p.)

# The area of a triangle

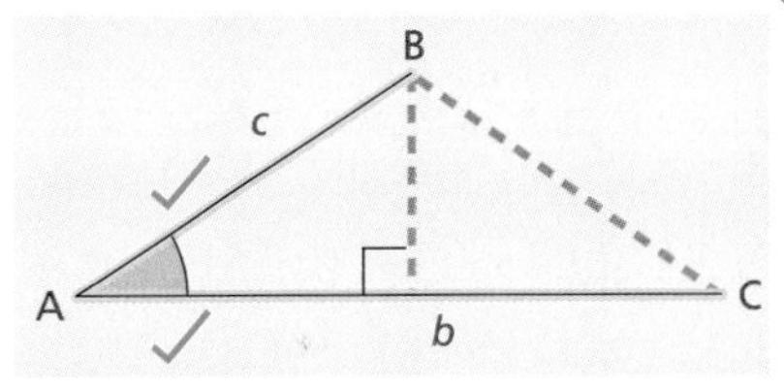


If we are given 2 sides and the included angle then, labelling the angle A and the two given sides $b$ and $c$, the area of the triangle ABC $= \frac{1}{2} \times AC \times AB\sin A$

base (AC) — perpendicular height of triangle (ABsinA)

i.e. Area of △ABC $= \frac{1}{2}bc\sin A$

NOTE If we had labelled the given angle $B$, then area $= \frac{1}{2}ac\sin B$
If we had labelled the given angle $C$, then area $= \frac{1}{2}ab\sin C$

**EXAMPLE**

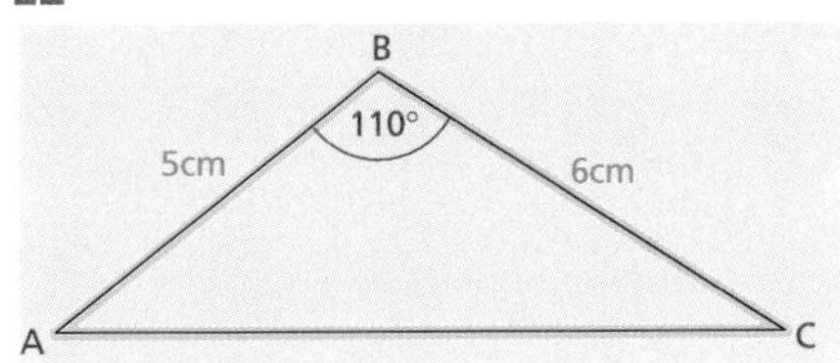


Area of triangle ABC $= \frac{1}{2} \times 5 \times 6 \times \sin 110^\circ$
$= 15\sin 110^\circ$
$= 14.1\text{cm}^2$ (1 d.p.)

# Quick test

**1** ***Find the unknown sides and angles. Give your answers to 1 d.p.***

***(a)*** Triangle ABC: ∠A = 51°, ∠C = 38°, AC = 7.3cm

***(b)*** Triangle ABC: ∠A = 29.3°, ∠B = 71.4°, BC = 8.9cm

***(c)*** Triangle ABC: ∠A = 55°, ∠C = 75°, AC = 5.3cm

***(d)*** Triangle ABC: ∠C = 64°, CB = 12.4cm, AB = 19.3cm

**2** ***Find the missing angle and sides of the triangle ABC where ∠A = 66°, ∠C = 44° and BC = 7cm.***

1. (a) ∠B = 91° AB = 4.5cm BC = 5.7cm (b) ∠C = 79.3° AB = 17.9cm AC = 17.2cm
(c) ∠B = 50° AB = 6.7cm BC = 5.7cm (d) ∠A = 35.3° ∠B = 80.7° AC = 21.2cm
2. ∠B = 70° AB = 5.3cm AC = 7.2cm

# The cosine rule

- **If you are given a non-right-angled triangle, always use the sine rule if you can. However, this will not be possible if you do not have a side and the opposite angle. This can happen in two ways.**

**1 You are given 2 sides and an included angle.**

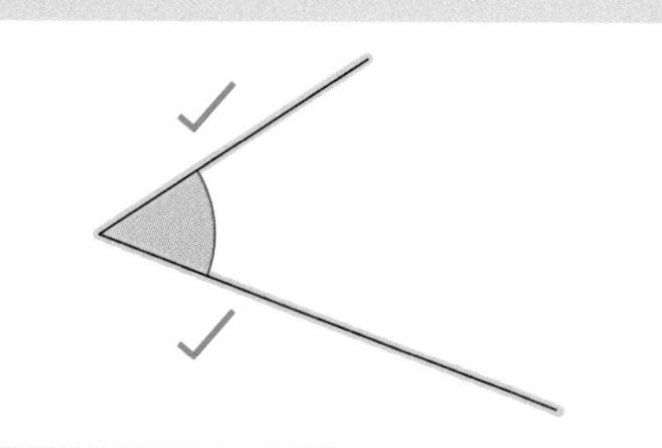

**2 You are given 3 sides.**

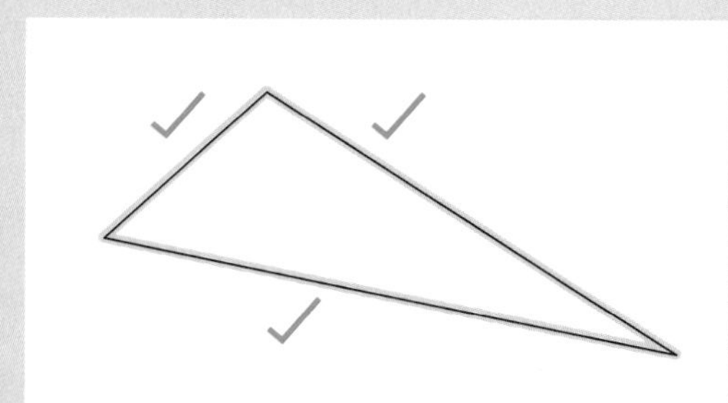

**In these two cases, you must use the cosine rule.**

## The cosine rule

$a^2 = b^2 + c^2 - 2bc\cos A$
$b^2 = a^2 + c^2 - 2ac\cos B$
$c^2 = a^2 + b^2 - 2ab\cos C$

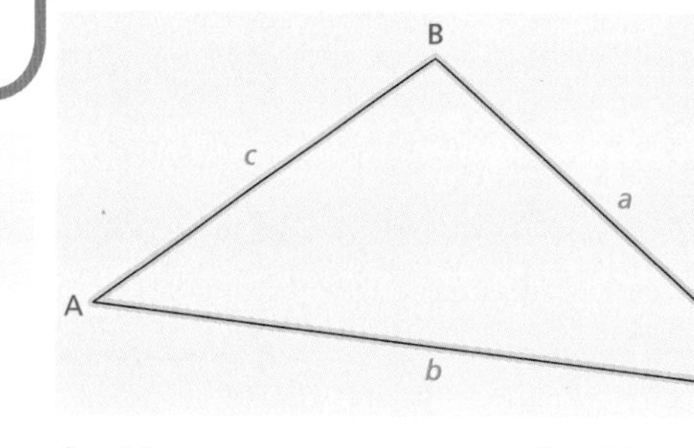


**EXAMINER'S TOP TIP**

**Think of the cosine rule as 'modified Pythagoras': $a^2 = b^2 + c^2 - 2bc\cos A$ is Pythagoras if angle A is 90° (NOTE $\cos A = 0$ in that case!)**

$\cos A = \dfrac{b^2 + c^2 - a^2}{2bc}$ $\cos B = \dfrac{a^2 + c^2 - b^2}{2ac}$ $\cos C = \dfrac{a^2 + b^2 - c^2}{2ab}$

NOTE If $90° < A < 180°$, then $\cos A < 0$

**EXAMPLE**

In triangle PQR, $PQ = 8$cm, $QR = 7$cm and $\angle PQR = 120°$.
Find the other two angles in the triangle.

Sketch the triangle.

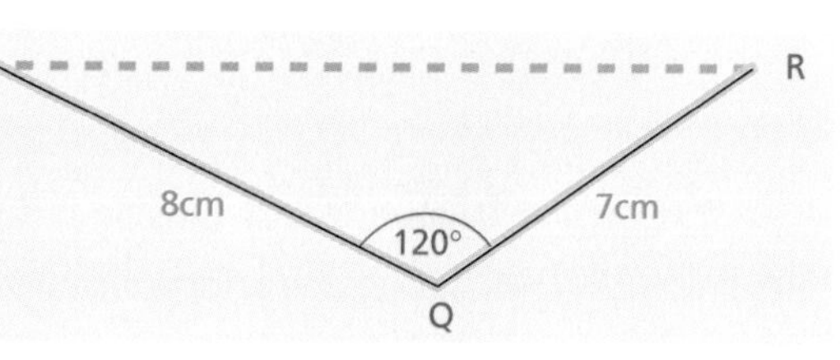


We must use the cosine rule as we haven't got a side and an opposite angle.

$PR^2 = 8^2 + 7^2 - \underbrace{2 \times 8 \times 7 \times \cos 120°}$

Work this out first.

$= 64 + 49 - 112 \times (-\tfrac{1}{2})$
$= 113 - -56 = 169$
$PR = 13$cm

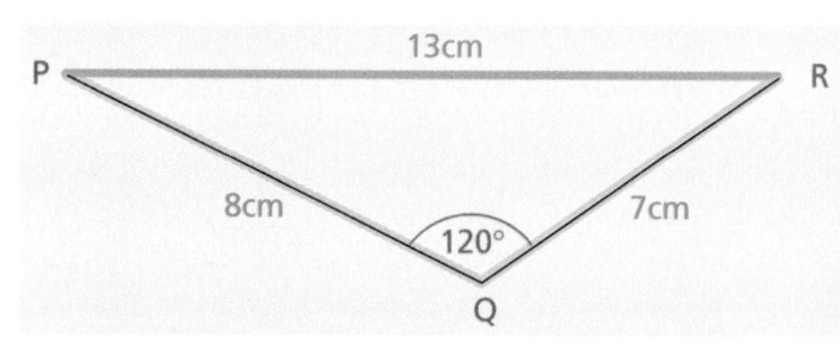


We now have a side and an opposite angle so we can use the sine rule.

$\dfrac{\sin QPR}{7} = \dfrac{\sin 120°}{13} \Rightarrow \sin QPR = \dfrac{7\sin 120°}{13} = 0.4663\ldots$

$\angle QPR = 27.8°$ *or* $180 - 27.8° = 152.2°$

Not possible as $152.2° + 120° > 180°$

$\angle PRQ = 180° - 120° - 27.8° = 32.2°$

**EXAMINER'S TOP TIP**

**Always write down both possible angles and then check to see if both are possible.**

# Further examples of the cosine rule

**EXAMPLE**
Find all the angles in the triangle whose sides are 5cm, 6cm and 7cm, giving your answers to 1 d.p.

Draw a sketch and then label the vertices.

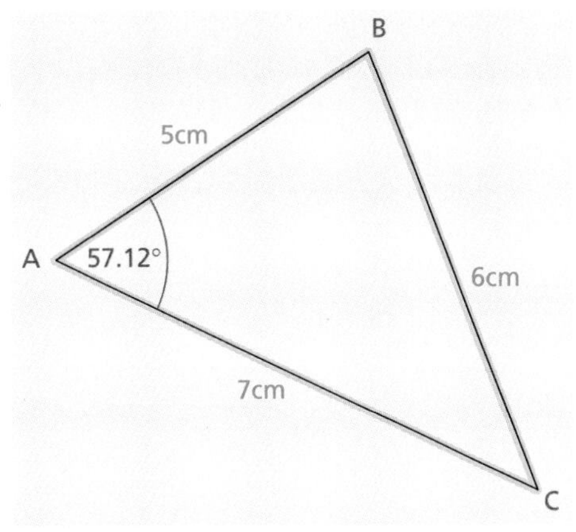


We have to use the cosine rule.

$\cos A = \dfrac{7^2 + 5^2 - 6^2}{2 \times 7 \times 5}$

$\cos A = \frac{38}{70} = \frac{19}{35}$

$A = 57.12^\circ$

**EXAMINER'S TOP TIP**
**Always work to 1 more figure than the degree of accuracy required in your answer.**

Now we can use the sine rule. In this kind of situation where we have the choice of **two** angles to find, *always* find the **angle opposite the shorter side** as this must be **acute**.

$\dfrac{\sin C}{5} = \dfrac{\sin 57.12^\circ}{6} \Rightarrow \sin C = \dfrac{5\sin 57.12^\circ}{6} = 0.6998\ldots$

$C = 44.415^\circ$ ($180^\circ - 44.415^\circ$ is *not* possible as $C$ must be acute.)

$B = 180^\circ - 57.12^\circ - 44.42^\circ = 78.5^\circ$

$A = 57.1^\circ$ (1 d.p.) $B = 78.5^\circ$ (1 d.p.) $C = 44.4^\circ$ (1 d.p.)

# Quick test

**1 Find the angle $\theta$ in each of these triangles.**

**(a)**

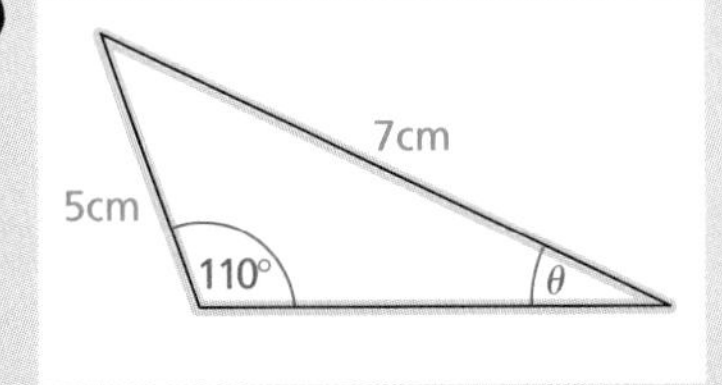


**(b)**

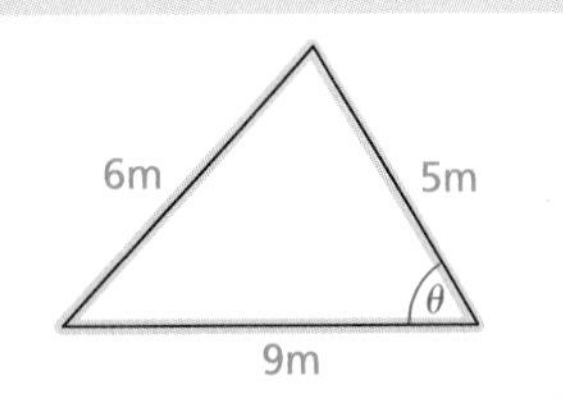


**(c)**

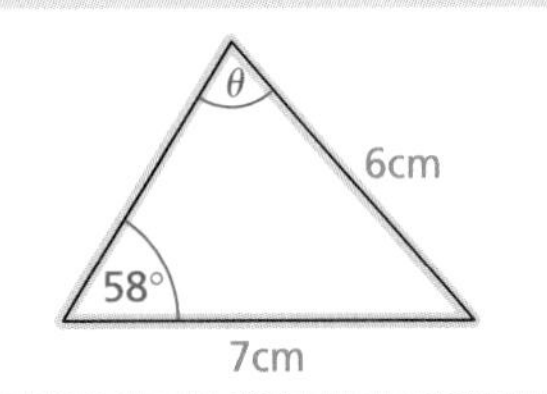


**2 Find the area of these triangles. Give your answers to 3 s.f.**

**(a)**

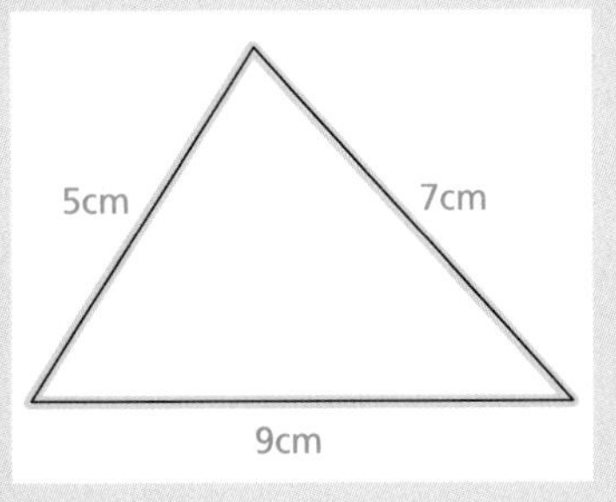


**(b)**

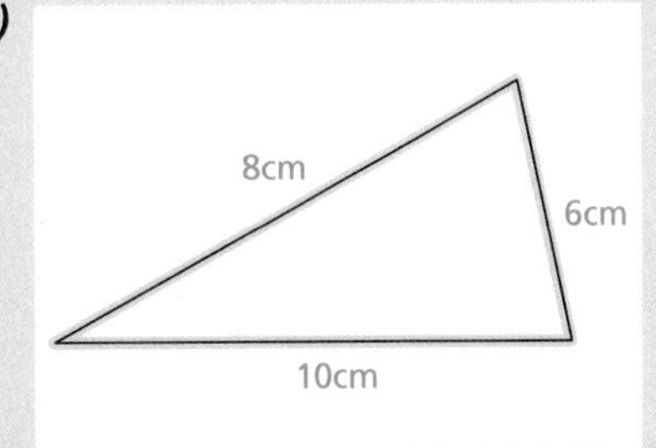


**(c)**

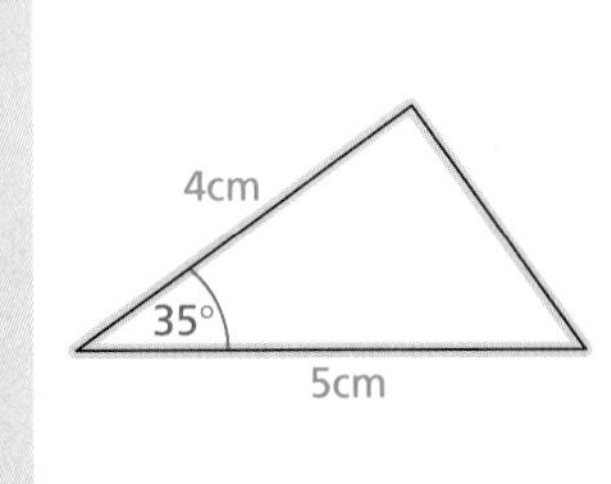


**(d)**

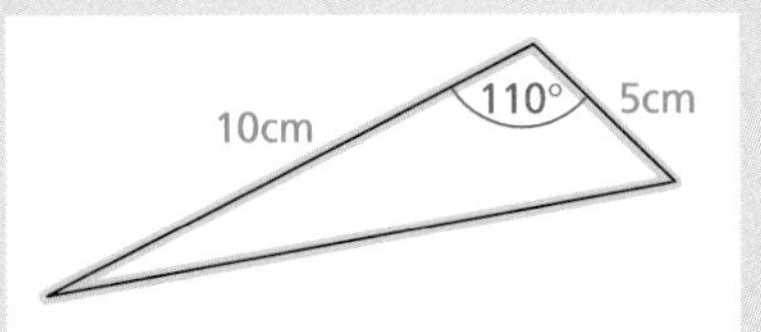


**(e)**

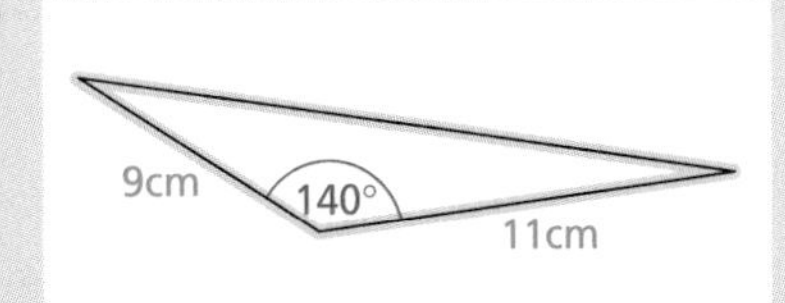


1. (a) 42.2° (b) 38.9° (c) 81.6° or 98.4° 2. (a) 17.4cm² (b) 24cm² (c) 5.74cm² (d) 23.5cm² (e) 31.8cm²

# Radian measure (or circular measure)

- **Angles are often measured in degrees. A radian is a much larger unit which is very useful in certain circumstances.**

**1 radian is the angle subtended at the centre of a circle by an arc whose length is equal to the radius of the circle.**

**1 radian is sometimes written $1^c$ (the c stands for circular measure). Look at the diagram. $\triangle$OPQ is approximately equilateral, so $1^c \approx 60°$ which gives us an idea of the size of 1 radian.**

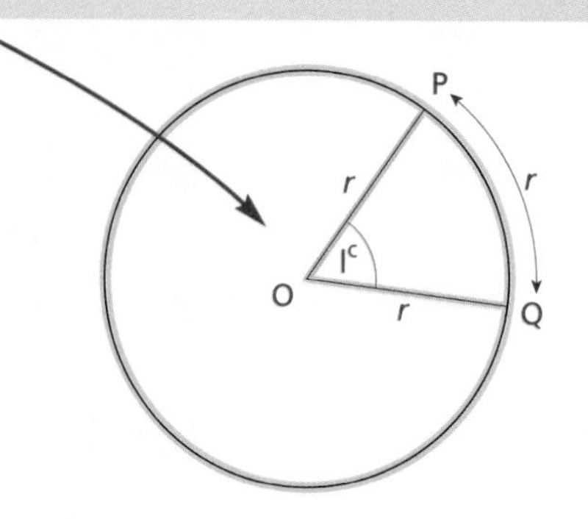


**For a more accurate value, we can use the fact that the circumference of a circle is $2\pi r$.**
**The complete angle around O must be $2\pi^c$**

**$2\pi^c = 360°$, so $1^c = \frac{360°}{2\pi} = \frac{180°}{\pi} \approx 57.3°$ (1 d.p.)**

## Common angles in radians

| | | | |
|---|---|---|---|
| $360° = 2\pi$ | $180° = \pi$ | $90° = \frac{\pi}{2}$ | $45° = \frac{\pi}{4}$ |
| $60° = \frac{\pi}{3}$ | $30° = \frac{\pi}{6}$ | $15° = \frac{\pi}{12}$ | |
| $36° = \frac{\pi}{5}$ | $18° = \frac{\pi}{10}$ | | |

**EXAMINER'S TOP TIP**
**Try to learn as many of these as you can.**

## The length of an arc

Suppose the circle centre O has radius $r$.
The arc PQ subtends an angle $\theta$ **radians** at O.
If $\theta = 1^c$, then PQ = $r$, if $\theta = 2^c$, then PQ = $2r$.
For a general angle $\theta$, PQ = $r\theta$
We usually denote an arc length by $s$.

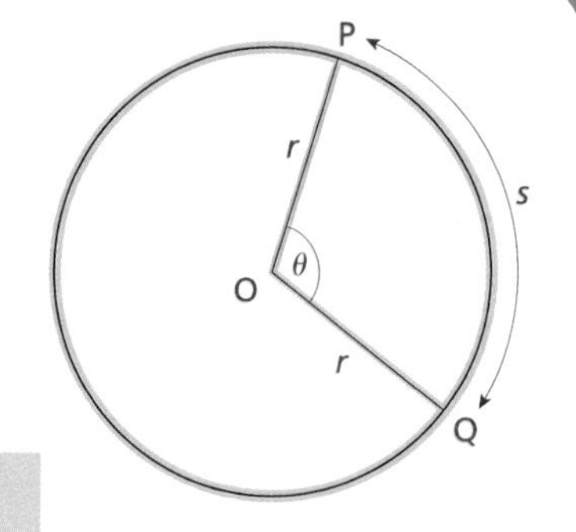


$s = r\theta$ $\quad\quad$ $\theta$ in **radians**

Check: if $\theta = 2\pi$ (360°) then $s = r \times 2\pi = 2\pi r$ = circumference of circle

## The area of a sector

Suppose the circle centre O has radius $r$.
The arc PQ subtends an angle $\theta$ **radians** at O.
Let area of sector OPQ = $A$

$$\frac{A}{\text{area of whole circle}} = \frac{\theta}{2\pi} \qquad \frac{A}{\pi r^2} = \frac{\theta}{2\pi}$$

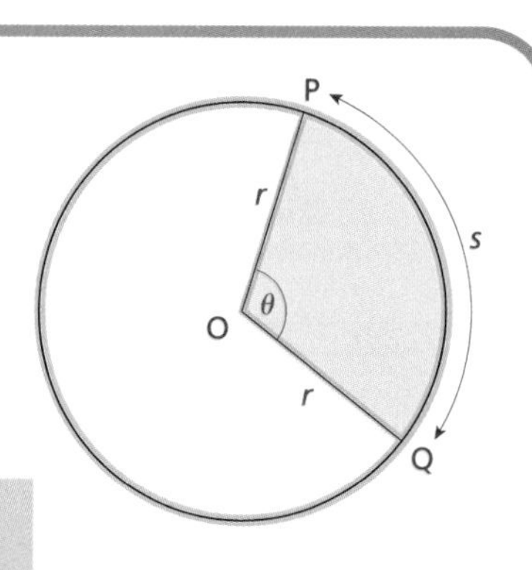


$A = \frac{1}{2}r^2\theta$ $\quad\quad$ $\theta$ in **radians**

Check: if $\theta = 2\pi$ (360°) then $A = \frac{1}{2}r^2 \times 2\pi = \pi r^2$ = area of whole circle

# The area of a segment

Suppose the circle centre O has radius $r$.
The arc PQ subtends an angle $\theta$ **radians** at O.

From the diagram,

Area of segment = area of sector OPQ – area of △OPQ

$= \frac{1}{2} r^2\theta - \frac{1}{2}r^2 \sin\theta$

For area of a triangle, **see page 49**.

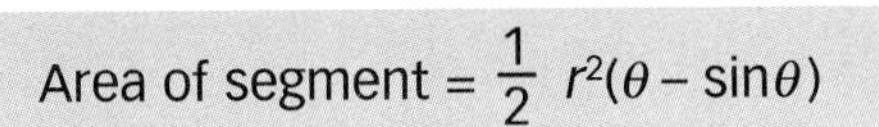

Area of segment $= \frac{1}{2} r^2(\theta - \sin\theta)$ $\theta$ in **radians**

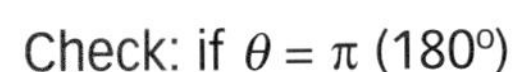

Check: if $\theta = \pi$ (180°)

area of segment $= \frac{1}{2} r^2(\pi - \sin\pi)$ ($\sin\pi = 0$)

$= \frac{1}{2} \pi r^2$ Area of a semicircle

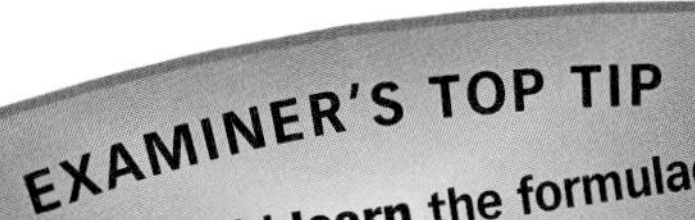

**EXAMINER'S TOP TIP**
You should **learn** the formulae for arc length, area of a sector and area of a segment.

**EXAMPLE**

P and Q are two points on the circumference of a circle centre O and radius 10cm. The length of the chord PQ is 12cm and $\angle POQ = \theta$ radians.

(a) Find $\theta$

(b) Find the area of the major segment bounded by PQ and the circle.

(a) Draw a diagram.

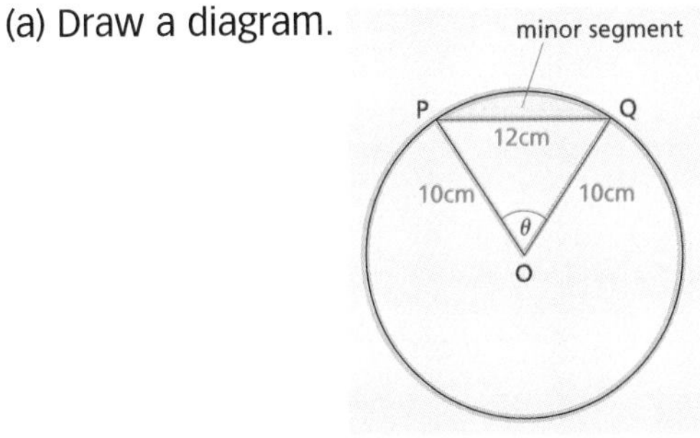


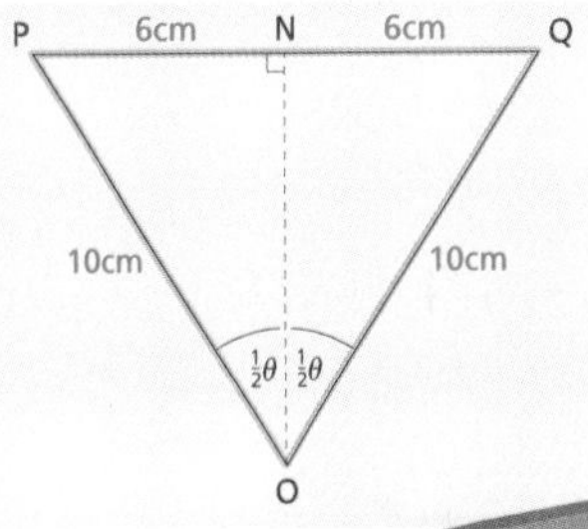


Triangle OPQ is isosceles, so we can split into 2 congruent **right-angled triangles** by dropping a perpendicular ON, which is a **line of symmetry** of triangle OPQ.

In triangle OPN, $\sin \frac{1}{2}\theta = \frac{6}{10} = 0.6$

$\frac{1}{2}\theta = 0.6435\ldots$ $\theta = 1.287^c$

NOTE We could find $\theta$ by using the cosine rule.

$$12^2 = 10^2 + 10^2 - 2 \times 10 \times 10\cos\theta$$
$$144 = 200 - 200\cos\theta$$
$$-56 = -200\cos\theta$$
$$0.28 = \cos\theta$$
$$1.287 = \theta$$

(b) Area of minor segment $= \frac{1}{2} \times 10^2(1.287 - \sin 1.287)$

$\approx 50(1.287 - 0.96)$

$= 16.35\text{cm}^2$

Area of major segment = area of circle – 16.35

$= \pi \times 10^2 - 16.35$

$= 100\pi - 16.35$

$= 297.8\text{cm}^2$

$= 298\text{cm}^2$ (3 s.f.)

**EXAMINER'S TOP TIP**
When working on this type of problem, ensure that your calculator is in **radian mode**.

# Quick test

**1** *Write these angles in radians, as multiples of $\pi$:*
*(a) 270° (b) 135° (c) 120° (d) 150° (e) 630°*

**2** *Write these angles in degrees:*
*(a) $\frac{5\pi}{12}$ (b) $\frac{3\pi}{2}$ (c) $5\pi$ (d) $\frac{7\pi}{8}$ (e) $2\frac{1}{2}\pi$*

**3** *Express these angles in radians to 3 s.f:*
*(a) 145° (b) 70° (c) 400°*

**4** *Find the angle, in degrees, that is subtended at the centre of a circle of radius 4cm by an arc of length 6cm.*

**5** *Find the area of the sector OPQ, where O is the centre of a circle of radius 5cm and PQ is an arc on the circle which is 10cm in length.*

1. (a) $\frac{3\pi}{2}$ (b) $\frac{3\pi}{4}$ (c) $\frac{2\pi}{3}$ (d) $\frac{5\pi}{6}$ (e) $\frac{7\pi}{2}$ 2. (a) 75° (b) 270° (c) 900° (d) 157.5° (e) 450° 3. (a) $2.53^c$ (b) $1.22^c$ (c) $6.98^c$ 4. 85.9° (3 s.f.) 5. 25 cm²

# Trigonometric graphs

**Basic graphs**

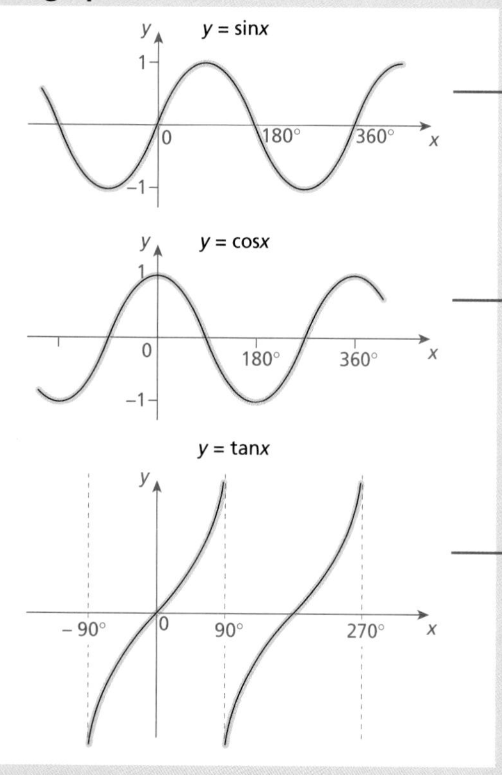


**Key points** (y = sin x)

- **Repeats every 360° (360° is its period)**
- **Takes values between –1 and 1 only**
- **Crosses $x$-axis at multiples of 180°**
- **$\frac{1}{2}$-turn symmetry about O, $\sin(-x) = -\sin x$**

**Key points** (y = cos x)

- **Repeats every 360° (360° is its period)**
- **Takes values between –1 and 1 only**
- **Crosses $x$-axis at odd multiples of 90°**
- **reflective symmetry in the $y$-axis, $\cos(-x) = \cos x$**

**Key points** (y = tan x)

- **Repeats every 180° (180° is its period)**
- **Takes all values**
- **Crosses $x$-axis at multiples of 180°**
- **Asymptotes (vertical) at odd multiples of 90°**
- **$\frac{1}{2}$-turn symmetry about O, $\tan(-x) = -\tan x$**

**NOTE You could be asked to sketch one of the above when $x$ is measured in radians. The sin and cos graphs have exactly the same shape except the cos graph is 90° behind the sin graph.**

**EXAMINER'S TOP TIP**
**Learn these graphs and the key points relevant to each.**

| | |
|---|---|
| **Thus $\cos(x - 90°) = \sin x$** | **–90° inside bracket moves graph forward 90° in $x$ direction** |
| **so $\cos(90° - x) = \sin x$** | **since $\cos(-x) = \cos x$.** |
| **Also $\sin(x + 90°) = \cos x$** | **+90° inside bracket moves graph backwards 90° in $x$ direction** |

## More complicated graphs

By using one of the basic graphs as a starting point, we can sketch the graph of a more complicated trigonometric graph using our knowledge of basic transformations.

**EXAMPLE**

Sketch the graph of $y = 2\sin(x + 90°) - 1$

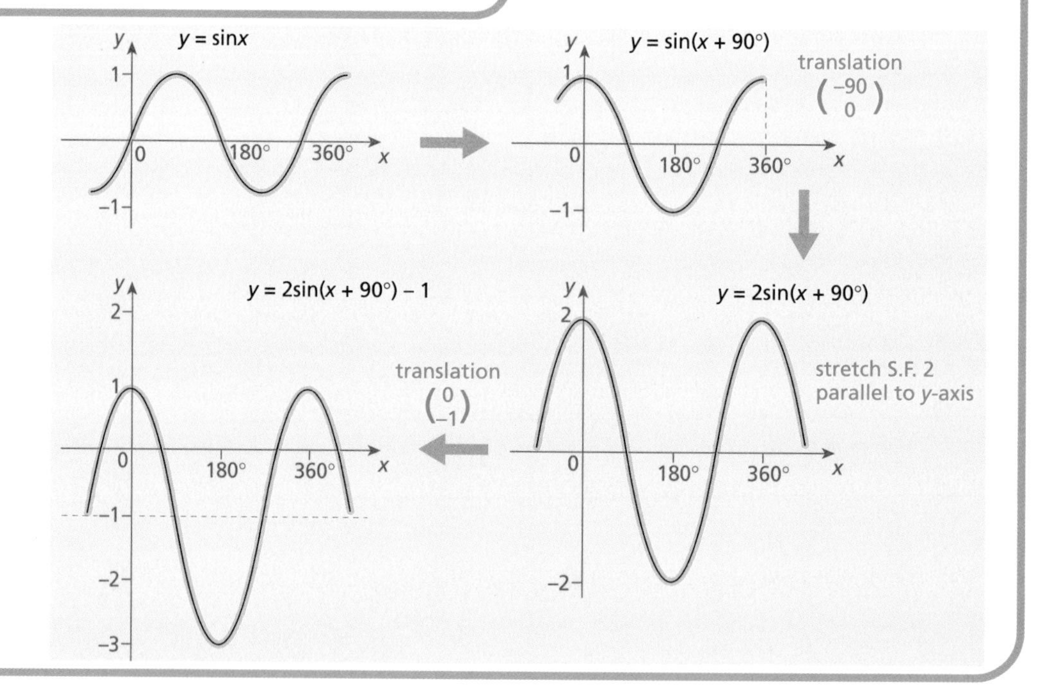

# Further examples of more complicated graphs

**EXAMPLE**

Sketch the graph of $y = 1 - \cos 2x$

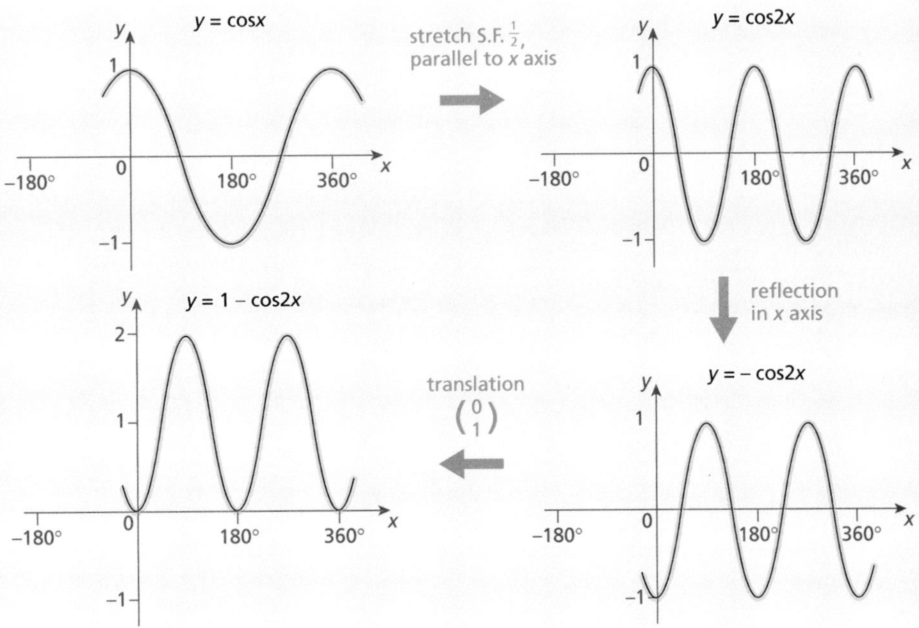


**EXAMINER'S TOP TIP**

It is important that the transformations are performed in the correct order. To help you with this, imagine you were evaluating the expression at a particular value of $x$ and note the order in which you perform the various operations on $x$

**EXAMPLE**

Sketch the graph of $y = \cos^2 x$

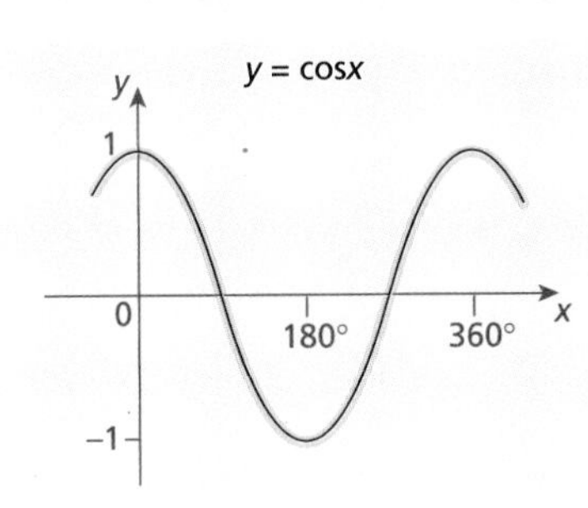


here we just square the y coordinate of each point

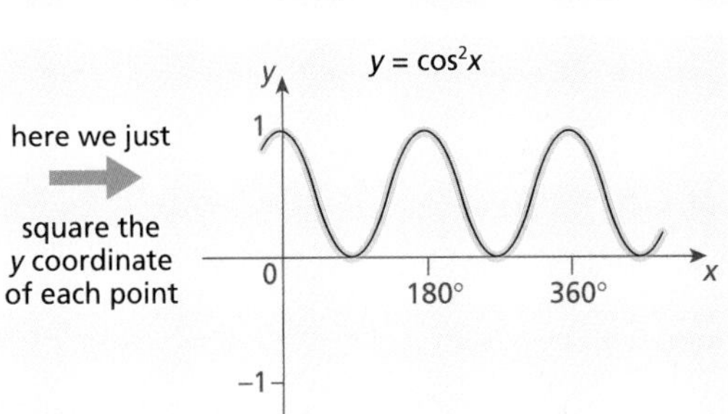


# Quick test

**1** ***Match the correct equation to each graph.***

***(a)*** $y = -\cos x$ ***(b)*** $y = 1 + \sin x$ ***(c)*** $y = 2\sin x$ ***(d)*** $y = 1 - \cos x$ ***(e)*** $y = \sin\frac{1}{2}x$ ***(f)*** $y = -\tan x$

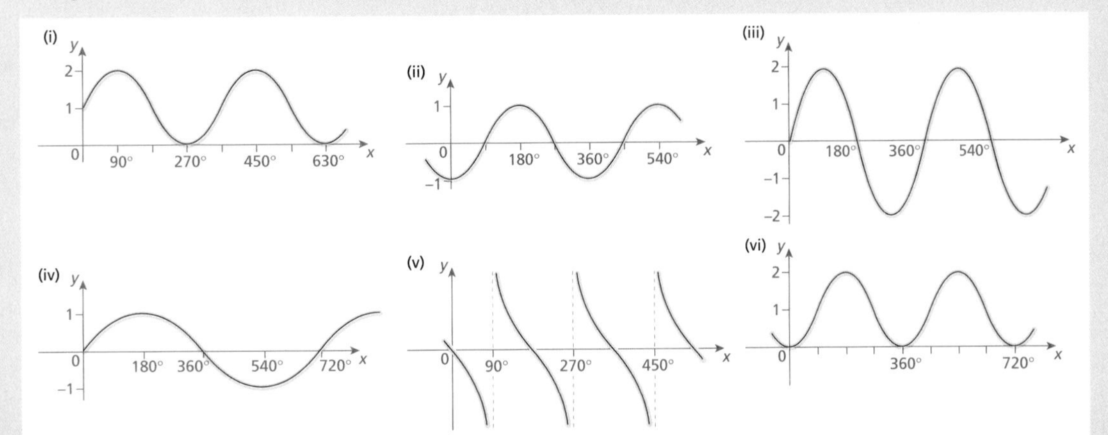


**2** ***On a single diagram, sketch the graphs of*** $y = 2\cos x$ ***and*** $y = \cos 2x$ ***for*** $0° \le x \le 360°$

***Hence state the number of solutions there are to the equation*** $\cos 2x = 2\cos x$***, for*** $0° \le x \le 360°$

1. (a) → (ii) (b) → (i) (c) → (iii) (d) → (vi) (e) → (iv) (f) → (v)

2.

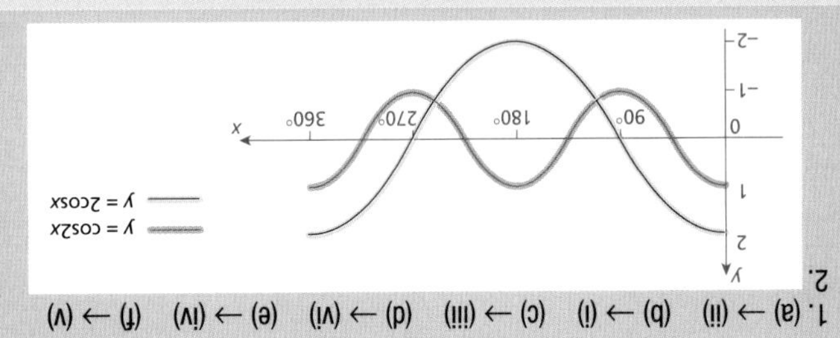


There are two points where they cross, so two solutions in the interval 0° to 360°

# Solving trigonometric equations

Change the range if necessary. → Ignore – sign, if present, and use calculator to find acute angle. → Using diagram below, find which quadrants the solutions will be in. → Use the diagram to find the required angles in range 0° to 360° → Use the period of the function (360° or 180°) to generate all possible angles within the changed range. → Readjust values, if necessary, to give solutions within the given range.

These two diagrams will be useful when solving trigonometric equations.
NOTE Anticlockwise is positive.

*Trigonometric functions which are positive in each quadrant.*

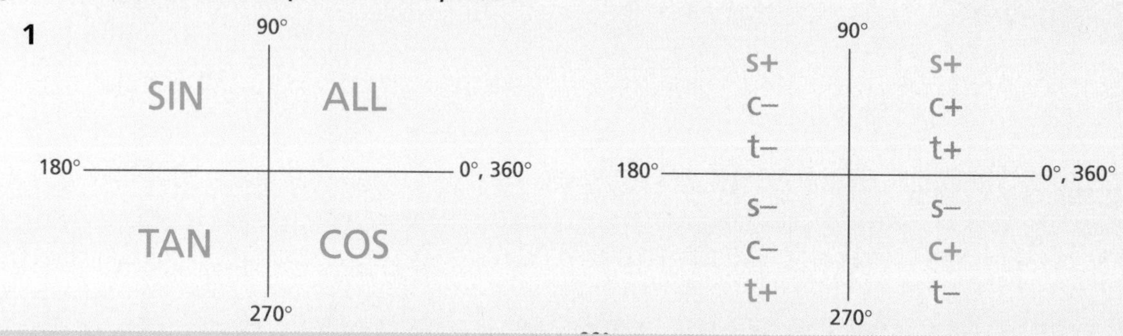


*Finding the angles which fit the equation using the acute angle, θ.*

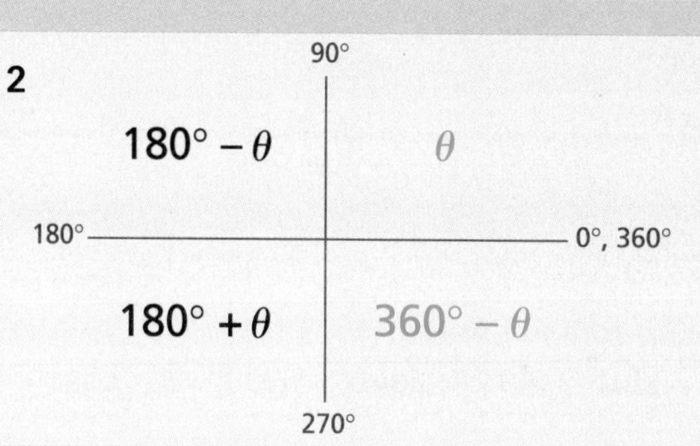


# How to solve trigonometric equations

**EXAMPLE**
Solve, for $0° \le x \le 360°$, $\sin x = -0.2$.

There is no need to change the range. Ignore the negative sign to give the angle $\theta = 11.5°$.
For sine to be negative, angles need to be in 3rd and 4th quadrants.

$x = 180° + 11.5°$ *or* $360° - 11.5°$
$= 191.5°$ *or* $348.5°$

**Check answers by substituting solutions back into the original equation.**

**EXAMPLE**
Solve, for $0° \le x \le 360°$, $\cos 2x = 0.7$.

New range is $0° \le 2x \le 720°$
$\theta = 45.6°$ The solution is in 1st or 4th quadrants.
$2x = 45.6°, (360° - 45.6°), 405.6°, 674.4°$ Generate last two by adding multiples of 360°
$x = 22.8°, 157.2°, 202.8°, 337.2°$
Check answers.

# Further trigonometric equations

**EXAMPLE**

Solve, for $-180^\circ \le x \le 180^\circ$,

$$2\tan(x + 100^\circ) + 1 = 0 \Rightarrow \tan(x + 100^\circ) = -\frac{1}{2}$$

New range is $-80^\circ \le x + 100^\circ \le 280^\circ$

$\theta = 26.6^\circ$ Solutions in 2nd and 4th quadrants

$x + 100 = (180^\circ - 26.6^\circ), (360^\circ - 26.6^\circ) = 153.4^\circ, 333.4^\circ$ (out of range), $-26.6^\circ$

$x = 53.4^\circ, -126.6^\circ$

Check answers.

**EXAMINER'S TOP TIP**

where possible, when working with radians, use multiples of $\pi$

**EXAMPLE**

Find the possible values of $x$ for which $\sin^2\left(x + \frac{\pi}{6}\right) = \frac{1}{2}$, for $-\pi \le x \le \pi$.

$\sin^2\left(x + \frac{\pi}{6}\right) = \frac{1}{2} \rightarrow \sin\left(x + \frac{\pi}{6}\right) = \pm\frac{1}{\sqrt{2}}$ NOTE Two square roots.

New range is $\frac{-5\pi}{6} \le \left(x + \frac{\pi}{6}\right) \le \frac{7\pi}{6}$

$\theta = \sin^{-1}\frac{1}{\sqrt{2}} = \frac{\pi}{4}\ (45^\circ)$

$\sin\left(x + \frac{\pi}{6}\right) = \frac{1}{\sqrt{2}}$ *or* $\sin\left(x + \frac{\pi}{6}\right) = \frac{-1}{\sqrt{2}}$

Solution in 1st or 2nd quadrant *or* solution in 3rd or 4th quadrants.

1st or 2nd:

$x + \frac{\pi}{6} = \frac{\pi}{4}$ or $\left(\pi - \frac{\pi}{4}\right)$

$x = \frac{\pi}{4} - \frac{\pi}{6}$ or $\frac{3\pi}{4} - \frac{\pi}{6}$

$= \frac{\pi}{12}$ or $\frac{7\pi}{12}$

3rd or 4th:

$x + \frac{\pi}{6} = \left(\frac{\pi}{4} + \pi\right)$ or $\left(2\pi - \frac{\pi}{4}\right)$ Both out of range.

$\sin\left(x + \frac{\pi}{6}\right) = \frac{-3\pi}{4}$ or $\frac{-\pi}{4}$ Generated by subtracting $2\pi$ from $\frac{\pi}{4} + \pi$ and $2\pi - \frac{\pi}{4}$

$x = \frac{-11\pi}{12}$ or $\frac{-5\pi}{12}$

Check answers by putting **calculator in radian mode** and substituting solutions.

**EXAMPLE**

Find the possible values of $x$ for which $1 - 2\sin x = 4 + 4\sin x$, for $0^\circ \le x \le 360^\circ$.

$1 - 2\sin x = 4 + 4\sin x$

$-3 = 6\sin x$

$\sin x = -\frac{1}{2}$

No need to change range. Ignore negative sign.

$\theta = 30^\circ$

Solution in 3rd or 4th quadrant.

$x = 30^\circ + 180^\circ$ or $360^\circ - 30^\circ$

$x = 210^\circ$ or $330^\circ$

Check solution.

## Quick test

1 ***Solve these for values of x for $0^\circ \le x \le 360^\circ$. Give answers to 1 d.p. where necessary.***

***(a) $\sin 2x = 0.3$*** ***(b) $\tan(x - 50^\circ) = -1$.***

2 ***Solve, for $-180^\circ < x < 180^\circ$, the equation $\cos(x - 10^\circ) = \frac{1}{2}$.***

3 ***Solve, for $0 < \theta < \pi$, the equation $\tan\left(2\theta + \frac{\pi}{4}\right) = -1$.***

1. (a) $8.7^\circ, 81.3^\circ, 188.7^\circ, 261.3^\circ$ (b) $5^\circ, 185^\circ$ 2. $70^\circ$ or $-50^\circ$ 3. $\frac{\pi}{4}$ or $\frac{3\pi}{4}$

# Trigonometric equations and identities

## Trigonometric ratios of 30°, 45° and 60°

Consider an equilateral triangle of side 2 units.

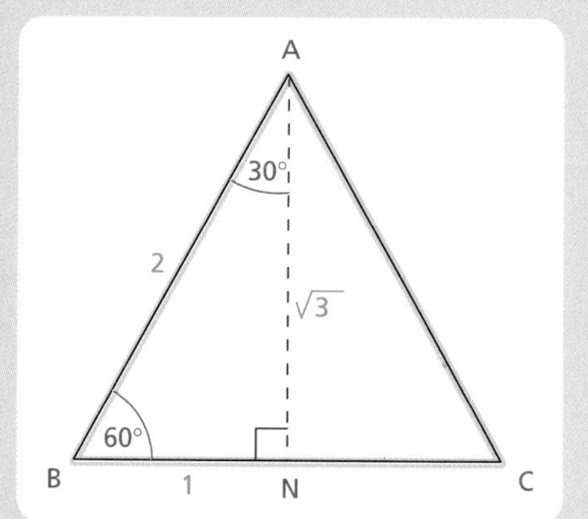


Drop a perpendicular from A onto BC. N is the midpoint of BC. BN = 1 and $\angle NAB = 30°$

In triangle ABN: $AN^2 + 1^2 = 2^2$ (Pythagoras' Theorem)

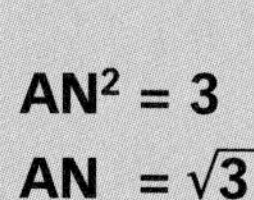

$AN^2 = 3$

$AN = \sqrt{3}$

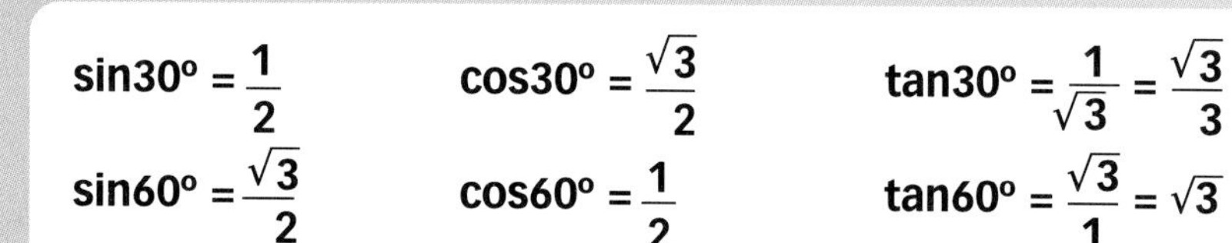

$\sin 30° = \frac{1}{2}$ $\quad \cos 30° = \frac{\sqrt{3}}{2}$ $\quad \tan 30° = \frac{1}{\sqrt{3}} = \frac{\sqrt{3}}{3}$

$\sin 60° = \frac{\sqrt{3}}{2}$ $\quad \cos 60° = \frac{1}{2}$ $\quad \tan 60° = \frac{\sqrt{3}}{1} = \sqrt{3}$

Consider an isosceles triangle which is also right-angled.

Suppose AC = BC = 1

Then $AB^2 = 1^2 + 1^2 = 2$

$AB = \sqrt{2}$

$\angle A = \angle B = 45°$

**EXAMINER'S TOP TIP**

These results are often used and should be learned, along with **radian** equivalents.

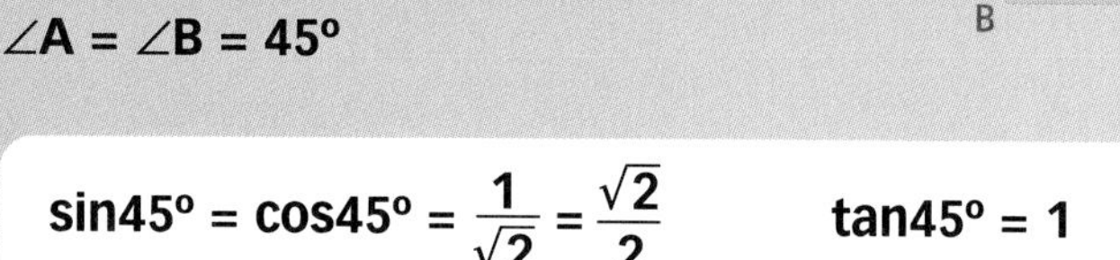

$\sin 45° = \cos 45° = \frac{1}{\sqrt{2}} = \frac{\sqrt{2}}{2}$ $\quad \tan 45° = 1$

## Two important identities

**EXAMINER'S TOP TIP**

Both these identities, together with their proofs, should be **learned**.

1 $\tan\theta = \frac{\sin\theta}{\cos\theta}$

To prove this, use SOHCAHTOA

$$RHS = \frac{\sin\theta}{\cos\theta} = \frac{(\frac{O}{H})}{(\frac{A}{H})} = \frac{O}{H} \times \frac{H}{A} = \frac{O}{A} = \tan\theta = LHS$$

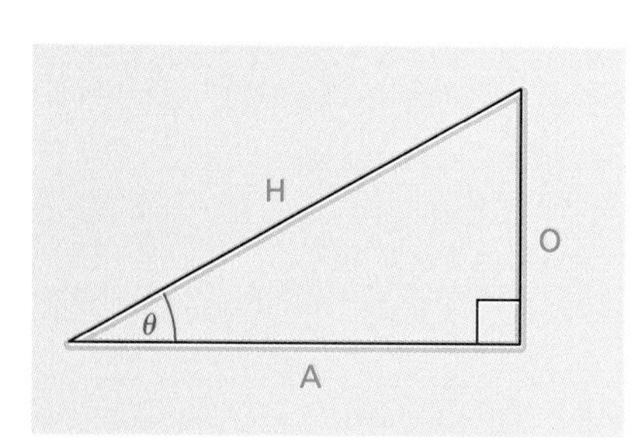


2 $\sin^2\theta + \cos^2\theta = 1$

Again, use SOHCAHTOA

$$LHS = \left(\frac{O}{H}\right)^2 + \left(\frac{A}{H}\right)^2 = \frac{O^2}{H^2} + \frac{A^2}{H^2}$$

$$= \frac{(O^2 + A^2)}{H^2}$$

$$= \frac{H^2}{H^2} \text{ (Pythagoras)}$$

$$= 1 = RHS$$

# Equations of form $a\cos\theta + b\sin\theta = 0$

**EXAMPLE**

Solve, for $0° \le \theta \le 360°$, $3\cos\theta + 5\sin\theta = 0$, giving answers to 1 d.p.

$$\frac{3\cos\theta}{\cos\theta} + \frac{5\sin\theta}{\cos\theta} = \frac{0}{\cos\theta}$$ Divide both sides by $\cos\theta$

$$3 + 5\tan\theta = 0$$
$$5\tan\theta = -3$$
$$\tan\theta = -\tfrac{3}{5} = -0.6$$

No need to change range. Acute angle is 30.96°
Solutions in 2nd and 4th quadrants.

$$\theta = 180° - 30.96° \text{ or } 360° - 30.96°$$
$$= 149.0° \text{ or } 329.0°$$

**EXAMPLE**

Solve, for $0° \le x \le 360°$, $2\cos\tfrac{1}{2}x = 3\sin\tfrac{1}{2}x$

$$\frac{2\cos\frac{1}{2}x}{\cos\frac{1}{2}x} = \frac{3\sin\frac{1}{2}x}{\cos\frac{1}{2}x}$$ Divide both sides by $\cos\tfrac{1}{2}x$

$$2 = 3\tan\tfrac{1}{2}x$$

$$\tan\tfrac{1}{2}x = \tfrac{2}{3}$$ Change range: $0° \le x \le 360° \rightarrow 0° \le \tfrac{1}{2}x \le 180°$

Acute angle is 33.7° Solutions in 1st and 3rd quadrants

$$\tfrac{1}{2}x = 33.7° \text{ or } 33.7° + 180° \text{ (out of range)}$$
$$x = 67.4°$$

# Equations using $\sin^2\theta + \cos^2\theta = 1$

**EXAMPLE**

Solve, for $0° \le \theta \le 360°$, $2\sin^2\theta + 5\cos\theta + 1 = 0$.

$$2\sin^2\theta + 5\cos\theta + 1 = 0$$

Change $\sin^2\theta$ into $(1 - \cos^2\theta)$

$$2(1 - \cos^2\theta) + 5\cos\theta + 1 = 0$$ <u>Collect terms</u> so that <u>square term has positive coefficient</u>.

$$2\cos^2\theta - 5\cos\theta - 3 = 0$$
$$(2\cos\theta + 1)(\cos\theta - 3) = 0$$
$$\cos\theta = -\tfrac{1}{2} \textit{ or } \cos\theta = 3$$ $\cos\theta = 3$ has no solutions.

No need to change range. Acute angle is 60° Solutions in 2nd and 3rd quadrants.

$$\theta = (180° - 60°) \text{ or } (180° + 60°) = 120° \text{ or } 240°$$

**EXAMINER'S TOP TIP**

**Any trigonometric equation which contains more than one trigonometric ratio, is solved by using an identity to reduce it to an equation in one ratio only.**

# Quick test

**1** ***Solve these for $0° \le x \le 360°$***

***(a) $2\sin x - 3\cos x = 0$***

***(b) $4\sin x\cos x = 3\cos x$ (Do not cancel cosx, factorise!)***

***(c) $2\sin^2 x - \sin x - 1 = 0$***

***(d) $\sin^2 x + \sin x\cos x = 0$ (Factorise!).***

**2** ***Solve these for $-180° \le \theta \le 180°$***

***(a) $\sin^2\theta + \cos\theta + 1 = 0$***

***(b) $4 - \sin\theta = 4\cos^2\theta$.***

1. (a) 56.3°, 236.3° (b) 48.6°, 90°, 131.4°, 270° (c) 90°, 210°, 330° (d) 0°, 135°, 180°, 315°, 360° 2. (a) ±180° (b) 0°, 14.5°, 165.5°, ±180°

# Exam-style questions

Use the questions to test your progress. Check your answers on page 95.

1 A ship S is 7 km away from a lighthouse L on a bearing of 080° and a ship T is 5 km away from the lighthouse on a bearing of 210°. Find:
(a) the distance of S from T [1]
(b) the bearing of S from T. [1]

2 A chord AB of a circle of radius 5cm subtends an angle of 2 radians at the centre of the circle. Find, to 1 d.p.,
(a) the length of the **major** arc AB [1]
(b) the area enclosed by the chord AB and the **minor** arc AB. [1]

3 P and Q are two points on the circumference of a circle centre O and radius $r$. The minor arc PQ subtends an angle of $\theta$ radians at O. If the area of the minor segment bounded by the chord PQ and the circle is one quarter of the area of the minor sector POQ, show that $4\sin\theta - 3\theta = 0$ [2]

4 Sketch on separate diagrams for $0° \leq \theta \leq 360°$,
(a) $y = 3\cos\theta$ (b) $y = \cos 2\theta$ (c) $y = \cos(\theta - 30°)$ [3]

5 (a) Sketch the curve with equation
$y = 3 + \cos x$ for $-360° \leq x \leq 360$ [2]
(b) On the same axes, sketch the curve with equation
$y = 3\sin x$ for $-360° \leq x \leq 360$ [2]
(c) On your diagram, shade the regions for which
$y < 3\sin x$ and $y > 3 + \cos x$ for $-360° \leq x \leq 360$ [2]

6 Solve, for $0° \leq x \leq 360°$, $3\cos^2 x = 2\sin x + 2$ [7]

7 Find the values of $x$, in the range $0 \leq x \leq \pi$, for which
(a) $\sin 3x = \frac{1}{2}$ [4]
(b) $\tan\left(x + \frac{\pi}{2}\right) = 1$ [4]

8 Given that $-180° < \theta \leq 360°$ and $\tan\theta = \tan 35°$, find the possible values of $\theta$ [3]

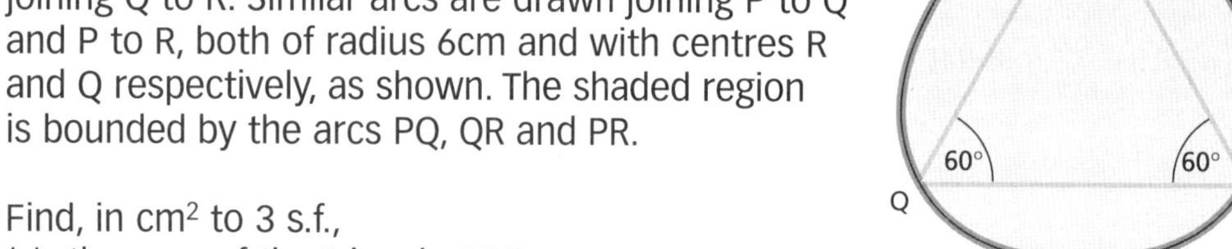

9 The triangle PQR is equilateral of side 6cm. A circular arc with centre P and radius 6cm is drawn joining Q to R. Similar arcs are drawn joining P to Q and P to R, both of radius 6cm and with centres R and Q respectively, as shown. The shaded region is bounded by the arcs PQ, QR and PR.

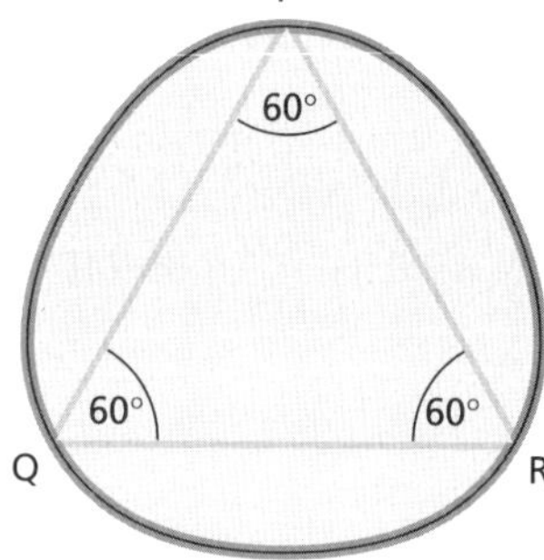

Find, in cm² to 3 s.f.,
(a) the area of the triangle PQR [2]
(b) the area of A. [6]

10 Solve, for $0 < \theta < \pi$,
$\tan\left(2\theta + \frac{\pi}{4}\right) = -1.$ [4]

11 Solve, for $-180° < x < 180°$,
$\cos(x - 10°) = 0.5$. [4]

12 The diagram shows a circle, centre O and radius r. The chord PQ subtends an angle $2\theta$ radians at O, where $0 < \theta < \frac{\pi}{2}$. The length of the minor arc PQ is 1.5 times the length of the chord PQ.

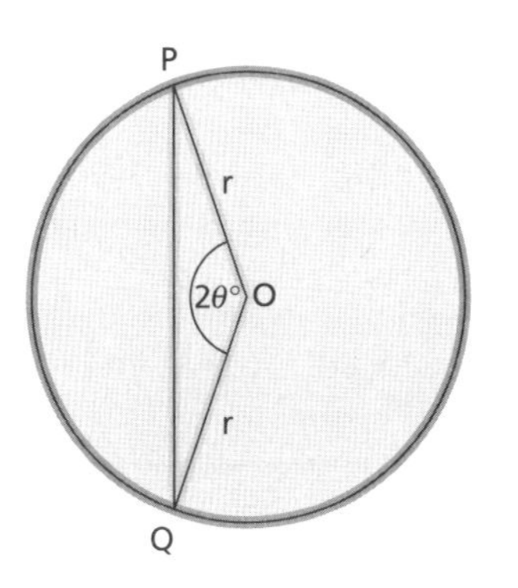


(a) Show that $2\theta - 3\sin\theta = 0$. [2]
(b) Show that the area of $\triangle$OPQ is $r^2\sin\theta\cos\theta$ [4]
(c) Hence show that, for this value of $\theta$,
$$\frac{\text{area of sector OPQ}}{\text{area of triangle OPQ}} = \frac{3}{2\cos\theta}$$ [4]

13 Two equal circles of radius 5cm are situated with their centres 6cm apart. Calculate the area which lies within both circles. [6]

14 The diagram shows an arc AB of a circle of radius 6cm which subtends an angle of 40° at the centre O. The line BC is a diameter of the circle.

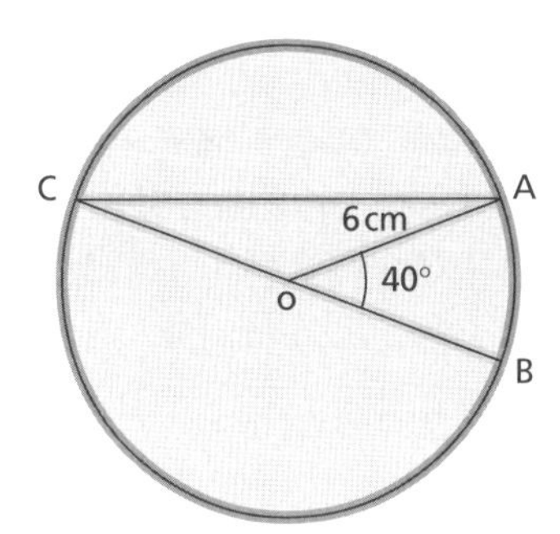


Find the area bounded by BC, the line CA and the arc AB. [6]

**Total: /71**

# Differentiation from first principles

A straight line has a constant gradient.

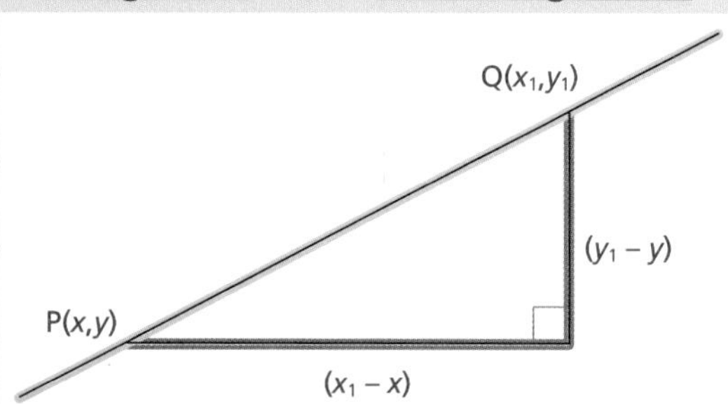


To find the gradient of the line, choose two points P ($x$, $y$) and Q ($x_1$, $y_1$) on the line.

Gradient of line = Gradient of PQ = $\dfrac{y_1 - y}{x_1 - x}$

A curve, however, has a gradient which changes as we move from point to point along the curve.

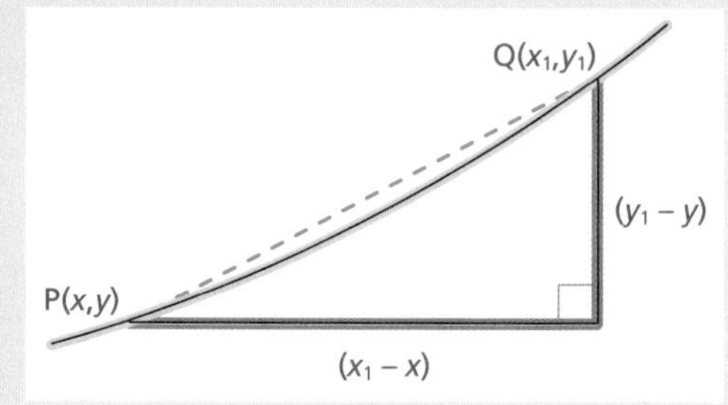


Suppose we wish to find the gradient at the point P ($x$, y) on some curve.

Suppose we choose another point Q ($x_1$, $y_1$) on the curve, fairly close to P, as shown.

Gradient of PQ $= \dfrac{y_1 - y}{x_1 - x}$ as before.

However, the gradient of PQ – the dotted line in the diagram – is clearly not the same as the gradient of the curve at P.

Let Q get closer and closer to P (without ever reaching P otherwise there would be no triangle from which to calculate the gradient) and see what happens to the gradient of PQ.

Gradient of curve at P = $\lim\limits_{Q \to P} \left(\dfrac{y_1 - y}{x_1 - x}\right)$ The limit of $\dfrac{y_1 - y}{x_1 - x}$ as Q approaches P.

We usually write $y_1 - y$ as $\delta y$ (change in $y$) and $x_1 - x$ as $\delta x$ (change in $x$).

**EXAMINER'S TOP TIP**
You need to learn this definition.

Gradient of curve at P = $\lim\limits_{\delta x \to 0} \left(\dfrac{\delta y}{\delta x}\right)$ This is differentiation from first principles.

NOTE The gradient of a curve at a point P is defined to be the gradient of the tangent to the curve at P.

The process of finding the gradient of the curve is called differentiation.

# Examples of differentiation

**EXAMPLE**

Differentiate $y = x^3$ from first principles.

Let P ($x$, $y$) be a point on the graph of $y = x^3$ and let Q ($x + \delta x$, $y + \delta y$) be another point close to P.

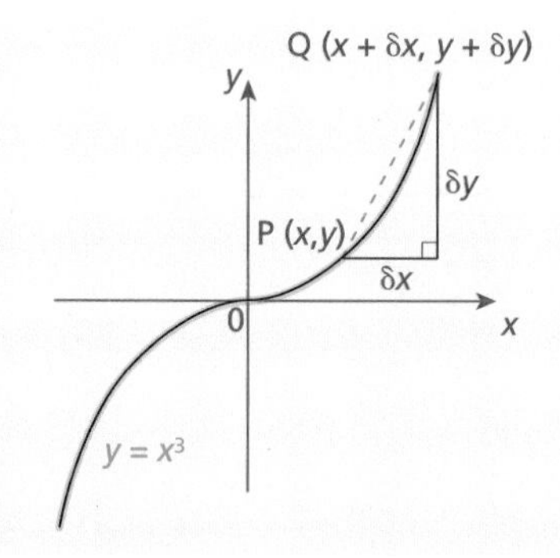


Since P lies on the curve, $y = x^3$

Since Q lies on the curve, $y + \delta y = (x + \delta x)^3$

## Further examples of differentiation

Subtracting top from bottom: $y + \delta y - y = (x + \delta x)^3 - x^3$ Expand the bracket using Binomial Theorem.

$$\delta y = x^3 + 3x^2\delta x + 3x(\delta x)^2 + (\delta x)^3 - x^3$$

$$\frac{\delta y}{\delta x} = 3x^2 + 3x\delta x + (\delta x)^2$$

$$\text{Gradient of PQ} = 3x^2 + 3x\delta x + (\delta x)^2$$

Let $\delta x \to 0$ and take the limit of this expression, giving

$$\text{Gradient of PQ} = 3x^2 \text{ (since } 3x\delta x + (\delta x)^2 \to 0 \text{ as } \delta x \to 0)$$

**EXAMPLE**

Differentiate $y = \frac{1}{x}$ from first principles.

Let P $(x, y)$ be a point on the graph of $y = \frac{1}{x}$ and let Q $(x + \delta x, y + \delta y)$ be another point close to P.

$y = \frac{1}{x}$ and $y + \delta y = \frac{1}{(x + \delta x)}$

$$\delta y = \frac{1}{(x + \delta x)} - \frac{1}{x} = \frac{x - (x + \delta x)}{x(x + \delta x)} = \frac{-\delta x}{x^2 + x\delta x}$$

$$\frac{\delta y}{\delta x} = \frac{-1}{x^2 + x\delta x}$$

Let $\delta x \to 0$ and take the **limit** of the RHS.

Gradient of curve at P $= \frac{-1}{x^2}$, since $x(\delta x)$ will tend to 0 as $\delta x$ tends to 0.

**EXAMINER'S TOP TIP**

**Although we drew a sketch in the first example, it is not necessary.**

## Notation and terminology

Once we have taken the limit of $\frac{\delta y}{\delta x}$ as $\delta x \to 0$, we write it as $\frac{dy}{dx}$

If $y = x^3$, $\frac{dy}{dx} = 3x^2$ This is the **gradient function** of $y = x^3$

If $y = \frac{1}{x}$, $\frac{dy}{dx} = \frac{-1}{x^2}$ This is the **gradient function** of $y = \frac{1}{x}$

The gradient function of a graph is a formula which allows us to find the gradient of the curve at any point.
Using function notation,

If $f(x) = x^3$, $f'(x) = 3x^2$ If $f(x) = \frac{1}{x}$, $f'(x) = \frac{-1}{x^2}$

$\frac{dy}{dx}$ is called the derivative of $y$ with respect to $x$.

$f'(x)$ is called the derivative of $f(x)$ with respect to $x$.

## Quick test

1. ***Differentiate $y = x^2$ from first principles.***
2. ***Differentiate $f(x) = 2x^3$ from first principles.***
3. ***Differentiate $y = x$ from first principles.***

1. $\frac{dy}{dx} = 2x$ 2. $f'(x) = 6x^2$ 3. $\frac{dy}{dx} = 1$

# Differentiation of $x^n$

- **We know that**

$\frac{d}{dx}(x^3) = 3x^2$

$\frac{d}{dx}(x^{-1}) = -x^{-2}$

NOTE **The notation $\frac{d}{dx}$(...) means differentiate what is in the bracket with respect to $x$**

**In general $\frac{d}{dx}(x^n) = nx^{n-1}$ This is true for all values of $n$**

NOTE **We can only appply this formula if we write the expression as a power first.**

## Examples of differentiation of $x^n$

**1** Differentiate these with respect to $x$

Write as powers **first**.

(a) $3x^2 + \frac{4}{x^2}$ (b) $4\sqrt{x} + \frac{1}{\sqrt{x}}$ (c) $\frac{2}{x^3} - \frac{4}{x} + 5$

(a) $\frac{d}{dx}\left(3x^2 + \frac{4}{x^2}\right) = \frac{d}{dx}(3x^2 + 4x^{-2}) = 6x - 8x^{-3} = 6x - \frac{8}{x^3}$

(b) $\frac{d}{dx}\left(4\sqrt{x} + \frac{1}{\sqrt{x}}\right) = \frac{d}{dx}(4x^{\frac{1}{2}} + x^{-\frac{1}{2}}) = 2x^{-\frac{1}{2}} - \frac{1}{2}x^{-\frac{3}{2}} = \frac{2}{\sqrt{x}} - \frac{1}{2\sqrt{x^3}}$

(c) $\frac{d}{dx}\left(\frac{2}{x^3} - \frac{4}{x} + 5\right) = \frac{d}{dx}(2x^{-3} - 4x^{-1} + 5x^0) = -6x^{-4} + 4x^{-2} + 0 \times 5x^{-1}$

$= \frac{-6}{x^4} + \frac{4}{x^2}$

**EXAMINER'S TOP TIP**

**Take care when dealing with terms such as $\frac{5}{x^2}$ and $\frac{3}{2x^3}$.**

**i.e. $5x^{-2}$ and $\frac{3}{2}x^{-3}$**

NOTE We cannot use $\frac{dy}{dx}$ unless $y$ is defined since $\frac{dy}{dx}$ means $\frac{d}{dx}(y)$, i.e. differentiate $y$ with respect to $x$

**2** Differentiate these with respect to $x$

| (a) $(2x-1)(3x+2)$ | (b) $\dfrac{x^3-1}{2x}$ | (c) $(2x^2-3)^2$ | (d) $\dfrac{(x-2)(x-3)}{\sqrt{x}}$ | (e) $\dfrac{(x-4)^2}{x}$ |
|---|---|---|---|---|

(a) $\dfrac{d}{dx}((2x-1)(3x+2)) = \dfrac{d}{dx}(6x^2+x-2) = 12x+1$

(b) $\dfrac{d}{dx}\left(\dfrac{x^3-1}{2x}\right) = \dfrac{d}{dx}\left(\dfrac{x^3}{2x}-\dfrac{1}{2x}\right) = \dfrac{d}{dx}\left(\dfrac{1}{2}x^2-\dfrac{1}{2}x^{-1}\right) = x+\dfrac{1}{2}x^{-2} = x+\dfrac{1}{2x^2}$

(c) $\dfrac{d}{dx}((2x^2-3)^2) = \dfrac{d}{dx}(4x^4-12x^2+9) = 16x^3-24x$

(d) $\dfrac{d}{dx}\left(\dfrac{(x-2)(x-3)}{\sqrt{x}}\right) = \dfrac{d}{dx}\left(\dfrac{x^2-5x+6}{x^{\frac{1}{2}}}\right) = \dfrac{d}{dx}\left(x^{\frac{3}{2}}-5x^{\frac{1}{2}}+6x^{-\frac{1}{2}}\right)$

$= \frac{3}{2}x^{\frac{1}{2}} - \frac{5}{2}x^{-\frac{1}{2}} - 3x^{-\frac{3}{2}}$

$= \dfrac{3\sqrt{x}}{2} - \dfrac{5}{2\sqrt{x}} - \dfrac{3}{\sqrt{x^3}}$

(e) $\dfrac{d}{dx}\dfrac{(x-4)^2}{x} = \dfrac{d}{dx}\left(\dfrac{(x^2-8x+16)}{x}\right) = \dfrac{d}{dx}(x-8+16x^{-1}) = 1-16x^{-2}$

$= 1-\dfrac{16}{x^2}$

**3** Find the gradient of the curve with equation $y = f(x)$ at the point where $x = a$ when:

| (a) $f(x) = \dfrac{x-4}{x}$; $a=-2$ | (b) $f(x) = \sqrt{(12x)}$; $a = \sqrt{3}$ |
|---|---|

(a)

$f(x) = \dfrac{x-4}{x^2} = \dfrac{x}{x^2} - \dfrac{4}{x^2} = x^{-1} - 4x^{-2}$

$f'(x) = -x^{-2} + 8x^{-3}$

$= -\dfrac{1}{x^2} + \dfrac{8}{x^3}$

Gradient = $f'(-2)$

$= -\dfrac{1}{(-2)^2} + \dfrac{8}{(-2)^3}$

$= -\dfrac{1}{4} - 1 = -\dfrac{5}{4}$

(b)

$f(x) = \sqrt{12}\,x^{\frac{1}{2}}$

$f'(x) = \sqrt{12} \times \dfrac{1}{2}x^{-\frac{1}{2}} = \sqrt[2]{3}\,x^{\frac{1}{2}}$

$= \dfrac{\sqrt{3}}{\sqrt{x}}$

Gradient = $f'(\sqrt{3})$

$= \dfrac{\sqrt{3}}{\sqrt{\sqrt{3}}}$

$= \dfrac{3^{\frac{1}{2}}}{3^{\frac{1}{4}}} = 3^{\frac{1}{4}}$

**EXAMINER'S TOP TIP**

1 You must multiply out or simplify fractions before differentiating expressions.

2 Every term must be written as a power before differentiating.

# Quick test

***1 Differentiate these with respect to x***

***(a)*** $2x^3 - 4x + 1$ ***(b)*** $2x + \dfrac{1}{2x}$ ***(c)*** $\dfrac{4}{x^2} - \dfrac{3}{\sqrt{x}}$ ***(d)*** $(x^2+1)(x-1)$ ***(e)*** $\dfrac{(x+2)(x+4)}{x}$ ***(f)*** $(1+\sqrt{x})^2$

***2 Find the gradient at x = 2 on the curve y = f(x) where***

***(a)*** $f(x) = \sqrt{20x}$ ***(b)*** $f(x) = \dfrac{x+1}{\sqrt{x}}$

1. (a) $6x^2 - 4$ (b) $2 - \dfrac{1}{2x^2}$ (c) $-\dfrac{8}{x^3} + \dfrac{3}{2\sqrt{x^3}}$ (d) $3x^2 - 2x + 1$ (e) $1 - \dfrac{8}{x^2}$ (f) $\dfrac{1}{\sqrt{x}} + 1$ 2. (a) $\sqrt{\dfrac{5}{2}} = \dfrac{\sqrt{10}}{2}$ (b) $\dfrac{\sqrt{2}}{8}$

# Second derivatives

- Suppose $y = f(x)$ then $\frac{dy}{dx} = f'(x)$ is called the first derivative of $y$ with respect to $x$.

  If we differentiate again, $\frac{d}{dx}\left(\frac{dy}{dx}\right) = f''(x)$ is the second derivative of $y$ with respect to $x$.

  $\frac{d}{dx}\left(\frac{dy}{dx}\right)$ is written as $\frac{d^2y}{dx^2}$.

  Similarly, $\frac{d}{dx}\left(\frac{d^2y}{dx^2}\right)$ is written as $\frac{d^3y}{dx^3}$, etc.

**EXAMINER'S TOP TIP**
You may need to revise your work on indices before tackling some of these problems.

EXAMPLE

Given that $y = \frac{1}{3x} - \frac{2}{x^2}$, find

(a) $\frac{dy}{dx}$ ⟶

(a) $y = \frac{1}{3x} - \frac{2}{x^2} = \frac{1}{3}x^{-1} - 2x^{-2}$

$\frac{dy}{dx} = -\frac{1}{3}x^{-2} + 4x^{-3} = -\frac{1}{3x^2} + \frac{4}{x^3}$

(b) $\frac{d^2y}{dx^2}$ ⟶

(b) $\frac{d^2y}{dx^2} = \frac{2}{3}x^{-3} - 12x^{-4} = \frac{2}{3x^3} - \frac{12}{x^4}$

## Gradient problems

EXAMPLE

**Find the coordinates of the points on the graph of $y = x^3 - 11x + 1$ where the gradient is 1.**

$y = x^3 - 11x + 1$

$\frac{dy}{dx} = 3x^2 - 11$

At the points required, $3x^2 - 11 = 1$

$3x^2 = 12$

$x^2 = 4$

$x = \pm 2$

When $x = 2$, $y = 2^3 - (11 \times 2) + 1 = 8 - 22 + 1 = -13$ — Point is $(2, -13)$

When $x = -2$, $y = (-2)^3 - (11 \times (-2)) + 1 = -8 + 22 + 1 = 15$ — Point is $(-2, 15)$

# Further gradient problems

**EXAMINER'S TOP TIP**

**$\frac{dy}{dx} = \tan\theta$, where $\theta$ is the angle that the tangent to the curve makes with the positive $x$-axis.**

EXAMPLE

The curve with equation $y = 50x - x^2$ represents the path of an arrow fired from the origin O.

(a) Find how far the arrow lands from its starting point.

(b) Find the angle to the horizontal at which the arrow is fired.

(c) Find the $x$-coordinates of the two points on the path where the arrow is moving at 45° to the horizontal.

(a) At B, $y = 0$, $50x - x^2 = 0$

$x(50 - x) = 0$

$x = 0$ *or* $x = 50$

The arrow lands 50m from its starting point.

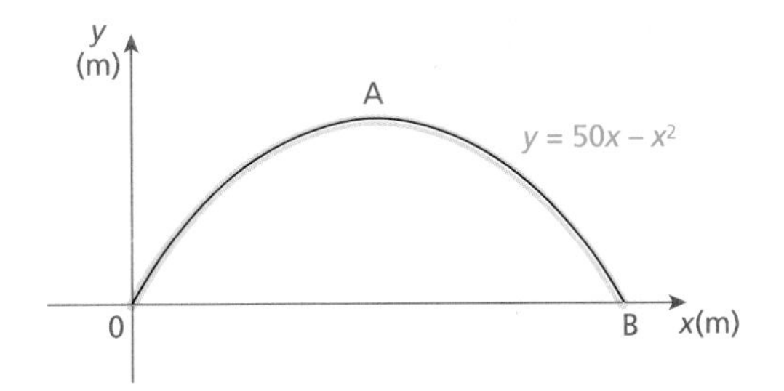


(b) $y = 50x - x^2$

$\frac{dy}{dx} = 50 - 2x$

At O, $x = 0$ so $\frac{dy}{dx} = 50$

$\tan\theta = 50 \Rightarrow \theta = 88.9^\circ$ (1 d.p.)

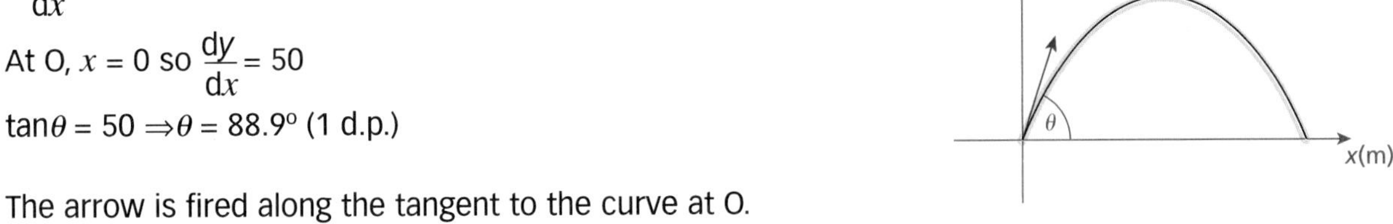


The arrow is fired along the tangent to the curve at O.

The gradient of this tangent is $\frac{dy}{dx}$ at O but it is also equal to $\tan\theta$, where $\theta$ is the angle between the tangent and the positive $x$-axis.

gradient $= \frac{a}{b} = \tan\theta$

(c)When moving at 45° to the horizontal on the way up, gradient of curve = +1

$\frac{dy}{dx} = +1$

$50 - 2x = 1$

$2x = 49$

$x = 24.5$m

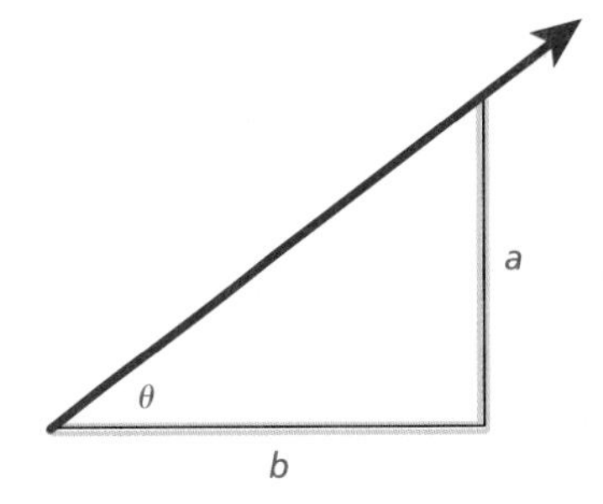


When moving at 45° to the horizontal on the way down, gr

$50 - 2x = -1$

$2x = 51$

$x = 25.5$m

# Quick test

**1** ***Given that $y = x^{\frac{3}{2}} + 3x^{\frac{5}{2}}$, find (a) $\frac{dy}{dx}$ (b) $\frac{d^2y}{dx^2}$.***

**2** ***A curve has equation $y = 7x^2 - x^3$. Find the x-coordinates of the points on the curve where the gradient is equal to 16.***

**3** ***A curve has equation $y = ax^2 + bx + c$, where a, b and c are constants. The curve passes through the point (1, 2) and has zero gradient at the point (2, 1). Find the values of a, b and c.***

1. (a) $\frac{3}{2}\sqrt{x} + \frac{15}{2}\sqrt{x^3}$ (b) $\frac{3}{4\sqrt{x}} + \frac{45\sqrt{x}}{4}$ 2. Gradient is equal to 16 when $x = 2$ and when $x = \frac{8}{3}$ 3. a = 1, b = −4, c = 5

# Applications of differentiation

- **How to apply differentation to tangents and normals.**

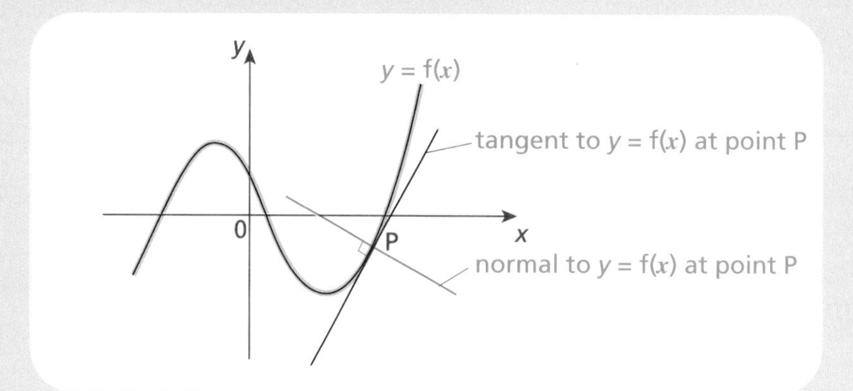


## Equation of the tangent

**What is the equation of the tangent to a given curve** $y = \mathrm{f}(x)$ at a given point P?

Suppose the $x$-coordinate of P is $p$
Then the $y$-coordinate of P is $\mathrm{f}(p)$

Also, $\dfrac{dy}{dx} = \mathrm{f}'(x)$
Gradient of curve at P = $\mathrm{f}'(p)$
Gradient of tangent at P = $\mathrm{f}'(p)$

Equation of tangent at P is
$y - \mathrm{f}(p) = \mathrm{f}'(p)(x - p)$

**EXAMINER'S TOP TIP**
One simple check that can be done is **to ensure that the coordinates of the point** where the tangent was drawn **satisfy the equation of the tangent.** If they do, it could be correct, **if they don't, it's definitely wrong!**

**EXAMPLE**
Find the equation of the tangent to the curve $y = 2x^2 - 4x + 3$ at the point where $x = 2$

When $x = 2$, $y = (2 \times 2^2) - (4 \times 2) + 3 = 3$
$\dfrac{dy}{dx} = 4x - 4$

Gradient of tangent at $x = 2$ is $(4 \times 2) - 4 = 4$

Equation of tangent is
$y - 3 = 4(x - 2)$
$y - 3 = 4x - 8$
$y = 4x - 5$ i.e. $4x - y - 5 = 0$

### Equation of the normal to a given curve $y = f(x)$ at a given point P

As before, the coordinates of P are $(p, f(p))$

Since the normal is perpendicular to the tangent, the gradient is $\dfrac{-1}{f'(p)}$

Equation of normal is $y - f(p) = \dfrac{-1}{f'(p)}(x - p)$

> **EXAMINER'S TOP TIP**
> It is usual to give the final equation in the form $ax + by + c = 0$, where $a$, $b$ and $c$ are integers.

**EXAMPLE**

Find the equation of the normal to the curve $y = \dfrac{2}{x^2}$ at the point where $x = 2$

When $x = 2$, $y = \dfrac{2}{2^2} = \dfrac{2}{4} = \dfrac{1}{2}$ and $y = \dfrac{2}{x^2} = 2x^{-2}$ $\dfrac{dy}{dx} = -4x^{-3} = \dfrac{-4}{x^3}$

Gradient of tangent at $x = 2$ is $\dfrac{-4}{2^3} = -\dfrac{1}{2}$. Invert and change sign.

Gradient of normal at $x = 2$ is 2.

Equation of normal is

$$y - \frac{1}{2} = 2(x - 2)$$
$$2y - 1 = 4(x - 2)$$
$$2y - 1 = 4x - 8$$
$$4x - 2y - 7 = 0$$

### A harder example

(a) Find the equation of the tangent to the curve with equation $y = x^3 - 9x^2 + 20x - 8$ at the point (1, 4).

(b) Find the points on the curve where the tangent is parallel to the line with equation $4x + y - 3 = 0$.

(a) $y = x^3 - 9x^2 + 20x - 8$

$\dfrac{dy}{dx} = 3x^2 - 18x + 20$

At the point (1, 4), $\dfrac{dy}{dx} = (3 \times 1^2) - (18 \times 1) + 20 = 5$

Equation of the tangent is $y - 4 = 5(x - 1)$

$$y - 4 = 5x - 5$$
$$0 = 5x - y - 1$$

(b) $4x + y - 3 = 0 \quad \Rightarrow \quad y = -4x + 3$ This has a gradient $-4$.

Find either by comparing with $y = mx + c$ or by differentiating: $\dfrac{dy}{dx} = -4$

We require gradient of curve to be $-4$, $\dfrac{dy}{dx} = -4$

$$3x^2 - 18x + 20 = -4$$
$$3x^2 - 18x + 24 = 0$$
$$x^2 - 6x + 8 = 0$$
$$(x - 2)(x - 4) = 0$$
$$x = 2 \text{ or } x = 4$$

When $x = 2$, $y = 2^3 - 9 \times 2^2 + 20 \times 2 - 8 = 8 - 36 + 40 - 8 = 4$

When $x = 4$, $y = 4^3 - 9 \times 4^2 + 20 \times 4 - 8 = 64 - 144 + 80 - 8 = -8$

Points are (2, 4) and (4, −8)

## Quick test

**1** ***Find the equations of the tangents to these curves at the points corresponding to the given values of x:***

***(a)*** $y = 3x^2 - x + 1$; $x = 0$ ***(b)*** $y = 9x - x^3$; $x = -3$ ***(c)*** $y = 3 - 4x - 2x^2$; $x = 1$.

**2** ***Find the equations of the normals to the curves in question 1 at the given points.***

1. (a) $x + y - 1 = 0$ (b) $18x + y + 54 = 0$ (c) $8x + y - 5 = 0$ 2. (a) $x - y + 1 = 0$ (b) $x - 18y + 3 = 0$ (c) $x - 8y - 23 = 0$

# Finding stationary points

- A stationary point on a curve is a point on the curve where the gradient is zero.
  NOTE $y$ is said to have a stationary value at such a point.

At a stationary point, $\frac{dy}{dx} = 0$

The tangent to a curve at a stationary point will be parallel to the $x$-axis.

There are four possibilities:

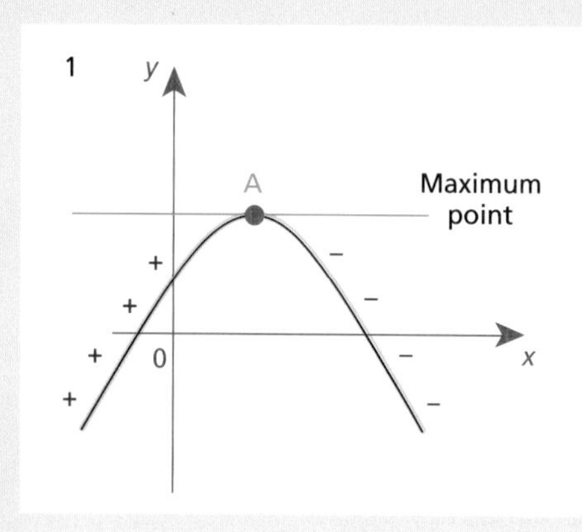


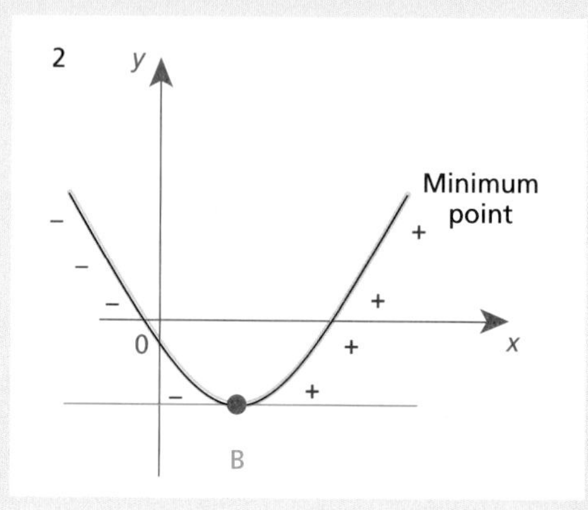


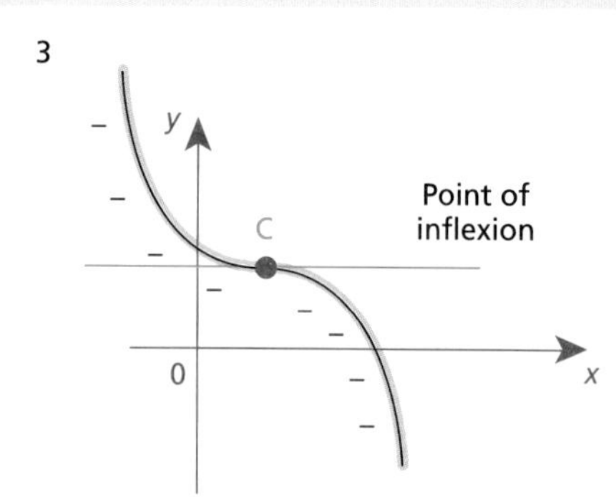


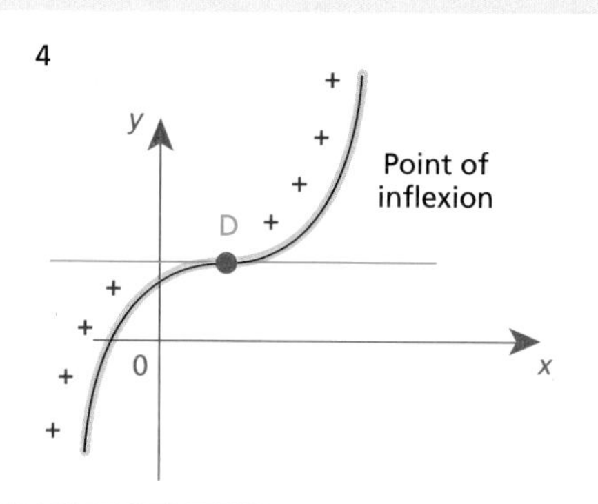


Points A and B are called turning points, since the graph turns on itself.

A is known as a (local) maximum point, as the curve reaches a peak there.

B is known as a (local) minimum point, as the curve reaches a trough there.

Points C and D are called stationary points of inflexion.

**EXAMINER'S TOP TIP**
A curve may have none, or many, stationary points.

## Different types of stationary point

To find all the stationary points on a curve:

Find $\frac{dy}{dx}$

Put $\frac{dy}{dx} = 0$ and solve this equation for $x$.

# Distinguishing between stationary points

There are two ways of distinguishing between the different types of stationary points.

1 By finding the gradient of the curve either side of the point. (See diagrams.)
At a maximum point, the gradient changes from positive to negative.
At a minimum point, the gradient changes from negative to positive.
At a point of inflexion, the gradient changes from positive to positive or negative to negative.

NOTE The above gradient changes assume that $x$ is increasing as we move from one side of the point to the other.

2 By using the value of the second derivative at the point.

The point is a maximum $\Leftrightarrow \frac{d^2y}{dx^2} < 0$ at the point.

The point is a minimum $\Leftrightarrow \frac{d^2y}{dx^2} > 0$ at the point.

The point is a point of inflexion $\Rightarrow \frac{d^2y}{dx^2} = 0$ at the point.

**EXAMINER'S TOP TIP**
**It is usually much easier to use method 2, although you must learn both methods.**

NOTE In the 3rd case, the implication only goes one way. $\frac{d^2y}{dx^2} = 0$ at a point does not mean that the point is a point of inflexion. It could be any of the three types. In this case, use method 1 to find what type it is.

EXAMPLE

(a) Find the turning points on the curve with equation $y = x^3 - 5x^2 + 3x + 2$

State whether $y$ has a maximum or minimum value at each.

(a) $y = x^3 - 5x^2 + 3x + 2$

$\frac{dy}{dx} = 3x^2 - 10x + 3$

For stationary points, $3x^2 - 10x + 3 = 0$

$(3x - 1)(x - 3) = 0$

$x = \frac{1}{3}$ or $x = 3$

When $x = \frac{1}{3}$, $y = \left(\frac{1}{3}\right)^3 - 5 \times \left(\frac{1}{3}\right)^2 + 3 \times \frac{1}{3} + 2 = \frac{1}{27} - \frac{5}{9} + 1 + 2 = \frac{1 - 15 + 81}{27} = \frac{67}{27}$

When $x = 3$, $y = 3^3 - 5 \times 3^2 + 3 \times 3 + 2 = 27 - 45 + 9 + 2 = -7$

Turning points are $\left(\frac{1}{3}, \frac{67}{27}\right)$ and $(3, -7)$

(b) $\frac{d^2y}{dx^2} = 6x - 10$ At $\left(\frac{1}{3}, \frac{67}{27}\right)$, $\frac{d^2y}{dx^2} = \left(6 \times \frac{1}{3}\right) - 10 = -8 < 0$, so point is maximum.

At $(3, -7)$, $\frac{d^2y}{dx^2} = (6 \times 3) - 10 = 8 > 0$, so point is a minimum.

## Quick test

**1 *Find the turning points on these curves, stating whether they are maximum or minimum points.***

**(a) $y = x(x^2 - 12)$**

**(b) $y = 4x^2 + \frac{1}{x}$**

**(c) $y = x(x - 8)(x - 15)$**

**2 *Find and classify the stationary values of y on these curves.***

**(a) $y = x^3(2 - x)$**

**(b) $y = 3x^4 + 16x^3 + 24x^2 + 3$**

1. (a) $(-2, 16)$, maximum $(2, -16)$, minimum (b) $\left(\frac{1}{2}, 3\right)$, minimum (c) $\left(3\frac{1}{3}, 181\frac{13}{27}\right)$, maximum $(12, -144)$ minimum
2. (a) $y = 0,0$ point of inflexion $y = \frac{2}{3}, \frac{27}{16}$, maximum (b) $y = 2,19$, point of inflexion $y = 0,3$, minimum

# Maximum and minimum problems

- We can use the theory developed for finding maximum or minimum points on a curve to solve real world problems which require us to maximise *or* minimise some quantity.
- Suppose we need to maximise or minimise some quantity $V$. Usually we are given (or can work out) a formula for $V$ in terms of 2 variables, $x$ and $y$, say.
- We are then given some constraint on $x$ and $y$ which allows us to write down an equation relating $x$ and $y$.
- We then use this equation to eliminate $x$ or $y$ from our formula for $V$, so that we end up with a formula for V in terms of one variable, say $x$.
- Suppose $V = f(x)$, then effectively we have a graph of $V$ against $x$ and we can find maximum or minimum points on the graph to solve the problem.

## Solving a real problem

Two opposite sides ends of a closed rectangular tank are squares of side $x$m and the total area of sheet metal forming the tank is 2400m$^2$

(a) Show that the total volume of the tank, $V$, is given by

$$V = \frac{1}{2}x(1200 - x^2)$$

(b) Find the dimensions of the tank which will give it maximum volume. Justify your answer.

(a)

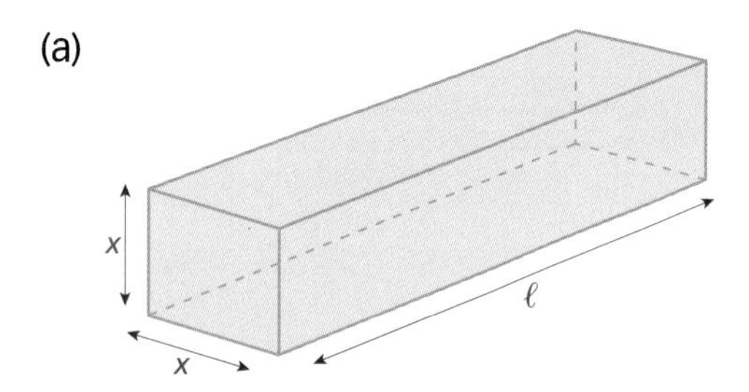


EXAMINER'S TOP TIP
A simple diagram will often help to clarify your thoughts.

Let the length by $\ell$ m

$V = x^2\ell$ — This is formula for $V$ in terms of two variables.

The total surface area is to be 2400 m$^2$ — This is the constraint.

$2x^2 + 4\ell x = 2400$ — This is equation relating the variables.

We use this equation to eliminate $\ell$ from the formula for $V$.

Make $\ell$ the subject.

$2\ell x = 1200 - x^2$

$$\ell = \frac{1200 - x^2}{2x}$$

Now substitute for $\ell$

$$V = x^2\left(\frac{1200 - x^2}{2x}\right) = \tfrac{1}{2}x(1200 - x^2) \text{ as required.}$$

(b) $V = 600x - \frac{1}{2}x^3$ — Multiply out before differentiating.

(b) $V = 600x - \frac{1}{2}x^3$ Multiply out before differentiating.

$\frac{dV}{dx} = 600 - \frac{3}{2}x^2$

For a maximum point, $\frac{dV}{dx} = 0$

$600 - \frac{3}{2}x^2 = 0$

$x^2 = 400$

$x = 20$ $x$ cannot be –20 here as it's a length.

To prove that this gives a maximum point, find $\frac{d^2V}{dx^2}$

$\frac{d^2V}{dx^2} = -3x$

When $x = 20$, $\frac{d^2V}{dx^2} = -60$ which proves it is a maximum point.

When $x = 20$, $\ell = \frac{1200 - 20^2}{2 \times 20} = \frac{800}{40} = 20$

So dimensions of tank which **maximise its volume** are $20 \times 20 \times 20$, a **cube** of side 20m

**EXAMINER'S TOP TIP**
Always evaluate the actual value of the second derivative.

NOTE To plot the graph of $V$ against $x$

$V = \frac{1}{2}x(1200 - x^2)$

Put $V = 0$ to find where it crosses the $x$-axis

$0 = \frac{1}{2}x(1200 - x^2)$

$x = 0$ or $x^2 = 1200$,

$x = \pm\sqrt{1200}$,

$= \pm 20\sqrt{3}$

The dotted part of the graph is irrelevant here as $x > 0$ and $V > 0$

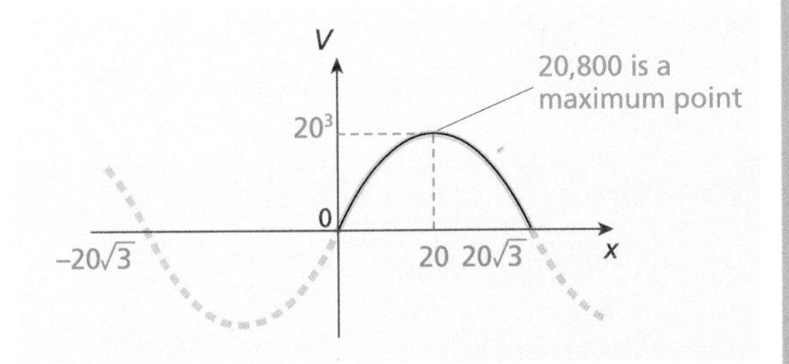


The total surface area of the tank must always be 2400m², so the graph tells us that if we have a small value of $x$, we get:

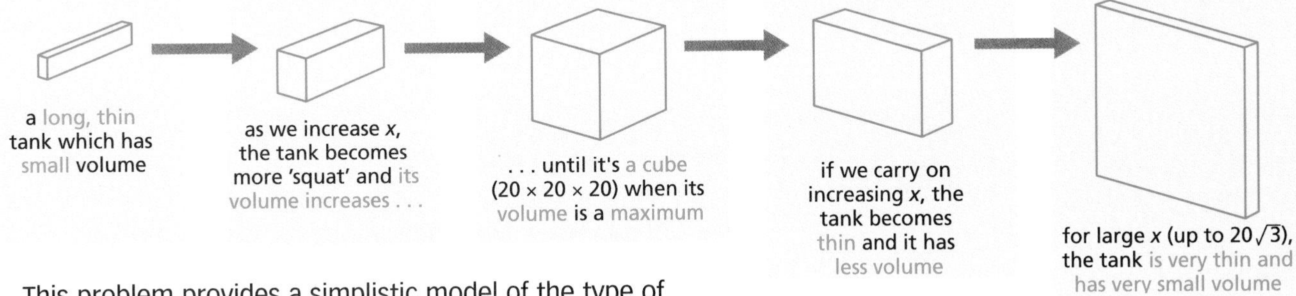


This problem provides a simplistic model of the type of **optimisation process** which occurs in industry on a regular basis.

# Quick test

**1** ***A cylinder, open at the top, is to be made so that its volume is 1 m³. Given that the radius of the base is r m***
***(a) Show that the total outside surface area is $(\pi r^2 + \frac{2}{r})$ m².***
***The manufacturer wishes to minimise this surface area.***
***(b) Find, in terms of r, the height of the cylinder which achieves this.***

**2** ***A man wishes to fence in a rectangular enclosure of area 128 m². One side of the enclosure is formed by part of a brick wall which is already in position. Find the least possible length of fencing required for the other three sides.***

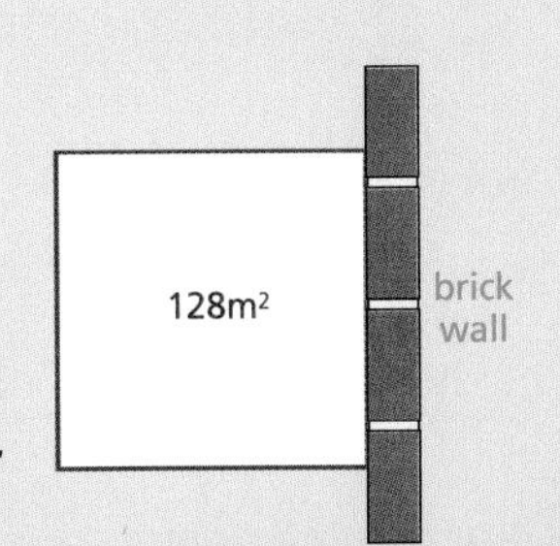


1. (b) $h = r$ 2. 32m

# Curve sketching

- **Suppose we want to sketch the graph of $y = f(x)$**
  **Finding the stationary points on the graph and being able to decide what type of point (maximum, minimum, or point of inflexion) they are, will obviously help to make the sketch.**

## Examples of curve sketching

**1** Find the maximum and minimum points on the graph of $y = x^3 - 6x^2 + 9x + 2$

Hence sketch the graph.

$y = x^3 - 6x^2 + 9x + 2$

$\frac{dy}{dx} = 3x^2 - 12x + 9$

For stationary points, $\frac{dy}{dx} = 0$

$$3x^2 - 12x + 9 = 0$$
$$x^2 - 4x + 3 = 0$$
$$(x - 3)(x - 1) = 0$$
$$x = 3 \text{ or } x = 1$$

When $x = 3$, $y = 3^3 - (6 \times 3^2) + (9 \times 3) + 2 = 2$

$\frac{d^2y}{dx^2} = 6x - 12$

When $x = 3$, $\frac{d^2y}{dx^2} = 18 - 12 > 0$

(3, 2) is minimum point.

When $x = 1$, $y = 1^3 - (6 \times 1^2) + (9 \times 1) + 2 = 6$

When $x = 1$, $\frac{d^2y}{dx^2} = 6x - 12 = 6 - 12 < 0$

(1, 6) is maximum point.

When $x = 0$, $y = 2$

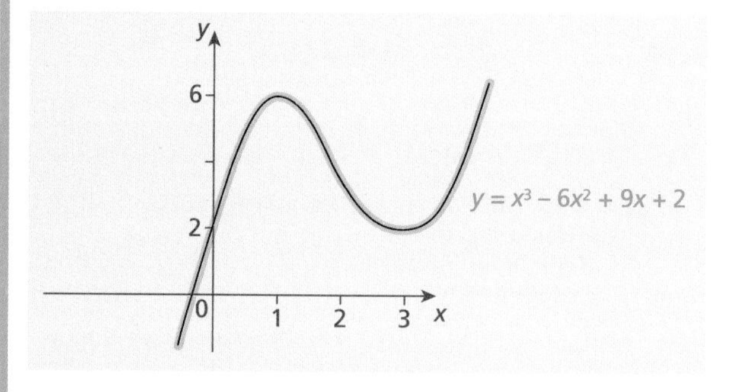


Putting $y = 0$ gives $x^3 - 6x^2 + 9x + 2 = 0$
We <u>cannot solve</u> a cubic equation like this <u>unless there is an obvious solution</u>. This does not help here. From the graph, there is only one negative solution.

**2** (a) Find any turning points on the graph of $y = f(x)$ where
$$f(x) = 4x - \frac{1}{4x^2}.$$
(b) Give the equation of any vertical asymptotes.
(c) Sketch the graph of $y = f(x)$.

**EXAMINER'S TOP TIP**
**When sketching graphs, try to find where the graph cuts the $x$-axis (put $y = 0$ and solve for $x$) and where it cuts the $y$-axis (put $x = 0$ and solve for $y$)**

(a) $y = 4x - \frac{1}{4x^2}$

$y = 4x - \frac{1}{4}x^{-2}$

$\frac{dy}{dx} = 4 + \frac{1}{2}x^{-3} = 4 + \frac{1}{2x^3}$

For turning points, $\frac{dy}{dx} = 0$

# Examples continued

**Examples** continued...

$$4 + \frac{1}{2x^3} = 0$$
$$8x^3 + 1 = 0$$
$$8x^3 = -1$$
$$x^3 = -\frac{1}{8}$$
$$x = \sqrt[3]{-\frac{1}{8}} = -\frac{1}{2}$$

When $x = -\frac{1}{2}$, $y = \left(4 \times -\frac{1}{2}\right) - \frac{1}{4 \times \left(-\frac{1}{2}\right)^2} = -2 - \frac{1}{1} = -3$

$$\frac{d^2y}{dx^2} = -\frac{3}{2}x^{-4} \quad \frac{-3}{2x^4}$$

When $x = -\frac{1}{2}$, $\frac{d^2y}{dx^2} = \frac{-3}{2\left(-\frac{1}{2}\right)^4} = -24 < 0$

So $\left(-\frac{1}{2}, -3\right)$ is maximum point.

(b) We can find vertical asymptotes by equating the denominator of any algebraic fractions to zero. Here, $4x^2 = 0 \Rightarrow x = 0$ is a vertical asymptote.

(c) Put $y = 0$

$$0 = 4x - \frac{1}{4x^2}$$
$$0 = 16x^3 - 1$$
$$1 = 16x^3$$
$$x^3 = \frac{1}{16}$$
$$x = \sqrt[3]{\frac{1}{16}} \approx 0.4$$

The dotted line is the line $y = 4x$

For large positive or negative values of $x$, the equation becomes $y \approx 4x$

We say $y = 4x$ is an oblique asymptote – this is not on the syllabus for AS!

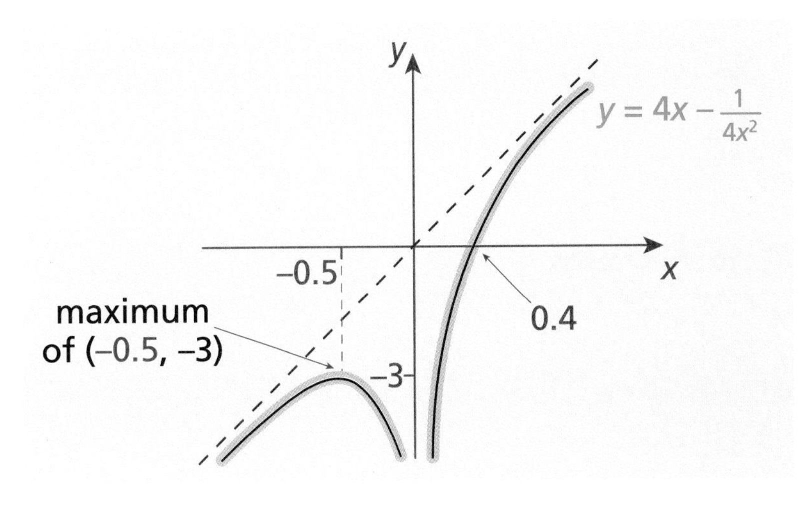


# Quick test

**1** **(a) Find the turning points on the graph of $y = 2x^3 + 3x^2 - 12x + 7$, distinguishing between maximum and minimum points.**

**(b) Show that the graph passes through (1, 0) and one other point on the x-axis.**

**(c) Sketch the curve.**

**2** **(a) If $y = x^4 - 2x^2 + 1$, find the values of $x$ for which $y$ is a minimum.**

**(b) Sketch the curve.**

**3** **Sketch the curve whose equation is given $y = 4x^3 - 3x^4$.**

1. (a) (1, 0) is a minimum, (−2, 27) is a maximum (b) The other point is $(-3\frac{1}{2}, 0)$ (c)

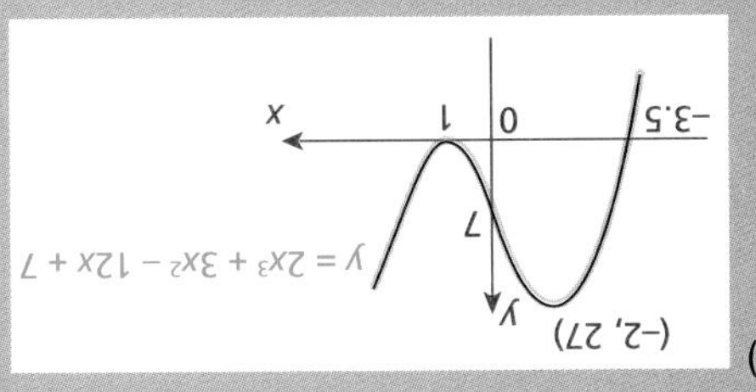


2. (a) $x = \pm 1$ (b)

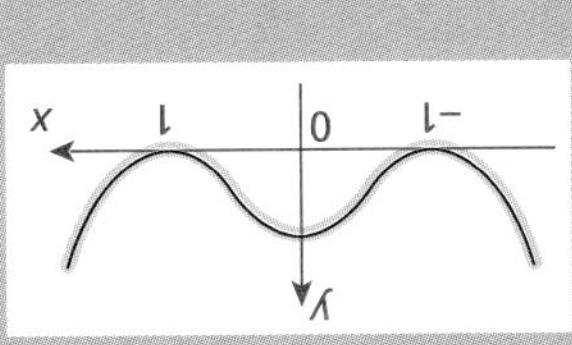


3.

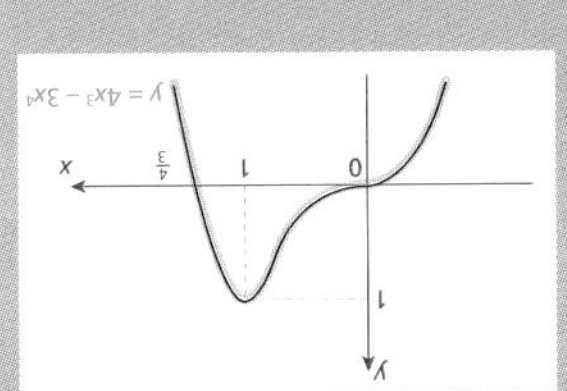

# Increasing and decreasing functions

- A function f($x$) is said to be increasing, for $a \le x \le b$, if $f'(x) > 0$ for all values of $x$, $a \le x \le b$ i.e. the gradient of an increasing function, $f'(x)$, is positive for all values of $x$, $a \le x \le b$
- A function f($x$) is said to be decreasing, for $c \le x \le d$, if $f'(x) < 0$ for all values of $x$, $c \le x \le d$
- If f($x$) is neither increasing or decreasing at $x = a$, then f($x$) is stationary at $x = a$, i.e. $f'(a) = 0$

## Examples

Here we are finding the values of $x$ for which $y$ is an **increasing** function.

EXAMPLE

A curve has equation $y = (x - 6)(x + 6)(3 - 2x)$.
Find the set of values of $x$ for which $y$ is an increasing function of $x$.

$y = (x - 6)(x + 6)(3 - 2x)$
$\quad = (x^2 - 36)(3 - 2x)$ We must multiply out first, in order to differentiate.
$\quad = 3x^2 - 2x^3 - 108 + 72x$

$\frac{dy}{dx} = 6x - 6x^2 + 72$

For $y$ to be increasing, $\frac{dy}{dx} > 0$

$6x - 6x^2 + 72 > 0$
$x - x^2 + 12 > 0$
$x^2 - x - 12 < 0$
$(x - 4)(x + 3) < 0$

**EXAMINER'S TOP TIP**
It is always easier to solve quadratic inequalities (or equations) which have a positive coefficient of $x^2$.

To solve this, draw a number line and mark the critical values of $x$ (4 and –3) on it.

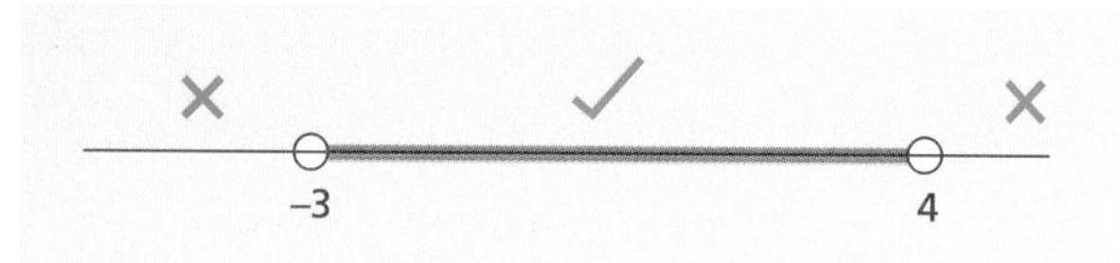


Test $x = 0$ to see if it satisfies the inequality:
$-4 \times 3 < 0$ so solution set is $-3 < x < 4$, $y$ is increasing between $x = -3$ and $x = 4$

NOTE If we sketch the graph of $y$ against $x$,
when $y = 0$, $(x - 6)(x + 6)(3 - 2x) = 0$,
$x = \pm 6$ or $\frac{3}{2}$

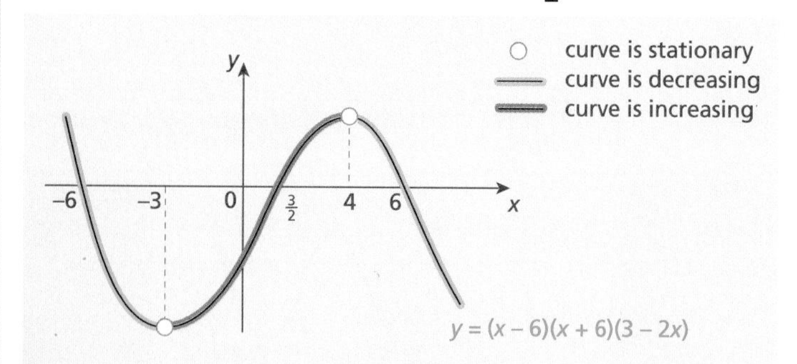

# Examples continued

Now we are finding values of $x$ for which y is a **decreasing** function.

**EXAMPLE**

$f(x) = 2x^2 - x^4$.

Find the set of values of $x$ for which $f(x)$ is a decreasing function of $x$.

$f(x) = 2x^2 - x^4$
$f'(x) = 4x - 4x^3$
For $f(x)$ to be decreasing, $f'(x) < 0$

$$4x - 4x^3 < 0$$
$$x - x^3 < 0$$
$$x^3 - x > 0$$
$$x(x^2 - 1) > 0$$
$$x(x + 1)(x - 1) > 0$$

> **EXAMINER'S TOP TIP**
> **Always** factorise. Do *not* cancel anything which could be zero. Here, dividing through by $x$ would not only lose a solution but would also leave us not knowing which inequality sign to use. (Dividing an inequality by a negative number reverses the inequality sign.)

The critical values of $x$ are 0, +1 and −1

−1 0 +1

Test $x = 2$
LHS gives $2(2 + 1)(2 - 1) > 0$,
so $x = 2$ satisfies the inequality.

We get alternating ✓ and ✗

✗ ✓ ✗ ✓
−1 0 +1

Solution set is $x > 1$ or $-1 < x < 0$, **i.e. f′(x) is decreasing when either $x > 1$** *or* **$-1 < x < 0$**

Again, a sketch of the graph is useful.

$y = 2x^2 - x^4 = x^2(2 - x^2)$
Put $y = 0$ $\quad 0 = x^2(2 - x^2) \Rightarrow x = 0$ (twice) or $x = \pm\sqrt{2}$

**Repeated root** indicates that the curve **touches the $x$-axis** at $x = 0$

From above, we have stationary points at $x = \pm 1$ and $x = 0$

The negative coefficient of $x^4$ (the **highest power**) indicates the graph goes down as $x \to \infty$
**NOTE** Since $f(x)$ consists of **even powers of $x$ only**, the **graph will be symmetrical about the $y$-axis**.
We can see that the graph decreases for $-1 < x < 0$ and $x > 1$ as above.

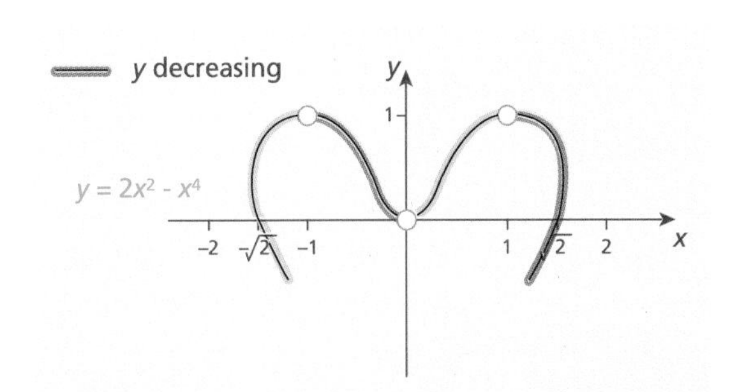


# Quick test

1. *Find the set of values of x for which the function f, defined as $f(x) = 2(x + 1)(x - 1)^2 + 1$ is an increasing function.*
2. *Find the set of values of x for which the function f, defined as $f(x) = 4x^5 - 5x^4$ is a decreasing function.*

1. $x < -\frac{1}{3}$ or $x > 1$ 2. $0 < x < 1$

# Exam-style questions

Use the questions to test your progress. Check your answers on page 95.

**1** Given that $y = \dfrac{(x-3)(3x+2)}{\sqrt{x}}$, find

**(a)** $\dfrac{dy}{dx}$ [1]

**(b)** $\dfrac{d^2y}{dx^2}$. [1]

**2** **(a)** Find the coordinates of the turning points on the curve with equation $y = x^3 - 9x^2 + 24x$. [1]

**(b)** What type of point is each one? [1]

**3** Given that $f(x) = (x - \frac{1}{x})^3$, find

**(a)** $f'(3)$ [1]

**(b)** $f''(3)$. [1]

**4** An open rectangular tank has a horizontal square base of side $x$-metres. The height of the tank is $y$ metres. The tank is made of thin sheet metal. The external surface area of the tank is $S$ m$^2$ and the volume is $V$ m$^3$

**(a)** Show that $S = \dfrac{4V}{x} + x^2$. [2]

Given that $V = 62.5$ and that $x$ varies,

**(b)** find $\dfrac{dS}{dx}$. [2]

**(c)** determine the value of $x$ for which $\dfrac{dS}{dx} = 0$ and find the corresponding value of $S$. [2]

**(d)** show that this value of $S$ is the minimum possible value. [1]

**5** Differentiate $y = x^2 + x$ from first principles. [1]

**6** The diagram shows a sketch of the curve with equation $y = 12x^{\frac{1}{2}} - x^{\frac{3}{2}}$ for $0 \le x \le 12$.

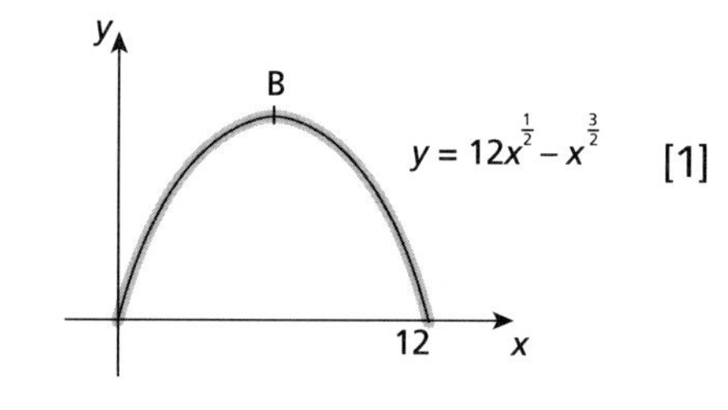


**(a)** Show that $\dfrac{dy}{dx} = \frac{3}{2}x^{-\frac{1}{2}}(4 - x)$. [1]

**(b)** At the point B on the curve, the tangent to the curve is parallel to the $x$-axis. Find the coordinates of point B. [1]

**7** The curve C with equation $y = x^3 - 5x^2 + 7x - 14$ meets the $x$- and $y$-axes at the points A and B respectively.

**(a)** State the coordinates of B. [2]

**(b)** Find the coordinates of the stationary points on C. [2]

**(c)** Find the set of values for which $y$ is decreasing. [3]

8 **(a)** Find the equation of the tangent to the curve with equation $y = 9x - x^3$ at the point where $x = 1$. [2]

**(b)** Find the coordinates of the point where this tangent meets the line $y = x$. [2]

9 A tangent to the parabola $y = \frac{1}{16}x^2$ is perpendicular to the line with equation $x - 2y - 3 = 0$.
**(a)** Find the equation of this tangent. [2]

**(b)** Find the coordinates of the point of contact where this tangent touches the curve. (Hint Solve them simultaneously.) [2]

**10** A curve has equation $y = x^2 + 3$.

**(a)** Show that the equation of the tangent to the curve at the point where $x = a$ is $y = 2ax - a^2 + 3$. [2]

**(b)** Hence find the coordinates of the two points on the curve, the tangents of which pass through the point (2, 6). [2]

**11 (a)** Find the equations of the normals to the parabola $4y = x^2$ at the points (–2, 1) and (–4, 4). [2]

**(b)** Show that the point of intersection of these two normals lies on the parabola. [2]

**12** A cylindrical biscuit tin has a close-fitting lid which, when fitted on the tin, overlaps the tin by 1 cm, as shown. The radii of the tin and the lid are both $x$ cm. The tin and the lid are made from a thin sheet of metal of area $80\pi$ cm$^2$ and there is no wastage. The volume of the tin is $V$ cm$^3$.

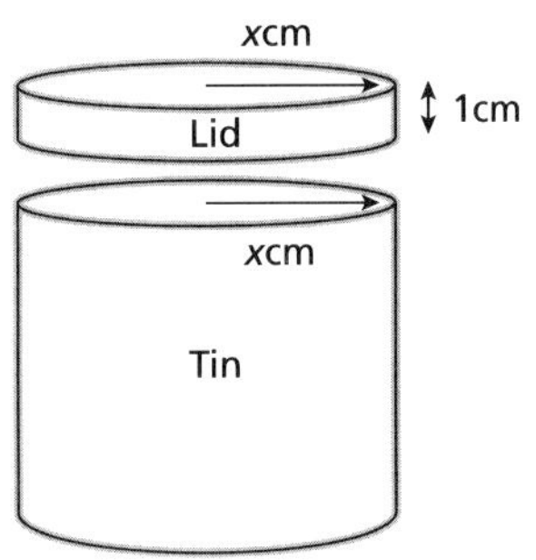


**(a)** Show that $V = \pi(40x - x^2 - x^3)$. [1]

Given that $x$ can vary,

**(b)** use differentiation to find the value of $x$ for which $V$ is stationary [1]

**(c)** prove that this value of $x$ gives a maximum value of $V$ [1]

**(d)** find this maximum value of $V$. [1]

**Total: /43**

# Integration
## – as the reverse of differentiation

- **We know that**

$\frac{d}{dx}(\frac{1}{2}x^2) = x$ $\quad\frac{d}{dx}(\frac{1}{3}x^3) = x^2$ $\quad\frac{d}{dx}(\frac{1}{4}x^4) = x^3$

**Reversing the process would give**

$x^1 \to \frac{1}{2}x^2$

$x^2 \to \frac{1}{3}x^3$

$x^3 \to \frac{1}{4}x^4$ **We call this reverse process integration.**

**In general,** $x^n \to \frac{1}{n+1}x^{n+1}$ **This rule applies, in fact, for all powers of $n$, except $n = -1$, which would involve $\frac{1}{0}$ which we cannot deal with.**

## Notation

We write

$$\int x^n dx = \frac{1}{n+1}x^{n+1} + c,\ n \neq -1$$

where $c$ is an arbitrary constant.

**EXAMINER'S TOP TIP**
**To check any integral, we can differentiate the answer and compare it with the function that we have integrated – it should be the same!**

## Indefinite integration

This process is called **indefinite integration** because of the presence of the **arbitrary constant** $c$.

**EXAMPLE**

$\int x^2 dx = \frac{1}{3}x^3$ *or* $\frac{1}{3}x^3 + 1$ *or* $\frac{1}{3}x^3 - 1$ *or* $\frac{1}{3}x^3 + \frac{1}{2}$, etc. since if we differentiate *any* of these, we get $x^2$

So $\int x^2 dx = \frac{1}{3}x^3 + c$ where $c$ stands for any number and we cannot be definite about what the number is.

**EXAMINER'S TOP TIP**
**Always use top-heavy fractions when integrating, as it is easy to divide by such a fraction by inverting and multiplying.**

**EXAMPLE**

Find these indefinite integrals.

(a) $\int x^5 dx$ (b) $\int x^{-3} dx$ (c) $\int x^{\frac{3}{2}} dx$

(a) $\int x^5 dx = \frac{1}{6}x^6 + c$ (b) $\int x^{-3} dx = -\frac{1}{2}x^{-2} + c$ (c) $\int x^{\frac{3}{2}} dx = \frac{2}{5}x^{\frac{5}{2}} + c$

**EXAMINER'S TOP TIP**
**All the rules that applied to differentiating powers of $x$ also apply to integrating powers of $x$**
- **All terms must be written as powers *first*.**
- **All brackets must be multiplied out *first*.**
- **All algebraic fractions must be divided out *first*.**

# Indefinite integration continued...

**EXAMPLE**

Integrate these with respect to $x$

(a) $2\sqrt{x}$ (b) $\dfrac{4}{x^3}$ (c) $\dfrac{1}{3x^2}$ (d) $(x+2)^2$

(e) $\dfrac{2x^2+3x^3-2}{x^2}$ (f) $\left(x-\dfrac{2}{x}\right)^2$ (g) $\dfrac{(x+2)(x-1)}{\sqrt{x}}$

(a) $\int 2\sqrt{x}\,dx = \int 2x^{\frac{1}{2}}dx = 2 \times \frac{2}{3}x^{\frac{3}{2}} + c = \frac{4}{3}x^{\frac{3}{2}} + c$

**NOTE** Top-heavy fractions!

(b) $\int \frac{4}{x^3}\,dx = \int 4x^{-3}dx = 4\int x^{-3}dx = 4 \times \frac{1}{-2}x^{-2} + c = -2x^{-2} + c$

<u>**Remember**</u>: To integrate a power of $x$, add <u>1</u> to the power and divide by the new power.

(c) $\int \frac{1}{3x^2}\,dx = \frac{1}{3}\int \frac{1}{x^2}\,dx = \frac{1}{3}\int x^{-2}dx = \frac{1}{3} \times \frac{1}{-1}x^{-1} + c = -\frac{1}{3}x^{-1} + c$

(d) $\int (x+2)^2dx = \int (x^2+4x+4)dx = \frac{1}{3}x^3 + (4 \times \frac{1}{2}x^2) + 4x + c = \frac{1}{3}x^3 + 2x^2 + 4x + c$

(e) $\int \frac{2x^2+3x^3-2}{x^2}\,dx = \int \left(\frac{2x^2}{x^2} + \frac{3x^3}{x^2} - \frac{2}{x^2}\right)dx$

$= \int 2 + 3x - 2x^{-2}dx$

$= 2x + 3 \times \frac{1}{2}x^2 - \frac{2}{-1}x^{-1} + c$

$= 2x + \frac{3}{2}x^2 + 2x^{-1} + c$

(f) $\int \left(x-\frac{2}{x}\right)^2dx = \int (x^2 - 4 + \frac{4}{x^2})dx = \int (x^2 - 4 + 4x^{-2})dx = \frac{1}{3}x^3 - 4x - 4x^{-1} + c$

(g) $\int \frac{(x+2)(x-1)}{\sqrt{x}}\,dx = \int \frac{x^2+x-2}{x^{\frac{1}{2}}}\,dx = \int (x^{\frac{3}{2}} + x^{\frac{1}{2}} - 2x^{-\frac{1}{2}})dx$

$= \frac{2}{5}x^{\frac{5}{2}} + \frac{2}{3}x^{\frac{3}{2}} - 4x^{\frac{1}{2}} + c$

# Quick test

**1** ***Find the following integrals:***

***(a)*** $\int x^{-1}(x-x^2)dx$ ***(b)*** $\int (1+x^{-2})^2dx$ ***(c)*** $\int (3x-2)(2x-3)dx$

***(d)*** $\int x(\sqrt{x}-2)^2dx$ ***(e)*** $\int \frac{3x^2-4}{2x^2}\,dx$ ***(f)*** $\int \frac{5}{8x^4}\,dx$

**2** ***Integrate the following with respect to x:***

***(a)*** $\dfrac{4}{3x^2}$ ***(b)*** $\sqrt[3]{x}$ ***(c)*** $2x^{-\frac{3}{2}} + x^{-\frac{5}{2}}$ ***(d) 1***

1. (a) $x - \frac{1}{2}x^2 + c$ (b) $x - 2x^{-1} - \frac{1}{3}x^{-3} + c$ (c) $2x^3 - \frac{13}{2}x^2 + 6x + c$ (d) $\frac{1}{3}x^3 - \frac{8}{5}x^{\frac{5}{2}} + 2x^2 + c$ (e) $\frac{3}{2}x + 2x^{-1} + c$ (f) $\frac{-5}{24}x^{-3} + c$ 2. (a) $\frac{-4}{3x} + c$ (b) $\frac{3}{4}\sqrt[3]{x^4} + c$ (c) $-4x^{-\frac{1}{2}} - \frac{2}{3}x^{-\frac{3}{2}} + c$ (d) $x + c$

# Simple differential equations

- An equation of the form

$$\frac{dy}{dx} = f(x)$$

is called a (1st order) differential equation.

EXAMPLES

$\frac{dy}{dx} = 4 \qquad \frac{dy}{dx} = 2x \qquad \frac{dy}{dx} = x^3 - 1$

# Solving a differential equation

**the general solution**

Consider the differential equation

$$\frac{dy}{dx} = 2x$$

This tells us that the gradient of some curve (or curves) is given by the formula $2x$

To solve the equation we have to find the equation of the curve (or curves). This is equivalent to integrating $2x$

$$\frac{dy}{dx} = 2x \quad \Rightarrow \quad y = \int 2x\,dx = x^2 + c$$

This is the general solution of the differential equation. It represents an infinite family of curves which are all parallel to each other.

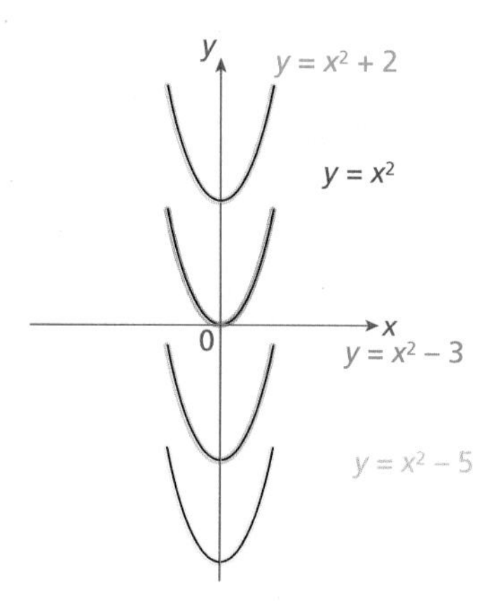


**EXAMINER'S TOP TIP**

Remember that the general solution of a differential equation *must* contain an arbitrary constant as it represents an infinite family of curves.

EXAMPLE

Find the general solution of the following differential equations:

(a) $\frac{dy}{dx} = 3$ (b) $\frac{dy}{dx} = 2x + 1$

(c) $\frac{dy}{dx} = (\sqrt{x} + 1)^2$ (d) $\frac{dy}{dx} = 2ax + b$. (*a* and *b* are constants.)

(a) $\frac{dy}{dx} = 3 \Rightarrow y = \int 3\,dx = 3x + c$ i.e. $y = 3x + c$

(b) $\frac{dy}{dx} = 2x + 1 \Rightarrow y = \int 2x + 1\,dx = x^2 + x + c$ i.e. $y = x^2 + x + c$

(c) $\frac{dy}{dx} = (\sqrt{x} + 1)^2 \Rightarrow y = \int (\sqrt{x} + 1)^2 dx = \int x + 2\sqrt{x} + 1\,dx = \int x + 2x^{\frac{1}{2}} + 1\,dx$ i.e. $y = \frac{1}{2}x^2 + \frac{4}{3}x^{\frac{3}{2}} + x + c$

(d) $\frac{dy}{dx} = 2ax + b \Rightarrow y = \int (2ax + b)\,dx = ax^2 + bx + c$ i.e. $y = ax^2 + bx + c$

# Solving a differential equation continued...



**EXAMPLE**

Suppose we have the differential equation $\frac{dy}{dx} = 2x$

This defines an infinite family of possible curves. However, sometimes we are given additional information which allows us to find a particular curve or solution.

**EXAMPLE**

$\frac{dy}{dx} = 2x$ *and* when $x = 1, y = 2$

The information about $x$ and $y$ values is sometimes called a boundary condition.

$y = \int 2x \, dx \Rightarrow y = x^2 + c$

To find the value of $c$, use the boundary condition.
Substitute $x = 1$ and $y = 2$ into the general solution: $2 = 1^2 + c \Rightarrow c = 1$
Particular solution is $y = x^2 + 1$

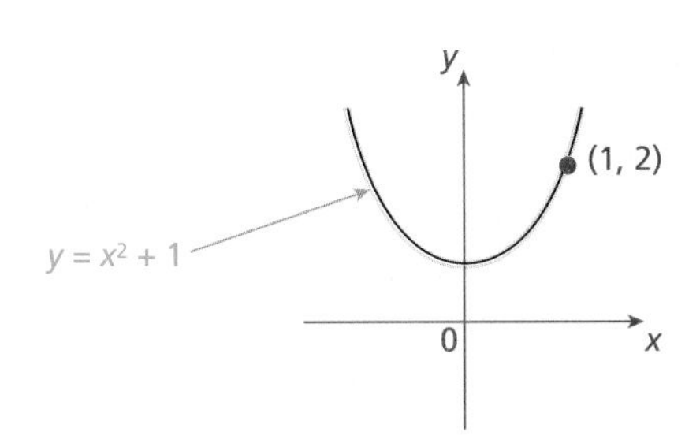


**EXAMINER'S TOP TIP**

**A boundary condition specifies a point (in the example, (1, 2)) and we then have to find the particular member of the family of curves that passes through that point.**

**EXAMPLE**

A curve passes through the point (2, –1) and its gradient at any point is given by $2 - 6x^2$.
Find the equation of the curve.

$\frac{dy}{dx} = 2 - 6x^2$

$\Rightarrow y = \int (2 - 6x^2) dx$

$\Rightarrow y = 2x - 2x^3 + c$

When $x = 2, y = -1$

So $-1 = 2 \times 2 - 2 \times 2^3 + c$

$-1 = 4 - 16 + c \Rightarrow 11 = c$

Equation of the curve is $y = 2x - 2x^3 + 11$

## Quick test

***1*** ***Given that $\frac{dy}{dx} = x^4 + 2x$ and that when $x = 0$, $y = 1$, find y in terms of x.***

***2*** ***Given that $\frac{dy}{dx} = x^3 + \frac{1}{x^3}$ and that $y = 4$ at $x = 1$, find***

***(a) y in terms of x***

***(b) the value of y at $x = 2$.***

***3*** ***A curve has equation $y = f(x)$***

***Given that $f'(x) = 2x - \frac{x^2}{2}$ and that the curve passes through the point (0, 1), find the value of f(3).***

1. $y = \frac{1}{5}x^5 + x^2 + 1$ 2. (a) $y = \frac{1}{4}x^4 - \frac{1}{2x^2} + \frac{17}{4}$ (b) $y = \frac{65}{8}$ 3. $f(3) = \frac{11}{2}$

# Definite integration

- We have seen that $\int f'(x)dx = f(x) + c$ where $c$ is an arbitrary constant, and this is known as indefinite integration.

**We now define a definite integral.**

**This is the upper limit.**

$$\int_a^b f'(x)dx = [f(x)]_a^b = f(b) - f(a)$$

**This is the lower limit of the integral.**

NOTE **A definite integral is a number.**

## Evaluating definite integrals

EXAMPLE

Evaluate $\int_2^4 (2x - 3)dx$

$\int_2^4 (2x - 3)dx \quad = [x^2 - 3x + c]_2^4$ The square brackets are standard notation and must be used.

$= (4^2 - 3 \times 4 + c) - (2^2 - 3 \times 2 + c)$

$= (16 - 12 + \not{c}) - (4 - 6 + \not{c})$

$= 4 - -2 = 6$

**EXAMINER'S TOP TIP**

Notice that the $c$ will always cancel out, so we never put it in when finding a definite integral.

EXAMPLE

Evaluate $\int_{-2}^{3} (-2x-1)(3x+1)dx$

$\int_{-2}^{3} (-2x-1)(3x+1)dx \quad = \int_{-2}^{3} (6x^2 - x - 1)dx$ These brackets are crucial.

$= \left[2x^3 - \frac{1}{2}x^2 - x\right]_{-2}^{3}$

$= (2 \times 3^3 - \frac{1}{2} \times 3^2 - 3) - (2 \times (-2)^3 - \frac{1}{2} \times (-2)^2 - (-2))$

$= (54 - \frac{9}{2} - 3) - (-16 - \frac{4}{2} + 2)$

$= 46\frac{1}{2} - (-16)$

$= 62\frac{1}{2}$

NOTE An alternative way of evaluating $\left[2x^3 - \frac{1}{2}x^2 - x\right]_{-2}^{3}$ is to do it term by term giving

$2(3^3 - (-2)^3) - \frac{1}{2}(3^2 - (-2)^2) - (3 - (-2)) \quad = 2(27 + 8) - \frac{1}{2}(9 - 4) - (3 + 2)$

$= 70 - \frac{5}{2} - 5 = 62\frac{1}{2}$

The advantage of using the term by term method of evaluation is that one can take out common factors straight away (in the example, the 2 and the $\frac{1}{2}$).

# Further examples

EXAMPLE

$y = 3x^{\frac{1}{2}} - 4x^{-\frac{1}{2}}, x > 0$

Show that $\int_1^3 y dx = a + b\sqrt{3}$, where $a$ and $b$ are integers to be found.

$$\int_1^3 y dx = \int_1^3 (3x^{\frac{1}{2}} - 4x^{-\frac{1}{2}}) dx$$
$$= \left[3 \times \tfrac{2}{3} x^{\frac{3}{2}} - 4 \times 2x^{\frac{1}{2}}\right]_1^3$$
$$= \left[2x^{\frac{3}{2}} - 8x^{\frac{1}{2}}\right]_1^3$$
$$= 2(3^{\frac{3}{2}} - 1^{\frac{3}{2}}) - 8(3^{\frac{1}{2}} - 1^{\frac{1}{2}})$$ Using term by term method of evaluation.
$$= 2\sqrt{27} - 2 - 8\sqrt{3} + 8$$
$$= 2 \times 3\sqrt{3} - 8\sqrt{3} + 6$$
$$= 6\sqrt{3} - 8\sqrt{3} + 6$$
$$= -2\sqrt{3} + 6 = 6 - 2\sqrt{3}$$ $a = 6, b = -2$

**EXAMINER'S TOP TIP**

**This type of question could easily appear on the non-calculator paper. It is therefore very important that you do not rely on your calculator to do basic arithmetic!**

EXAMPLE

Given that $y^{\frac{1}{2}} = x^{\frac{1}{3}} + 3$, find the *exact* value of $\int_1^8 y dx$

$$\int_1^8 y dx = \int_1^8 (y^{\frac{1}{2}})^2 dx = \int (x^{\frac{1}{3}} + 3)^2 dx = \int_1^8 (x^{\frac{2}{3}} + 6x^{\frac{1}{3}} + 9) dx$$
$$= \left[\tfrac{3}{5} x^{\frac{5}{3}} + 6 \times \tfrac{3}{4} x^{\frac{4}{3}} + 9x\right]_1^8$$
$$= \tfrac{3}{5}(8^{\frac{5}{3}} - 1^{\frac{5}{3}}) + \tfrac{9}{2}(8^{\frac{4}{3}} - 1^{\frac{4}{3}}) + 9(8 - 1)$$

$8^{\frac{5}{3}} = (8^{\frac{1}{3}})^5 = 2^5 = 32$

$$= \tfrac{3}{5}(32 - 1) + \tfrac{9}{2}(16 - 1) + 9 \times 7$$

and $8^{\frac{4}{3}} = (8^{\frac{1}{3}})^4 = 2^4 = 16$

$$= \frac{93}{5} + \frac{135}{2} + 63 = 18\frac{3}{5} + 67\frac{1}{2} + 63 = 149.1$$

# Quick test

**1** ***Evaluate these definite integrals.***

***(a)*** $\int_4^9 (2x^{\frac{1}{2}} + 3x^{-\frac{1}{2}}) dx$ ***(b)*** $\int_1^2 (x-1)(x-2) dx$

***(c)*** $\int_0^2 (\sqrt{x} - 2)^2 dx$ ***(d)*** $\int_{-1}^2 (4 - 5x)x^3 dx$

**2** ***Find the values of these.***

***(a)*** $\int_4^9 x^{\frac{1}{2}}(2x-3) dx$ ***(b)*** $\int_{-1}^2 \frac{(x-1)}{x^4} dx$

1. (a) $31\frac{1}{3}$ (b) $-\frac{1}{6}$ (c) $10 - \frac{16}{3}\sqrt{2}$ (d) $-18$ 2. (a) $\frac{654}{5}$ (b) $-\frac{62}{81}$

# Finding the area under a curve 1

## Using integration

- Suppose we have a curve $y = f(x)$ and we wish to find the area under the curve from 0 up to some $x$ value as shown in the diagram.

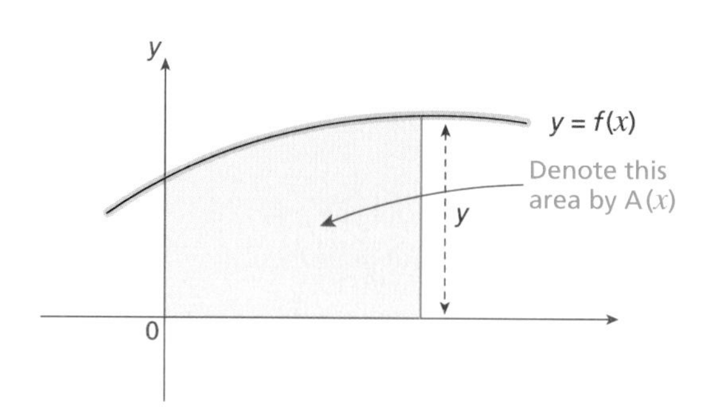


The rate at which this area is growing at some particular point is precisely equal to the $y$-coordinate at the point. This is the key point to understanding why we use integration to find area. (If $y$ is a large value, then the area is growing quickly at that point, if $y$ is a small value, then the area is growing slowly at that point.)

The rate of change of area is $\frac{dA}{dx}$.

$$\frac{dA}{dx} = y \Rightarrow A = \text{ i.e. } \int y \, dx$$

$$A(x) = F(x) + c \text{ where } F(x) = \int y \, dx$$

Suppose we want to find the area under the curve between $x = a$ and $x = b$,.

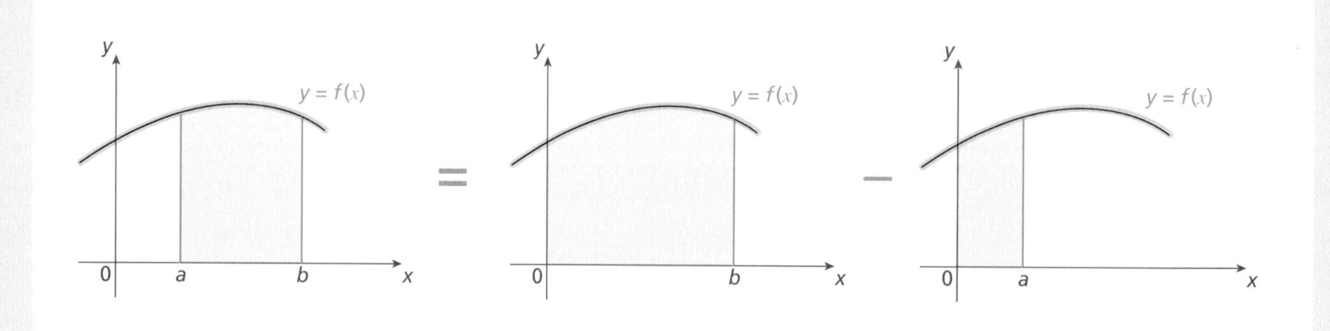


Required area = A($b$) – A($a$)

$= (F(b) + c) - (F(a) + c) = F(b) - F(a)$

i.e. $\text{Area} = \int_a^b y \, dx$

**EXAMINER'S TOP TIP**
Although you will not be expected to justify this result, you must know it!

This is a definite integral whose value is the area bounded by the curve, the $x$-axis and the lines $x = a$ and $x = b$.

# Examples of finding the area under a curve



**EXAMPLE**

The definite integral, $\int_1^2 x^2 dx$, is equal to the area under the curve $y = x^2$ between the $x$-axis and the lines $x = 1$ and $x = 2$

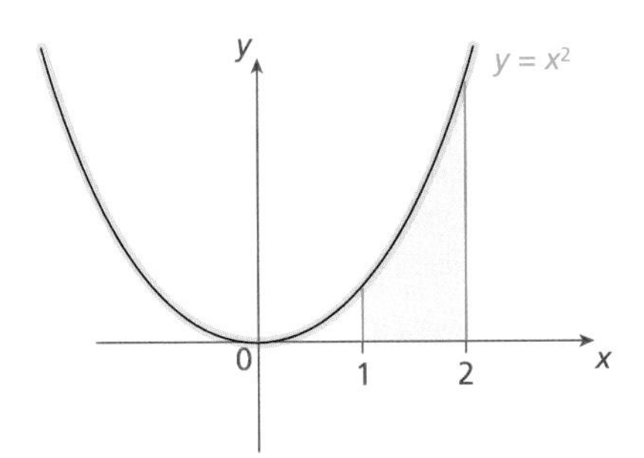


By evaluating this definite integral, we can find the **exact** value of this area.

Area = $\int_1^2 x^2 dx = \left[\frac{1}{3}x^3\right]_1^2 = \frac{1}{3}(2^3 - 1^3) = \frac{7}{3}$ square units

**EXAMPLE**

Find the area of the region bounded by the curve $y = x^2 - 9$ and the $x$-axis.

Notice that we have not been told what the limits are, so a sketch will help.

- Find out where the graph crosses the $x$-axis by putting $y = 0$
  $0 = x^2 - 9 \Rightarrow x^2 = 9 \Rightarrow x = \pm 3$
- Find out where the graph crosses the $y$-axis by putting $x = 0$
  $y = 0^2 + 9 = -9$

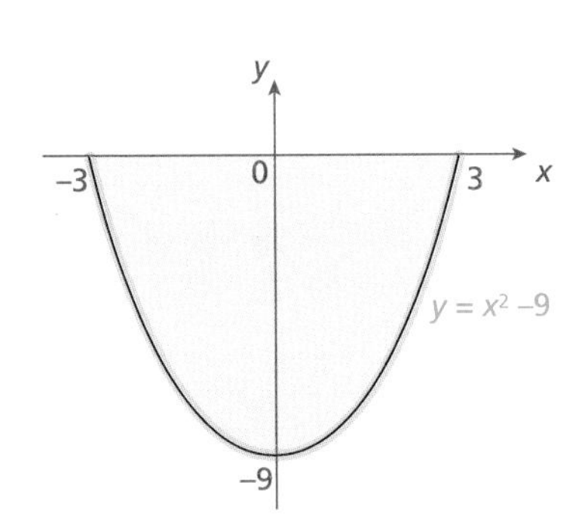


Area = $\int_{-3}^{3} y dx = \int_{-3}^{3} (x^2 - 9dx) = \left[\frac{1}{3}x^3 - 9x\right]_{-3}^{3}$

$= \frac{1}{3}(3^3 - (-3)^3) - 9(3 - (-3))$

$= \frac{1}{3}(27 - -27) - 9(3 + 3)$

$= \frac{1}{3} \times 54 - 54 = -36$

**NOTE**

The negative sign means that the area is below the $x$-axis
So, area = 36 square units.

**EXAMINER'S TOP TIP**

Although a sketch isn't essential, in most cases it will help to clarify the situation.

## Quick test

**1** ***Find the area enclosed by the x-axis and the following curves and straight lines:***

***(a)*** $y = 3x^2, x = 1, x = 3$

***(b)*** $y = x^2 + 1, x = -2, x = 5$

***(c)*** $y = x^2(x - 1)(x - 2), x = -2, x = -1$

***(d)*** $y = \frac{3}{x^2}, x = 1, x = 6.$

**2** ***Find the area under*** $y = 4x^3 + 8x^2$ ***from*** $x = -2$ ***to*** $x = 0.$

**3** ***Sketch the curve*** $y = x^2 - 5x + 6$***. Find the area cut off below the x-axis.***

1. (a) 26 (b) $51\frac{1}{3}$ (c) $22\frac{7}{60}$ (d) $2\frac{1}{2}$ 2. $5\frac{1}{3}$ 3. $\frac{1}{6}$

# Finding the area under a curve 2

## Using integration 2

EXAMPLE

**Find the total area enclosed by the curve with equation $y = x(x - 1)(x - 2)$ and the $x$-axis.**

**Here a sketch is essential.**

**Put $y = 0$**

$$0 = x(x - 1)(x - 2) \Rightarrow x = 0, x = 1, x = 2$$

**Put $x = 0$**

$$y = 0$$

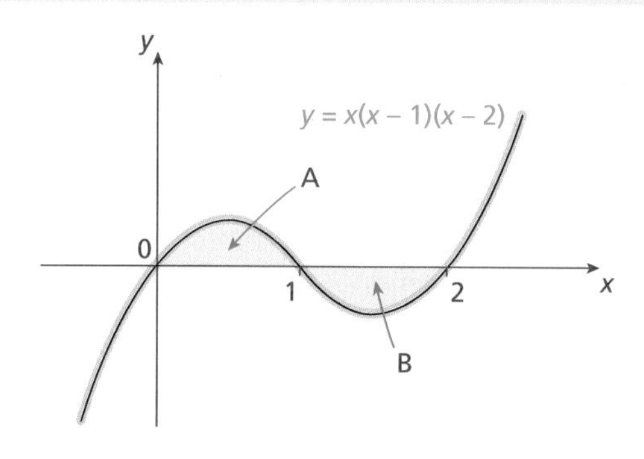


**The highest power of $x^3$ has a positive coefficient (+1) so as $x \to \infty$, $y \to \infty$, i.e. the graph goes up.**

**Since part of the area is above the $x$-axis and positive, and part is below the $x$-axis and negative, if we integrate from $x = 0$ to $x = 2$ we will not get the total area.**

**EXAMINER'S TOP TIP**

**This example shows clearly the importance of sketching the graph!**

**We therefore find each area separately.**

$$A = \int_0^1 x(x - 1)(x - 2)dx = \int_0^1 x(x^2 - 3x + 2)dx = \int_0^1 (x^3 - 3x^2 + 2x)dx$$

$$= [\tfrac{1}{4}x^4 - x^3 + x^2]_0^1$$

$$= \frac{1}{4} - 1 + 1 = \frac{1}{4}$$

$$B = \int_1^2 x(x - 1)(x - 2)dx = [\tfrac{1}{4}x^4 - x^3 + x^2]_1^2$$

$$= \frac{1}{4}(2^4 - 1^4) - (2^3 - 1^3) + (2^2 - 1^2)$$

$$= \frac{15}{4} - 7 + 3 = -\frac{1}{4}, \text{ so actual area is } \frac{1}{4}$$

**A + B = total area = $\frac{1}{4} + \frac{1}{4} = \frac{1}{2}$ square unit**

NOTE **If we had tried to find area in one go, by finding $\int_0^2 x(x - 1)(x - 2)dx$, we would have got an answer of 0 $(\frac{1}{4} + -\frac{1}{4})$.**

# Finding the enclosed area

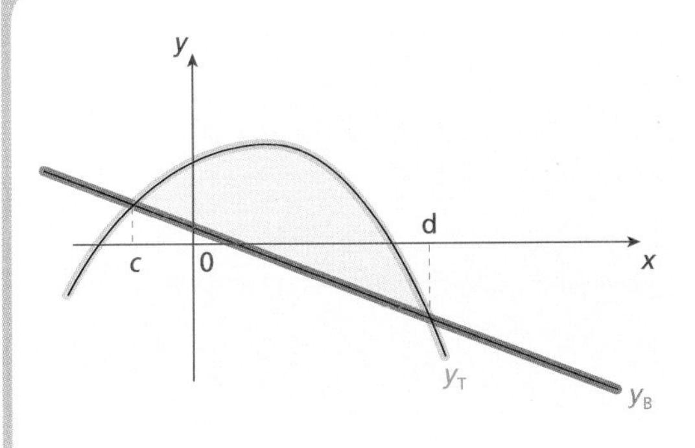


Suppose we wish to find the area enclosed between a curve and a straight line, as shown in the diagram. Suppose we denote the top boundary of the area (in this case, the curve) by $y_T$ and the bottom boundary of the area (in this case, the line) by $y_B$.

- First find the $x$-coordinates of the points where the curve and the line meet. We do this by putting $y_T = y_B$ and solving for $x$
- Suppose the solutions are $x = c$ and $x = d$ ($c < d$)

Area enclosed = $\int_c^d (y_T - y_B)\,dx$ **Learn this!**

**EXAMINER'S TOP TIP**

**When using the above result, always simplify ($y_T - y_B$) before integrating.**

**EXAMPLE**

Find the area enclosed between the curve $y = 2x - x^2$ and the straight line $y = -2x$.

- Sketch the two graphs. For $y = 2x - x^2$ put $y = 0 = x(2 - x) \Rightarrow x = 0$ *or* $x = 2$
  The $-x^2$ shows that the parabola is inverted.

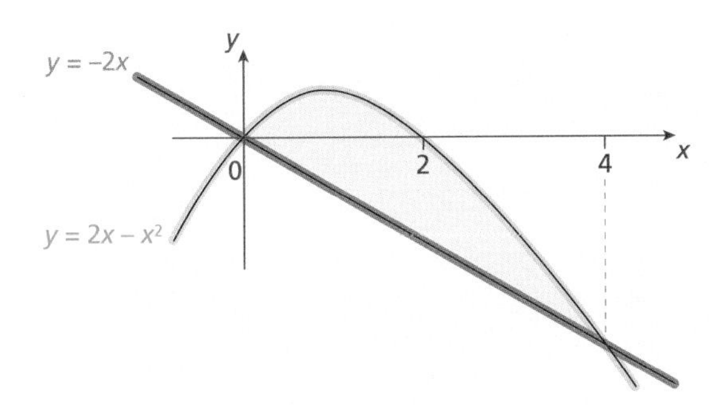


Here, $y_T = 2x - x^2$ (curve is top edge of area) $y_B = -2x$ (line is bottom edge of area).

- Find points of intersection. Put $y_T = y_B$
  $2x - x^2 = -2x$
  $0 = x^2 - 4x = x(x - 4) \Rightarrow x = 0$ *or* $x = 4$
- Area enclosed = $\int_0^4 ((2x - x^2) - (-2x))\,dx = \int_0^4 (4x - x^2)\,dx = \left[2x^2 - \frac{1}{3}x^3\right]_0^4$

$$= 2 \times 4^2 - \tfrac{1}{3} \times 4^3$$
$$= 32 - \tfrac{64}{3}$$
$$= \tfrac{32}{3} \text{ square units}$$

## Quick test

**1** ***Find the area of the region bounded by the curve $y = \sqrt{x}$ and the line $y = x$.***

**2** ***Find the area enclosed between the curve $y = x(4 - x^2)$ and the x-axis.***

**3** ***Find the area enclosed between the curve with equation $y = x^2 - 6x + 2$ and the straight line with equation $x + y - 2 = 0$.***

**4** ***Find the area cut off from the curve with equation $y = 3x - x^2 - 4$ by the line with equation $y = -4$***

1. $\frac{1}{6}$ 2. 8 3. $20\frac{5}{6}$ 4. $4\frac{1}{2}$

# Numerical integration

**Approximation of a definite integral**

- **Suppose that we have a definite integral which either cannot be evaluated or is very difficult to evaluate exactly. How could we find an approximation to it?**

## The trapezium rule

EXAMPLE

Find an approximation to the definite integral $\int_0^4 (16 - x^2)^{\frac{1}{2}}dx$ using the trapezium rule with four strips.

The exact evaluation of this integral is beyond the scope of this book. However, we can approximate it like this.

$\int_0^4 (16 - x^2)^{\frac{1}{2}}dx$ = Area under $y = (16 - x^2)^{\frac{1}{2}}$ between $x = 0$ and $x = 4$

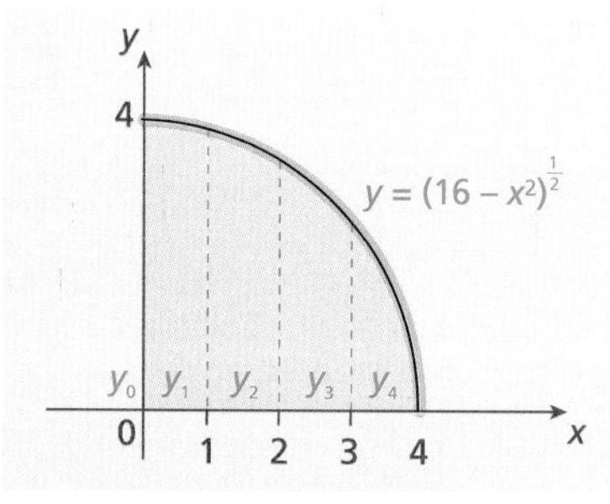


We can approximate this area using the trapezium rule.

Area under a curve is approximately $\frac{h}{2}\{y_0 + y_n + 2(y_1 + y_2 + \ldots + y_{n-1})\}$ where there are $n$ strips and the width of each strip is $h$

We are told to use four strips, so each strip = $\frac{4}{4}$ = 1 unit.

| $x$ | $y = (16 - x^2)^{\frac{1}{2}}$ |
|---|---|
| 0 | $y_0 = 4$ |
| 1 | $y_1 = \sqrt{15}$ |
| 2 | $y_2 = \sqrt{12}$ |
| 3 | $y_3 = \sqrt{7}$ |
| 4 | $y_4 = 0$ |

**EXAMINER'S TOP TIP**

**Using a table is usually a good idea.**

Area under curve $\approx \frac{1}{2}\{4 + 0 + 2(\sqrt{15} + \sqrt{12} + \sqrt{7})\} = 11.98\ldots = 12.0$ (3 s.f.)

Hence $\int_0^4 (16 - x^2)^{\frac{1}{2}}dx \approx 12.0$ (3 s.f.)

**NOTE**

We can see from the diagram that **due to the shape of the curve**, this is going to be an **underestimate of the true area**, i.e. of the true integral.

In fact, the area is one quarter of a circle of radius 4, i.e. $\frac{1}{4} \times \pi \times 4^2 = 12.566\ldots$

We could **improve the accuracy** of our approximation by using **more strips**.

# Further examples

**EXAMPLE**

The table gives the values of a function $f(x)$ for certain values of $x$

| $x$ | 1 | 1.5 | 2 | 2.5 | 3 | 3.5 | 4 |
|---|---|---|---|---|---|---|---|
| $f(x)$ | 4.1 | 4.7 | 5.1 | 4.8 | 5.1 | 5.4 | 5.9 |

Use the trapezium rule, with six strips, to estimate the value of $\int_1^4 f(x)dx$

$\int_1^4 f(x)dx$ = area under $f(x)$ between $x = 1$ and $x = 4$

$\approx \frac{0.5}{5}\{4.1 + 5.9 + 2(4.7 + 5.1 + 4.8 + 5.1 + 5.4)\}$

$= 0.25(10 + 50.2) = 15.05$

Hence $\int_1^4 f(x)dx \approx 15.05$

**EXAMINER'S TOP TIP**

**The number of y values is always one more than the number of strips.**

**EXAMPLE**

Using the table of values in the example above, use the trapezium rule with six strips to estimate the value of $\int_1^4 [f(x)]^2dx$

$\int_1^4 [f(x)]^2dx$ = area under $[f(x)]^2$ between $x = 1$ and $x = 4$

$\approx \frac{0.5}{2}\{4.1^2 + 5.9^2 + 2(4.7^2 + 5.1^2 + 4.8^2 + 5.1^2 + 5.4^2)\}$

$= 76.06$

**EXAMPLE**

(a) Estimate the definite integral $\int_1^4 \sqrt{x}\,dx$ using the trapezium rule with six strips.

(a) Range of the integral = upper limit – lower limit

$= 4 - 1 = 3$

Width of strip $= \frac{3}{6} = 0.5$

$\int_1^4 \sqrt{x}\,dx$ = area under $\sqrt{x}$ between $x = 1$ and $x = 4$

$\approx \frac{0.5}{2}\{1 + 2 + 2(\sqrt{\tfrac{3}{2}} + \sqrt{2} + \sqrt{\tfrac{5}{2}} + \sqrt{3} + \sqrt{\tfrac{7}{2}})\}$

$= 4.66148\ldots$

(b) Evaluate $\int_1^4 \sqrt{x}\,dx$ exactly.

(b) $\int_1^4 \sqrt{x}\,dx = \int_1^4 x^{\frac{1}{2}}dx = \left[\frac{2}{3}x^{\frac{3}{2}}\right]_1^4$

$= \frac{2}{3}(4^{\frac{3}{2}} - 1^{\frac{3}{2}})$

$= \frac{2}{3}(8 - 1)$

$= \frac{14}{3} = 4.66\ldots$

(c) Hence, find the percentage error in your estimate.

(c) percentage error $= \frac{\text{error}}{\text{actual value}} \times 100\%$

$= \frac{(4.666666 - 4.661488\ldots)}{4.6666666666} \times 100\%$

$= 0.1\%$ (1 d.p.)

| $x$ | $\sqrt{x}$ |
|---|---|
| 1 | 1 |
| 1.5 | $\sqrt{\tfrac{3}{2}}$ |
| 2 | $\sqrt{2}$ |
| 2.5 | $\sqrt{\tfrac{5}{2}}$ |
| 3 | $\sqrt{3}$ |
| 3.5 | $\sqrt{\tfrac{7}{2}}$ |
| 4 | 2 |

# Quick test

**1** ***Using the table of values, estimate $\int_{10}^{50} y\,dx$ using the trapezium rule with four strips.***

| $x$ | 10 | 20 | 30 | 40 | 50 |
|---|---|---|---|---|---|
| $y$ | 1.21 | 3.98 | 7.97 | 13.08 | 19.22 |

**2** ***Use the trapezium rule with five strips to estimate the value of $\int_0^{\frac{\pi}{6}} \sqrt{\sin x}\,dx$ giving your answer to 3 d.p.***

1. 352.45 2. 0.244

# Exam-style questions

Use the questions to test your progress. Check your answers on page 95.

**1** Use the trapezium rule with three strips to find an estimate for $\int_{\frac{1}{2}}^{2} \frac{1}{x}\,dx$. [1]

**2** Given that $\frac{dy}{dx} = 2x^2 - 10x + 12$, $x \geq 0$, and $y = 2$ when $x = 1$, find the value of $y$ when $x = 4$. [2]

**3** The diagram shows the curve $y = \frac{1}{2}(x^2 + 1)$ and the line $y = x + 2$, which meet at the points A and B.

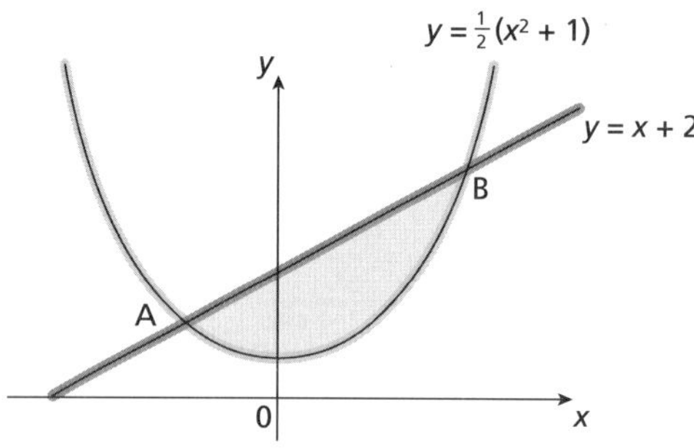


**(a)** Find the coordinates of A and B. [2]

**(b)** Find the area of the shaded region. [1]

**4** Find the area enclosed by the curve with equation $y = 6x^2$ and the line with equation $5x + y + 1 = 0$. [2]

**5** $f(x) = x^3 - 5x^2 - 8x + 12$. Find the area of the region bounded by the curve $y = f(x)$, the $x$-axis and the lines $x = -1$ and $x = 1$. [3]

**6** The curve $y = x^{\frac{3}{2}}$ is shown together with the line $x = 8$ which meets the curve at P and the $x$-axis at Q.

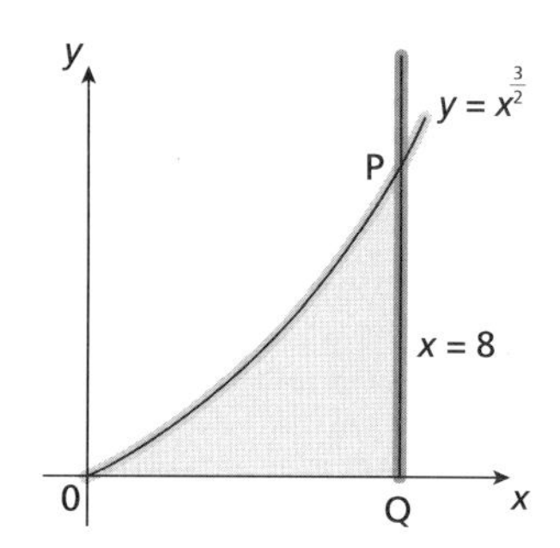


**(a)** Find the length of PQ, giving your answer in surd form. [2]

**(b)** Find the shaded area, giving your answer in surd form. [2]

**7** The line $y = 2$ meets the curve $y = 6 - x^2$ at two points P and Q, as shown. Find the area of the shaded region. [2]

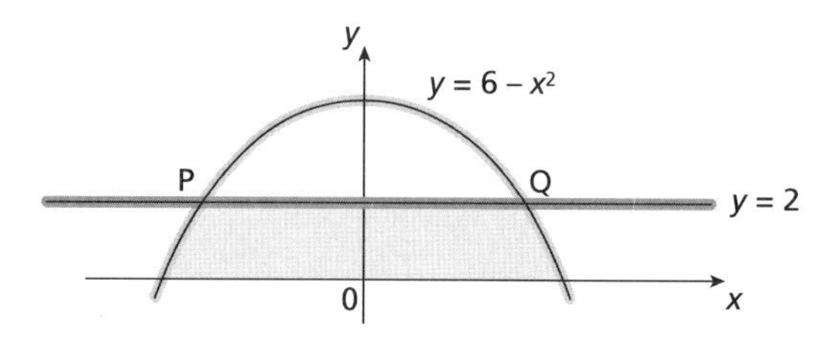

**8** The diagram shows the region R bounded by the curve with equation $y = x^2 + 2$, the $x$- and $y$-axes and the line joining the point (2, 6) to the point (26, 0).

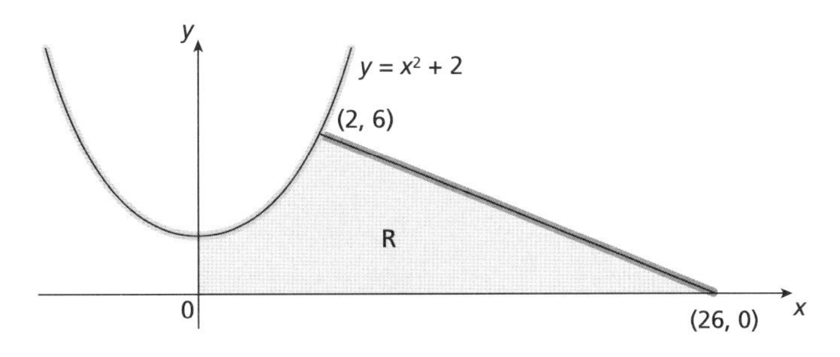


**(a)** Find the area of R. [2]

**(b)** Show that the line joining (2, 6) to (26, 0) is normal to the curve at the point (2, 6). [2]

**9** The tangent to the curve with equation $y = 4 - x^2$ at the point P (1, 3) meets the $x$-axis at the point Q, as shown.

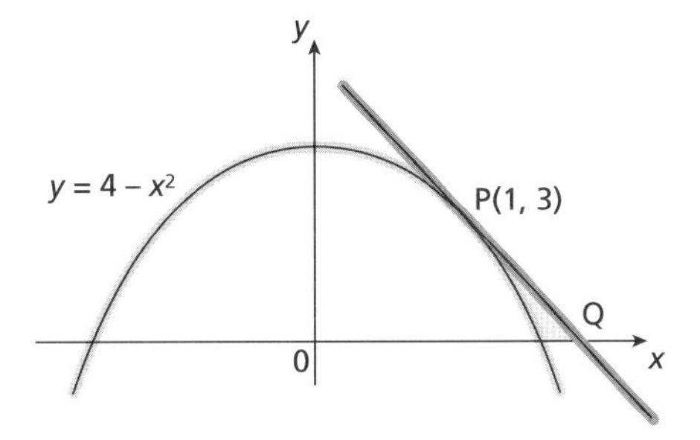


**(a)** Find the $x$-coordinate of Q. [2]

**(b)** Find the area of the shaded region. [2]

**10** Given that $\frac{dy}{dx} = 2 + \frac{1}{x^2}$ and that when $x = 1$, $y = 2$, find:

**(a)** $y$ in terms of $x$ [2]

**(b)** the value of $y$ when $x = -1$. [2]

**11 (a)** Find the equation of the normal to the curve $y = 2 + 5x - x^2$ at the point where $x = 3$. [3]

**(b)** Show that the normal meets the curve again at (1, 6). [2]

**(c)** Find the area of the region bounded by the curve and the normal. [2]

**Total: / 36**

# Answers

## Algebra and functions

**1** **(a)** $2^{(2x+2)}$

**(b)** $x = -\frac{1}{5}$

**2** $3\sqrt{3}$

**3** **(a)** A = 3, B = 2, C = –7

**(b)** –7

**(c)** $-2 + \sqrt{2\frac{1}{3}}, -2 - \sqrt{2\frac{1}{3}}$

**4** **(a)** $1 \pm \sqrt{13}$

**(b)** $x < 1 - \sqrt{13}$ *or* $x > 1 + \sqrt{13}$

**5** (–2, –3) *or* $(\frac{1}{2}, 2)$

**6** **(a)** $p = 5, q = -6$

**(b)** $(x - 1)(x + 2)(2x + 3)$

**7** **(b)** $x = 2$ *or* $x = 0$

**8** $x = \frac{1}{16}$ *or* $x = 64$

**9** **(a)** (i) 3 (ii) $\frac{1}{9}$ (iii) 1

**(b)** $y = -1$

**10** **(a)** $x > 10\frac{1}{2}$m

**(b)** $x(x - 5) < 104$

**(c)** $10\frac{1}{2} < x < 13$

**11** **(a)** A = 8, B = –3

**(b)** $x = \pm\frac{1}{2}$ *or* $x = -\frac{2}{3}$

**12** **(a)**

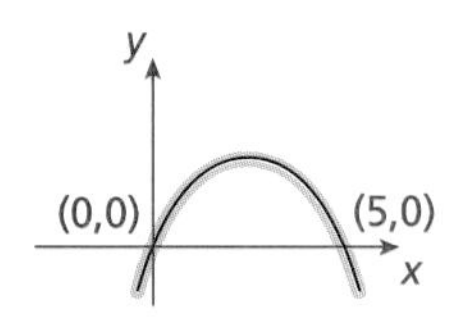


**(b)**

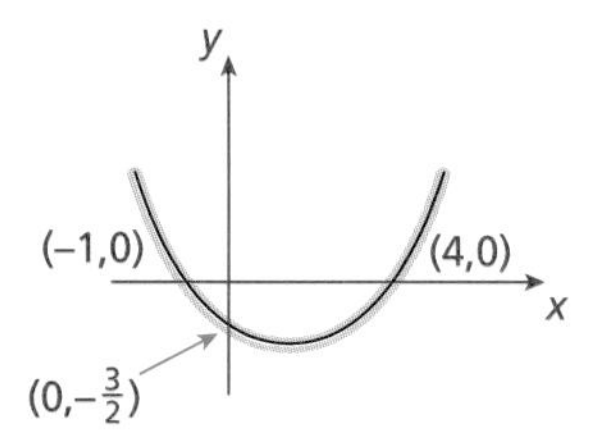


**13** $x = -3$ *or* $x = 1$

**14** **(a)** $x = -2.58$

**(b)** $x = 2.32$ *or* $x = 1.58$

**15** **(a)** $p + q$

**(b)** $2q - p$

**(c)** $3p + q$

**(d)** $3p + 4q$

**(e)** $\frac{q}{p}$

**16** $x = 2$

**17** $x = 10$ ($x \neq 3$ as $x > 6$)

## Coordinate geometry

**1** **(a)** $x + 2y = 6$

**(b)** $4y = x + 9$

**(c)** 1.12

**(d)** 18.75 units$^2$

**2** **(a)** 6.71

**(b)** $y = -\frac{1}{2}x + 18$

**(d)** $(\frac{3}{2}, \frac{69}{4})$

**3** (2, 0) *or* (4, 6)

**4** **(a)** $7x + 5y - 18 = 0$

**(b)** $\frac{162}{35} \approx 4.63$ units$^2$

**5** **(a)** centre (8, 6)

**(b)** radius 2

**(c)** 8, 12

**6** **(a)** (0, 5)

**(b)** radius 5

**7** **(a)** $x^2 + y^2 - x - 3y - 4 = 0$

**(b)** (0, –1) (1, 4)

**8** **(a)** P = (1, 3) Q = (–4, –2)

**(b)** $5\sqrt{2}$

**9** 5 square units

**10** **(a)** (4, 3)

**(c)** $x - y - 1 = 0$

**(d)** $(x - 4)^2 + (y - 3)^2 = 8$

**(e)** R is (6, 5) *or* R is (2, 1)

**(f)** $x + y = 11$

## Sequences and series

**1** **(a)** $15 - 4k$

**(b)** $-8k^2 + 30k - 30$

**(c)** $k = 4$ *or* $k = -\frac{1}{4}$

**2** **(a)** (i) $k = \frac{3}{2}$ (ii) $p = 63$ (iii) $q = 189$

**(b)** 126

**3** **(a)** $u_2 = 4, u_3 = 6, u_4 = 8$ **(c)** $4N^2 + 2N$

**4** **(a)** 14.9 **(b)** 689

**5** **(a)** $a = 5, d = 3.5$

**(b)** 16

**6** **(a)** $16 + 32x + 24x^2 + 8x^3 + x^4$

*and* $16 - 32x + 24x^2 - 8x^3 + x^4$

**7** **(a)** $a^4 + 4a^3b + 6a^2b^2 + 4ab^3 + b^4$

**(b)** 1

**8** **(a)** 1080

**(b)** 15

**9** **(a)** $x^3 - 3x + 3x^{-1} - x^{-3}$

**(c)** $x^5 - 5x^3 + 10x - 10x^{-1} + 5x^{-3} - x^{-5}$

**(d)** 393

**10** $x = -\frac{1}{2}$ *or* $x = 1$

**11 (a)** $d = 1.5$

**(b)** $u_1 = -3$

**(c)** $n = 21$

**12 (a)** $k = 2, n = 22$

**(b)** 12 320

## Trigonometry

**1 (a)** 10.9km

**(b)** 059.4°

**2 (a)** 21.4cm

**(b)** $13.6\text{cm}^2$

**4 (a)**

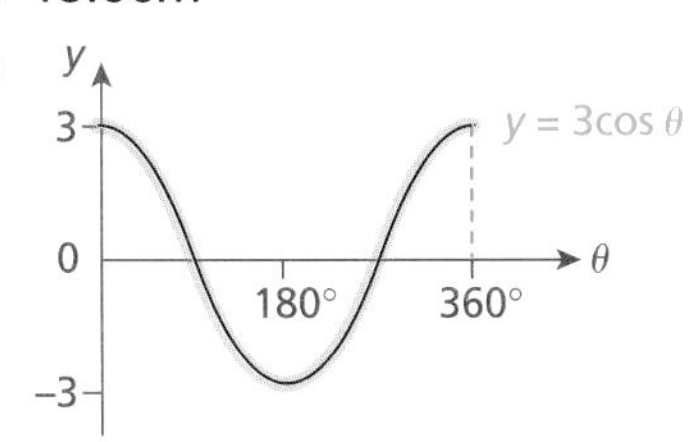


**(b)**

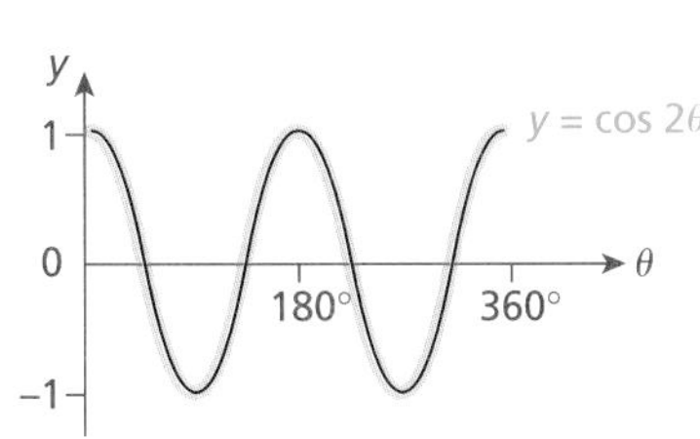


**(c)**

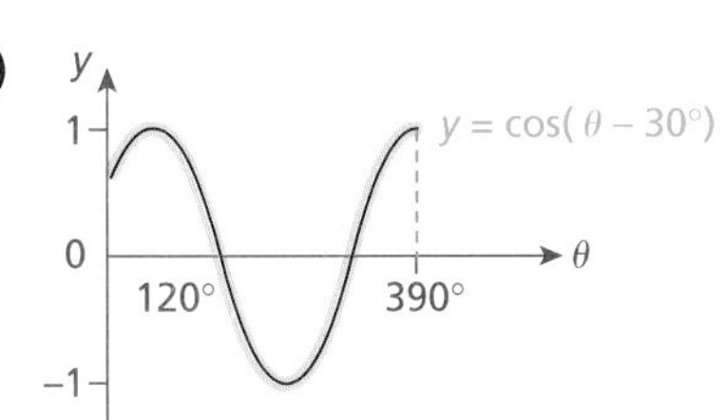


**5**

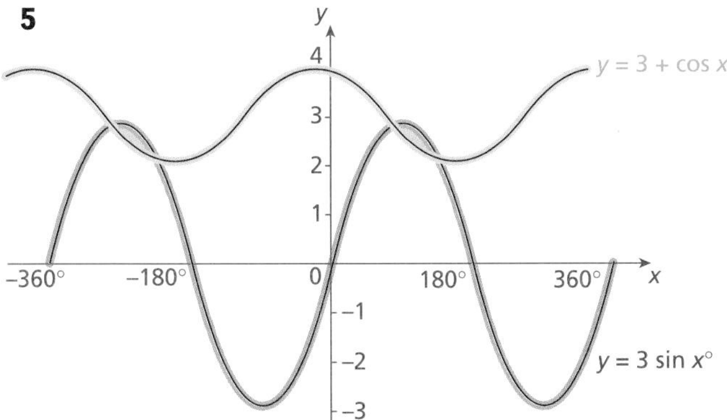


**6** 19.5°, 160.5°, 270°

**7 (a)** $\frac{\pi}{18}, \frac{5\pi}{18}, \frac{13\pi}{18}, \frac{17\pi}{18}$

**(b)** $\frac{3\pi}{4}$

**8** −145°, 35°, 215°

**9 (a)** $15.6\text{cm}^2$

**(b)** $25.4\text{cm}^2$

**9 (a)** 15.

**10** $\theta = \frac{\pi}{4} = \frac{3\pi}{4}$.

**11** $x = 70°$ or $-50°$

**13** $22.4\text{ cm}^2$

**14** $24.1\text{ cm}^2$

## Differentiation

**1 (a)** $\frac{9}{2}x^{\frac{1}{2}} - \frac{7}{2}x^{-\frac{1}{2}} + 3x^{-\frac{3}{2}}$

**(b)** $\frac{9}{4}x^{-\frac{1}{2}} + \frac{7}{4}x^{-\frac{3}{2}} - \frac{9}{2}x^{-\frac{5}{2}}$

**2 (a)** (2, 20) (4, 16)

**(b)** (2, 20) is maximum (4, 16) is minimum

**3 (a)** $23\frac{19}{27}$

**(b)** $18\frac{14}{81}$

**4 (b)** $2x - \frac{250}{x^2}$

**(c)** $x = 5, S = 75$

**5** $\frac{dy}{dx} = 2x + 1$

**6 (b)** (4, 16)

**7 (a)** (0, −14)

**(b)** (1, −11) *and* $(\frac{7}{3}, -12.2)$

**(c)** $1 < x < \frac{7}{3}$

**8 (a)** $6x - y + 2 = 0$

**(b)** $(-\frac{2}{5}, -\frac{2}{5})$

**9 (a)** $2x + y + 16 = 0$

**(b)** (−16, 16)

**10 (b)** (1, 4) (3, 12)

**11 (a)** $x - y + 3 = 0$ $x - 2y + 12 = 0$ (6, 9)

**12 (b)** $\frac{10}{3}$

**(d)** $\frac{2300\pi}{27}$

## Integration

**1** $\frac{35}{24}$

**2** 5

**3 (a)** (−1, 1), (3, 5)

**(b)** $5\frac{1}{3}$

**4** $\frac{1}{216}$

**5** $20\frac{2}{3}$

**6 (a)** $16\sqrt{2}$

**(b)** $256\frac{\sqrt{2}}{5}$

**7** 8.93

**8 (a)** $78\frac{2}{3}$

**9 (a)** $\frac{5}{2}$

**(b)** $\frac{7}{12}$

**10 (a)** $y = 2x + 1 - \frac{1}{x}$

**(b)** 0

**11 (a)** $y = x + 5$

**(c)** $\frac{4}{3}$

# Index